IMPLEMENTING
SUPPLIER
PARTNERSHIPS

▲

HOW TO
LOWER COSTS
AND IMPROVE
SERVICE

▼

TIMOTHY VAN MIEGHEM

PRENTICE HALL
Englewood Cliffs, New Jersey 07632

Prentice-Hall International (UK) Limited, *London*
Prentice-Hall of Australia Pty. Limited, *Sydney*
Prentice-Hall Canada, Inc., *Toronto*
Prentice-Hall Hispanoamericana, S.A., *Mexico*
Prentice-Hall of India Private Limited, *New Delhi*
Prentice-Hall of Japan, Inc., *Tokyo*
Simon & Schuster Asia Pte. Ltd., *Singapore*
Editora Prentice-Hall do Brasil, Ltda., *Rio de Janeiro*

© 1995 by
PRENTICE HALL
Englewood Cliffs, NJ

10   9   8   7   6   5   4   3   2   1

Library of Congress Cataloging-in-Publication Data

Van Mieghem, Timothy.
    Implementing supplier partnerships : how to lower costs and
improve service / Timothy Van Mieghem.
        p.   cm.
    Includes index.
    ISBN 0–13–180365–4
    1. Industrial procurement.   I. Title.
HD39.5.V36   1995
658.7'2—dc20   94–43262
                                                                                    CIP

PRENTICE HALL
Career and Personal Development
A division of Simon & Schuster
Englewood Cliffs, NJ 07632

Printed in the United States of America

To my partner in life: my wife, Annette

ABOUT THE AUTHOR

Timothy Van Mieghem is a Senior Manager at Gibson & Associates, Inc., specializing in assisting clients in negotiating supplier partnerships. His clients have included *Fortune* 500 companies as well as dozens of middle market businesses.

Tim has taught executive classes on negotiations, communications, and presentations as critical parts of the partnership process.

Prior to joining Gibson & Associates, he worked as a consultant at Arthur Andersen & Company's Operational Consulting Practice. He also worked as director of a chain of seven food stores.

Tim is a Certified Public Accountant and earned a bachelor's degree from Marquette University in Milwaukee, Wisconsin.

Acknowledgments

Although many people have contributed to this book and to the development of supplier partnerships in general, there are three people whom I would like to recognize and thank for their help, support, and inspiration.

The first person is Jeff Temple. Over the past two years, Jeff has written, edited, critiqued, and brainstormed with me on many occasions and has improved the message and delivery of this book immeasurably. He has implemented dozens of partnership agreements himself, and his insights have been invaluable.

The second person is Kevin Spengel, one of the finest salesperson and sales trainer I have met. His understanding of the importance of addressing audience needs and concerns has become one of the foundations of implementing a successful supplier partnership. Whether winning the support of your company or negotiating with the supplier on a specific issue, selling is involved, and Kevin's contribution to this area is inspired.

Finally, I have had the privilege of working with one of the founders and innovators in this field. The instruction, example, support, and freedom that Wes Gibson has provided to me and our clients has made this book and its contents possible.

In addition, I would like to thank all of my friends and co-workers at Gibson & Associates who have made my professional life exciting and pleasurable.

Contents

Chapter 1
An Introduction to the Partnership Process—1

Chapter 2
Steps and Tools to Begin the Partnership Process—11

CHAPTER 3

CONDUCTING COMPANY AND SUPPLIER INTERVIEWS—25

CHAPTER 4
WINNING COMPANY-WIDE SUPPORT—43

CHAPTER 5
GATHERING PROFILE DATA AND RESEARCHING SUPPLIERS—69

CHAPTER 6
HOW TO DEVELOP NEGOTIABLE ISSUES—81

CHAPTER 7
HOW TO DEVELOP A SUPPLIER PRESENTATION TO ENCOURAGE PARTNERSHIPS—103

CHAPTER 8
GAINING INFORMATION LEVERAGE THROUGH THE PROFILE—121

CHAPTER 9
EVALUATING SUPPLIER PROPOSALS—149

CHAPTER 10
PREPARING FOR NEGOTIATIONS—181

CHAPTER 11
CONDUCTING NEGOTIATIONS——195

CHAPTER 12
AWARDING THE BUSINESS—213

CHAPTER 13

CONVERTING TO YOUR NEW SYSTEM—229

CHAPTER 14
DEVELOPING MONITORING AND EVALUATION SYSTEMS—241

CHAPTER 15
THE ROLE OF CONSULTANTS—255

APPENDIX A
NEGOTIABLE ISSUES—267

APPENDIX B
PROJECT TASK LIST—299

INDEX—313

FOREWORD

Over the years the relationship between supplier and customer has focused hard—and with laser precision—on many of the wrong things. Price alone is almost always the least important factor in determining the overall cost of the product or service to the buyer and its ultimate value to the organization. Price can only account for out-of-pocket costs actually paid to suppliers. Other factors, too often overlooked, can include the cost of value added services, rework, factory down time, customer dissatisfaction, returns, inspection, additional administration, and diminished reputation.

More important, these costs exclude the opportunity costs of not doing business with suppliers who can provide significant additional benefits. We have found, time and again, that the company that eliminates the traditional barriers with its suppliers receives the most value from its purchasing dollars. This value can come from joint strategic planning, joint product design, coordinated marketing, joint customer research, collective research and development, cross selling, paperwork reductions, management information and systems support, and increased customer good will. These opportunities separate true supplier alliances from the one-sided relationships that typically and routinely soil the name "partnership."

A true strategic alliance requires that you seek not only to find cost reductions and service enhancements for your company, but that you seek to find similar benefits for the supplier, or to find the supplier who is interested in your business because of its strategic importance. At the point where you cease to seek mutually beneficial solutions to problems and challenges, you cease to have the partner alliance relationship this book will help you develop.

Supplier partnerships have been discussed by many and truly implemented by few over the past seven to ten years. Tim has summarized the wisdom gleaned from helping clients implement partnerships with their suppliers. This presents me with a paradox. As a consultant I am concerned that this book will abate the need for our consulting services. As a CEO, I am excited to see a book that provides the reader with the tools to accomplish something of value for his or her company. Either way, adopting this open view of suppliers will strengthen your company and your ability to compete in the open market, as well as helping your suppliers achieve the same. Everybody wins.

***Wesley Jay Gibson**
Founder and Executive Partner
Gibson & Associates, Inc.
Oakbrook, Illinois*

PREFACE

This book is not just for purchasing executives. It presents a detailed, strategic sourcing plan with benefits far beyond those of traditional purchasing functions. Whether you are an executive, line manager, purchasing agent or manager, or department leader, you can champion and begin implementing a supplier partnership and help everyone in your organization understand the goals and expectations of this type of program.

One way to look at this issue is to compare the purchasing function to the customer service function. Companies that provide outstanding customer service—such as Nordstrom, Disney, or Land's End—have a tremendous competitive advantage. Yet the core of the great customer service in each of these companies exploits both a philosophical approach and a well-executed systematic process. In each case, outstanding customer service neither begins with nor is driven by the customer service department.

Similarly, an outstanding network of supplier alliances will provide tremendous competitive advantages. From the executive level to front-line buyers, you can help your company view your suppliers as partners and allies, as resources that can add value beyond delivering a basic material or service. In addition, world-class supplier partnerships can only be derived from a well-executed, systematic process. This book will help you understand this process from a general level, and it will provide you with the details necessary to implement a partnership program.

As outstanding customer service provides its company with a competitive advantage, supplier partnerships produce measurable and lasting results in three critical areas:

- ▼ Reducing, controlling, and understanding costs. (Over the past eight years, my clients who have implemented supplier partnerships have reduced their purchasing costs from 10 to 400 times over the cost to implement the partnership programs.)

- ▼ Enhancing services provided by the supplier for your company's internal customers as well as your end customers.

- ▼ Improving quality—of parts, materials, and services; of information; of processes and procedures; and, most dramatically, of the purchasing process itself.

Most companies achieve some level of success in these three areas, but many do not execute the steps that are necessary if purchasing is to add the most value to the company: the lowest total cost philosophy. *Lowest total cost* means selecting suppliers based not only on price but on a balanced analysis of *all* factors that have costs associated with them. Only by rigidly adhering to this approach can companies be assured that they are effectively managing their purchasing. The strategic partnership approach discussed in this book is a process tool that, if implemented thoroughly, will give you the confidence that you are paying the lowest total cost and therefore adding the most economic value to your company.

ARE PARTNERSHIPS RIGHT FOR YOU?
▼

You may already have a well-run purchasing operation; or maybe you are not so sure if you do. Perhaps you have a current supplier who is powerful or monopolistic. Are supplier partnerships right for you? The following questions and characteristics will help you gauge your situation.

Implementing Supplier Partnerships will walk you through every step that leads to the highest level of supplier partnerships. If quality, service, and cost issues are important to your company, and if you want your suppliers to help you with those issues, then read this book. In addition to the discussing the action steps required to implement partnerships, this book will

▼ Provide you with the tools to implement world-class supplier partnerships.

▼ Explain the importance of each step, thus helping you customize this process to the specific needs of your company.

▼ Provide multiple options on how to accomplish each task as well as the task's goal.

▼ Help you manage every detail of this process, from winning company-wide support to converting to new suppliers.

▼ Help you use this process with your suppliers so they support you in any Total Quality Management (TQM), Just-in-Time (JIT), Quick Response, Deming Quality Principles, Team Quality Circles, ISO 9000–9004, or other programs.

▼ Help you open communication lines with your suppliers. This point is so important that if you never actually negotiate to get all you deserve from your suppliers but do open the lines of communication, you will be successful. For example, some purchasing departments use this approach by including suppliers in cost-cutting tasks.

▼ Help you go beyond cost savings. The strongest issues and benefits in partnerships relate to services. High levels of customer service not only help retain current customers but help you attract new customers as well.

▼ Help you go beyond service enhancements. How much would you give up in price to gain these services? A 10% markup, or 3% or 5%? Not only can you add significant value to your company by enhancing the services you offer your customers, you can also reduce your cost of purchased goods.

▼ Help you minimize paperwork, optimize procedures, streamline processes and periodic supplier inspections, and utilize preapproved quality programs (e.g., ISO 9000). These and other opportunities provide the majority of cost savings and lead-time reductions through close communication and cooperation with suppliers.

Over the past eight years, I have helped over thirty clients implement long-term partnerships with their suppliers and carriers. Through these partnerships, my clients have increased their profitability and competitive edge significantly. My clients' initial interest has typically been cost reduction, but these clients testify consistently that service enhancements are worth even more than reduced prices over the long run. In fact, 75% of the issues negotiated with suppliers and potential partners are service related. In short, this partnership approach to purchasing is a state-of-the-art method that reduces overall company costs for both customer and supplier.

How to Use This Book
▼

In addition to defining and explaining what a world-class supplier partnership is, this book walks you through the implementation process. To communicate the ideas and individual tasks involved in implementing a partnership, this book includes the following:

▼ A flowchart at the beginning of each chapter. These charts provide a quick picture of how the detailed steps and examples in the chapter fit into the whole partnership process.

▼ Basic project descriptions, philosophies, and tasks.

▼ A complete appendix of negotiable issues, including descriptions, what to ask the supplier for, and how to sell the supplier on the issue.

▼ Stories or narrations designed to highlight important ideas or concepts.

▼ Examples of letters, profiles, reports, or other documents used throughout the project.

▼ Work programs, to-do lists, and step-by-step instructions to guide you through specific steps or procedures.

The examples provided and specific issues discussed in this book are timely and relevant to many diverse business situations. Of course, you should customize the ideas presented based on the unique characteristics of your company and situation.

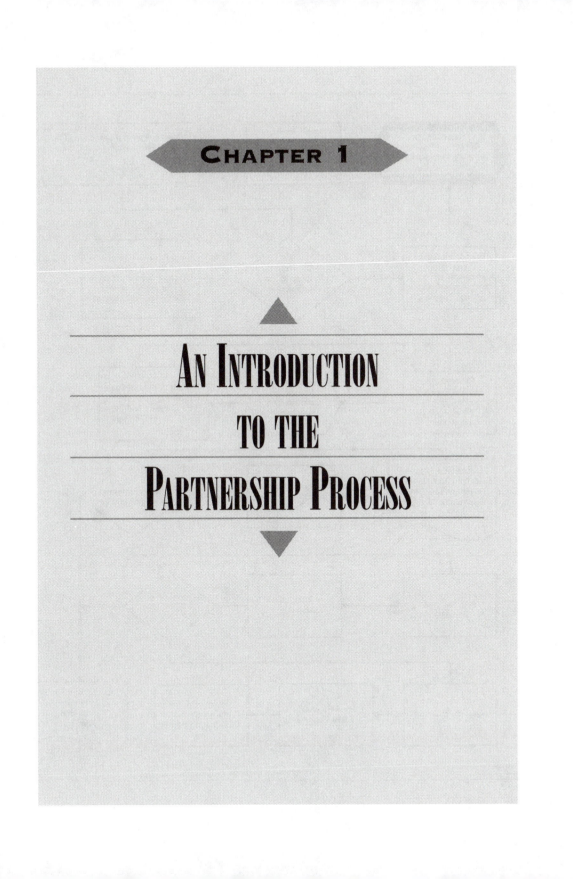

CHAPTER 1

AN INTRODUCTION TO THE PARTNERSHIP PROCESS

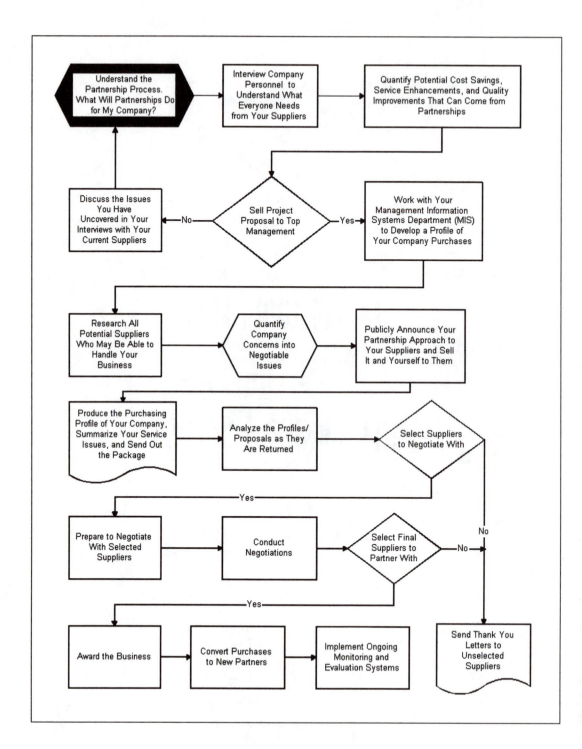

DEFINING SUPPLIER PARTNERSHIPS
▼

Partnering with suppliers is both a widely used and widely misunderstood concept. When implemented successfully, companies realize some powerful results: significant cost reductions, dramatically improved services, and many product and process quality improvements. These goals are important to any company and are typically part of the purchasing function. However, many companies are finding that by reworking traditional buying processes, dramatic results that were once thought unbelievable can be achieved. This book is about how to achieve the highest results for your company.

For example, I recently visited a forklift manufacturing plant, where an accepted step in the process of making a forklift included drilling holes in a pre-manufactured part. The dramatic realization that the specifications of that part should be updated came after years of thoughtless rework. When the supplier for that part learned of the rework through the rumor mill, it quickly suggested an update to the blueprints that would eliminate this drilling, thus reducing the time and cost required to produce the forklifts. As this example shows, although you alone may not have the time to check every step of the manufacturing process or any other process in your company, you can work with each of your suppliers, developing strong alliances that include ongoing reviews of each department within each other's plants and systems.

Developing or negotiating this close relationship is only one aspect of a partnership or alliance project. In general, a supplier partnership is a mutually beneficial relationship in which both parties understand each others' needs and capabilities and then work together to satisfy those needs. Most companies agree with that approach theoretically and work to implement it with varying degrees of success. However, there are often vast differences between the basic philosophy and reality.

Eight Common Supplier Relationship Profiles

Which of the following attitudes toward supplier relationships is typical of your company?

1. The supplier is the enemy.

   - The supplier is viewed as a disliked enemy.
   - Information is closely guarded and is often falsely presented.
   - There is no trust on either side.

- Price is the major negotiable issue.
- Problems are addressed (if they are addressed) by finger-pointing.
- There is no commitment of service or supply.
- The only relationship is between the buyer and the supplier's sales representative.

2. With partners like you, who needs enemies?

   - The supplier is dwarfed, dominated, and totally dependent on the buyer (monopsony).
   - Information is used only to minimize the supplier's profits.
   - The vendor is seen as a pawn rather than a resource.
   - The buyer dictates the price and service parameters.
   - Problems are often addressed by threats of pulling business.

3. The supplier is viewed as an opponent. (This view is common in government contract businesses.)

   - Information is shared only when necessary.
   - Each side trusts the other as ethical but has opposing goals and thus acts completely for its own best interest.
   - Price is the major negotiable issue.
   - Problems are addressed only within the confines of the supplier's customary practices.
   - The only commitment is for the current contract or purchase order.
   - The primary relationship is between the company's buyer and the supplier's sales representative.

4. Sure we're partners, aren't we?

   - The buyer views the supplier's sales representative as a friend or a partner.
   - The supplier knows the buyer's favorite football team, golf handicap, and kids' names but has only superficial knowledge of business quality and service needs.
   - Trust is based on personal feelings rather than knowledge.
   - Price—and everything else—is rarely professionally negotiated.

- Problems are blamed on the buyer's operations, not the supplier's shortcomings.
- There is a vague feeling of commitment, but it is not contractual, and the buyer might feel that the sales representative's superiors do not reinforce that commitment.
- The primary relationship is between the company's buyer and the supplier's sales representative.

5. The supplier is viewed as a partner only because of his or her long-standing status as a vendor.
   - The vendor knows the operating quirks of the buyer's business but has no idea about longer term goals and is not proactive in helping the buyer achieve them.
   - Trust is part of the status quo—but will it continue if the playing field changes?
   - Pricing is based on historical prices—not the marketplace—and there is no commitment to aggressive cost reduction.
   - Formal negotiations neither occur nor seem necessary.
   - Problems are accepted as a cost of doing business.
   - There is a genuine commitment to each other's business, but commitment is not tied to any specifics.

6. The supplier is viewed as a friendly parasite.
   - The supplier is viewed as the only option—"he's so small, his survival depends on our business."
   - The information flow is good on a day-to-day basis (the supplier's business depends on it), but exchange of longer term strategic information is rare.
   - Trust is present, but the supplier may get defensive or suspicious if the buyer seeks to expand sourcing options.
   - Pricing is based on what the supplier needs to remain profitable—not what the buyer should be paying.
   - Formal negotiations are rarely executed.
   - There is a genuine commitment to each other's business, but confusion develops if needs change.

7. We are on the right track.

  - The supplier is viewed as an integral part of the buyer's business.
  - The information flow allows both parties to gain a better understanding of each other's business.
  - Trust is built by close relationships with key individuals in each company.
  - Multiple price, service, and quality issues are negotiated for a blanket purchase order (PO) or contract.
  - Problems are addressed quickly by the supplier.
  - The commitment to the supplier is longer term (one to three years).
  - Relationships include technical and operations people as well as the sales representative and buyer.

8. We have a complete strategic alliance.

  - The supplier is viewed as a resource to gain competitive advantage.
  - Information exchange is regular and procedural; it helps the supplier reduce costs internally and allows the supplier to be measured and monitored.
  - Trust is built by both personal relationships and exchange of specific information (financial statements, quality measurements, cost analyses, etc.).
  - Every price, service, and quality issue is negotiated to specific agreements and developed into a binding contract.
  - Problems rarely occur because of proactive communication flow and performance monitoring.
  - Commitment to the supplier is even longer term (three to five or more years).
  - Relationships include top management as well as all key operational people and are diligently maintained over the life of the long-term agreement.

In general, the success of a supplier partnership program might best be summed up in the First Law of Partnerships:

> The degree to which cost, service, and quality goals are achieved is driven by the degree to which a true partnership process is implemented.

How to Determine Whether to Establish Supplier Partnerships

As with any plan or program, you must determine if it makes sense for you and your company before any resources are invested. The following key indicators will help you determine if a coordinated supplier partnership program may provide cost savings or service improvements to your company.

Identify the Number of Suppliers Used for Each Commodity

As used here, the term *commodity* can mean either a raw material (such as paper or steel), a category of parts (such as electrical components), or a purchased service (such as security services). The more suppliers you use, the more dramatic your opportunity to achieve cost savings and enhanced service. The traditional approach to purchasing has been to use multiple sources. In assessing your opportunity, note that as you spread your purchases over more suppliers, you are paying for the reduced risk of doing so with lower discounts, minimized status for service priorities, and a more complex purchasing department. Although it is not necessary to eliminate multiple suppliers, for some commodities you may achieve additional efficiencies and higher discounts through supplier consolidation.

Examine the Range of Low and High Prices

If you buy similar products from more than one supplier and they do not all charge the same amount, there is a good possibility that you can negotiate that the lowest rate charged by any supplier can be applied to all similar purchases from other suppliers. In addition, many suppliers attempt to maximize their profits through pricing variances such as rush charges and order quantity pricing. In some cases, these charges have little relationship to the vendor's actual costs and are prime targets for negotiation. In short, the greater the variance between the highest and lowest prices paid for a product or service, the greater the potential savings.

Review the Length of Current Contracts with Suppliers

If you negotiate annually or more often, then there may be additional opportunities for cost savings and service enhancements through offering suppliers a longer term commitment. Many companies do not have contracts—they simply buy on a spot basis. Again, this is a practice that typically is ripe for change.

Compare the Industry Average to Your Costs

For each commodity group, compare your total cost to industry averages. This comparison may reveal areas replete with opportunities for change. This age-old practice is known as benchmarking. Although entire books have been written on this subject, you can gain many of the benefits by following a few key steps:

1. Compute your cost of purchased goods as a percentage of sales for each of your main commodity types or product areas. For example, determine how much you spend for raw materials, transportation, packaging, utilities, distribution, warehousing, and other areas. Then take each amount and divide the total dollars spent by the total sales for the company. This gives you a ratio that you can compare with other companies.

2. Locate companies against which you can compare your ratios. In the past, many people have considered that direct competitors are the only appropriate companies for comparison. Time has shown, however, that you can compare your company to any company that is similar in size, is in a similar industry, engages in some similar manufacturing practices, or has another common thread with your company. Sources you can use to find these companies include purchasing associations, the *Thomas Registry*, personal knowledge of competitors and industry peers, and consulting firms that specialize in benchmarking services.

3. Collect the data from the companies you have identified. Once you have located the companies, you can gather the specific data you are looking for. The two primary methods of collecting these data are (1) reviewing companies' annual reports and public information and interviewing their accounting department; and (2) entering into an exchange of information. Most likely, you will not find companies willing to provide proprietary information unless you are willing to provide them with helpful information in return.

4. Assess your data. Remember that the ratios and other information you have collected on your target companies are a point of reference, not goals. You do not want to limit your aspirations by what other companies have done. With the partnership process, you have the opportunity to forge new developments by working closely with your suppliers.

5. Relate your data to the partnership process. If you find that the benchmarks you uncover in the industry show that you are paying more for your purchases than other companies, you can summarize that information to evidence your company's need for negotiating long-term supplier partnerships.

One last word of caution: Developing a supplier partnership is itself a form of benchmarking. Because the process of implementing supplier partnerships requires that you commit long term to a group of hand-selected suppliers, you will secure prices and services that will provide industry benchmarks for other companies.

Determine the Size of Your Potential Supplier Base

Although this process provides benefits even if you have a monopolistic supplier, the most dramatic enhancements and cost savings typically spring from supplier competition. You can use the following sources to understand how many suppliers you can invite to participate in your partnership process:

▼ The *Thomas Registry,* or other industry sourcing periodicals. The *Thomas Registry* lists, by subject, participating suppliers throughout the United States. For example, if you look up "corrugated suppliers" in the *Thomas Registry,* you will find a list of companies that provide boxes, packaging, and other corrugated supplies.

▼ Industry associations. In many disciplines, you can find an association that supports the professionals in that field. Most public libraries have reference books that list all of the known associations in the United States by subject. Once you locate the associations that relate to the different commodity or product areas you are researching, you can tell them to ask for a list of recommended or preferred suppliers.

▼ Personal interviews. Even though they may not buy from different suppliers, your own purchasing staff may be aware of many optional suppliers.

Remember that additional suppliers only add competition to your negotiating process, reducing your ability to negotiate rate reductions. Developing a formal alliance with your monopolistic suppliers may in itself provide service enhancements and mutual cost reductions.

Determine the Uniqueness of Your Business

One of the most powerful features of supplier partnerships is near-universal applicability. If your company is unique and requires specialized services and products from suppliers, this partnership process will help you address those needs with your suppliers. Remember, the supplier is the expert in their business, not you. Many customers avoid a formal partnership program because they mistakenly think that a supplier will not be interested in their business due to its uniqueness.

SUMMARY
▼

As with many emerging strategies, supplier relationships often claim the status of a partnership. However, a true partnership must contain some basic traits:

▼ There are open communication lines at all levels of the company.

▼ Joint strategic planning sessions incorporate cost-saving and quality-enhancing innovations.

▼ There is a long-term commitment of volume to the supplier.

▼ Trust is built by both personal relationships and an open exchange of information.

▼ Price, service, and quality issues are addressed and negotiated up front.

These characteristics identify a true partnership and indicate that the customer-supplier relationship provides the highest quality service and products at the lowest overall company cost to the customer, while providing a fair profit to the supplier. Although these characteristics are desirable to any company, it is important to analyze the potential advantages to determine the actual benefits of a supplier partnership. The primary indicators include

▼ The number of suppliers you currently use by product area

▼ The range of prices you pay for similar products

▼ The length of any contracts you might currently have with any suppliers

▼ How much your company pays for products compared to your competition

▼ The number of potential suppliers

▼ The uniqueness of your business.

This chapter has focused on defining partnerships and determining the opportunities provided by them. Chapter 2 will discuss the major steps in implementing a supplier partnership.

CHAPTER 2

STEPS AND TOOLS TO BEGIN THE PARTNERSHIP PROCESS

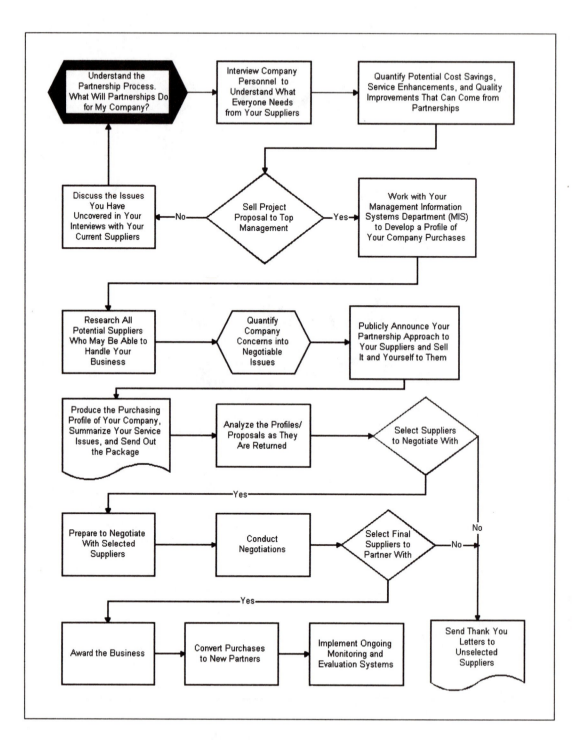

In Chapter 1, we reviewed the reasons for implementing a supplier partnership. Regardless of which reasons justify supplier partnerships for your company, the same basic steps produce the most competitive supplier partnerships.

MAJOR STEPS TO ENSURE A SUCCESSFUL PARTNERSHIP PROGRAM
▼

The steps discussed in this section, when combined, generate a process that will allow you to achieve the highest degree of measurable success. The process is not rigid—no single approach can be applied in the same way to any two different companies. Your company's market situation, people, history, and strategic goals must be used to customize the process to your company. You could even eliminate some of the major steps and still achieve dramatic results. However, investing the resources and attention to implement each step completely is the best way to do the following:

- ▼ Manage the change process as it affects your company internally.

- ▼ Manage the change process as it affects your suppliers and customers externally.

- ▼ Achieve maximum results and benefits.

- ▼ Manage any risk to which you may be exposed.

In short, executing all of the steps completely (while considering your individual situation) is the difference between a top-notch job, which separates you from your competition, and a mediocre job. As you read, pay close attention to how each step is explained in terms of (1) selling the supplier on your company and on the benefits of becoming your partner, and (2) eliminating service or pricing risks to your company.

Gathering Data

This step involves researching the service, quality, and cost needs of each department in your company. Begin by informally interviewing each department head and a number of line workers. Focusing on documenting and understanding the needs and desires of each department in your company will guide the partnership process for two main reasons. First, this focus will help you sell the project because all the important people will see that their concerns and thoughts are addressed. Second, it will provide the groundwork for the actual specific issues you will negotiate with the suppliers. (This step is covered in detail in Chapter 3.)

In addition to service and quality issues, we will gather data to solicit detailed pricing proposals from suppliers, negotiate pricing and related discounts, and measure the results of newly negotiated pricing against the pricing under current purchasing practices. These data will give you power, knowledge, leverage, and confidence to negotiate effectively and to make management decisions about specific issues and suppliers, and they will give you the confidence to know you are making the appropriate decisions.

Developing a Supplier Presentation

This is a key step in finding companies whose interests match your own. It provides a forum with which to present your company to your potential supplier partners, describe your goals and expectations of the process, and begin generating interest among suppliers. Almost as if you were selling your company, you tell your company's story and persuade the audience that you will be an outstanding potential customer. You also set the tone for the supplier selection process and establish the control and direction of the program.

Developing a Purchasing Profile

This accomplishes two goals. First, it gives the potential supplier a complete and honest assessment of your specific material needs and service issues. Second, it provides a format for the vendors to submit their proposals. The profile contains service issues as well as a complete list of material needs (descriptions and quantities). In other words, by showing the supplier historically what products your company purchases, the supplier can accurately bid on pricing and service levels. This also reduces the risk of a partnership failing because the supplier didn't understand what it was getting into. In addition, by showing the total usages and requirements in detail, a supplier will be better informed and, therefore, more comfortable in making commitments to your company.

Developing Specific Negotiable Issues

At this point, you have developed a database of every service and pricing concern of your company. To use this information, you need to quantify each issue in terms of what you ideally want, what you are willing to accept, what the supplier's interests and objections will be, what evidence will satisfy those objections, and basic facts you can use in describing the issue. This is the step at which you maximize your ability to execute this project. If you know what you can accept in a supplier negotiation and how you will sell the supplier that it is in his or her best interest to provide it, and if you practice communicating all of this, you are prepared to succeed.

Zig Ziglar, the popular motivational speaker, states that if you want to win, you have to prepare to win. And if you prepare to win, then you can legitimately expect to win. This step is the muscle of your project.

Conducting Negotiations

You are finally up to bat. This is the part of the project at which you negotiate, in detail, every service and pricing issue important to you and your company. After each issue is covered, both the supplier and your executives sign a memo documenting their understanding of the agreement reached on each issue negotiated. This memo will be the basis for a partnership contract.

Awarding the Business

Each department head will go over the service and pricing concessions of the various suppliers and help you decide to which suppliers to award the business. This step is completed with an awarding meeting, during which you will negotiate any closing issues and, with much fanfare, award the supplier your business. This is a good psychological start to what could be a long partnership. However, it is not your final step.

Converting Your Business to Your New Partners

The first two months of your new partnership are critical to its long-term success. This initial period, when you convert your purchases from your old supplier to your new partner, provides the first impression of your supplier partner for the rest of your company. Communication between you and the supplier partner, initial strategy meetings, plant tours, and conversations with your designers and manufacturers will smooth this transition greatly. In the long run, the success of the partnership will be based on effective conversion of business.

Developing Monitoring and Evaluation Systems

The best negotiated contracts in the world mean nothing if there is no actual performance. After the initial systems and transitions are completed and installed, the relationship must be maintained, and the quality, service, and cost must be measured. In this step, you will develop the tools, reports, tasks, and routines that you will use to monitor and evaluate the ongoing performance of your new partner suppliers.

HOW TO GAIN SUPPORT FROM KEY INDIVIDUALS
▼

Although we will discuss this topic in detail in Chapter 4, it is important to discuss it in general at this point because if you are the president of your company and seeking to implement this approach, the staff and managers involved must first share your vision and understand the benefits of change. If you are the purchasing director, the president, the chief financial officer, and the chief operations officer will want to know why they should devote additional time and resources to a job that you alone are supposed to handle.

Selling the Project

The key in selling this project is to control the expectations of your audience. If you begin with a proclamation and try to "give religion" to your company, you might scare people away. Keep in mind the following key ideas:

1. Be discreet. Divulging your intentions early can put too much pressure on you to deliver quickly, at best. At worst, you will scare away support and be dismissed as an unprepared goon.

2. Before you begin, be sure you understand the flow of this project and the reasons for every step. Remember, what you are proposing goes against business as usual and may not receive an open, unquestioning embrace.

3. Gather input from others in the following areas (be sure to include line workers as well as executives in each area to get a full understanding of the issues):

  ▼ Purchasing

  ▼ Customer Service

  ▼ Sales and Marketing

  ▼ Transportation

  ▼ Financial/Accounting

▼ Manufacturing

▼ MIS

▼ Distribution

▼ Engineering

(This step is covered in detail in Chapter 3.)

4. Organize your thoughts into a presentation. If you are selling upward or across your company, you want to appear professional, thoughtful, prudent, and confident. If you are selling downward, you will face difficulty if you are commanding downward. Be ready to list services you hope to enhance, specifics and quantified objectives, the resources you will require, and the time frame you expect. (This is covered in detail in Chapter 4.)

5. Make sure your plan is credibile. Research articles that describe how other companies have benefited from the process. Gather information on your competitors and show how you can gain an advantage—or that you may be lagging behind them today.

6. Analyze the fit with your company's strategic plan. Your company may be growing at 30% a year. It may be highly leveraged and have immediate cash flow needs. It may be facing an uncertain future due to changing government regulations. It may have goals to increase profit margins, grow market share, cut costs, etc. Be prepared to discuss from a strategic context how a supplier partnership program will help your company achieve these goals.

PREPARING YOUR PEOPLE FOR YOUR PARTNERSHIP PROGRAM
▼

To complete the aforementioned steps, you need some special programs. As you implement these programs, you will draw on the experience of your co-workers, management, and peers. These experiences will translate into critical issues you will negotiate, stories you will relate to suppliers, and basic knowledge you can use to show suppliers the business reasons for your requests. Although the major steps in the process may vary somewhat based on your specific situation, the following tools are essential in implementing effective partnerships.

Offering Training and Practice

Many business settings and supplier relationships nurture an adversarial overtone in negotiations. However, you need to communicate complex and vital ideas to suppliers. Any additional communicative distraction, any not-so-tactful comment, any unprepared topic, or any misjudgment of supplier interests and objections could tarnish or diminish the results of this process. Thus, practice is vital. Most companies, because of supposed time constraints or simple lack of execution, fall far short of appropriate levels of practice and training. The results are either poorly structured partnerships or a destroyed belief in the partnership process. By devoting the time for practice, you will be several steps ahead of most of your competition. You can get this training from an internal person at your company, from professional training companies, or from operational consultants who have experience implementing these programs. Specifically, for each person involved in this project, include the following types of training and practice:

NEGOTIATION SKILLS

Many negotiation training courses focus on tactics. Your course should focus primarily on developing the issues to be negotiated. It should define ultimate goals as well as the minimum acceptable offers. Conversely, it should anticipate supplier interests and objections and develop responses and sales strategies. In this way, individuals can hone their skills using tactics and practices that typify suppliers.

COMMUNICATION SKILLS

Whereas negotiation training will fine-tune the *why* and *what* of negotiating, this course will help define the *how*. The focus is on minimizing distractions and maximizing the selling of your ideas.

PRESENTATION SKILLS

During the supplier presentation, you and other executives will present your company to each of your potential supplier partners. To sell these suppliers on your company, you will need to deliver this presentation professionally. To ensure your ability to do this, work with a facilitator or professional speaker.

Teamwork

Quality experts have long sung the praises of team building within organizations. Cross-functional or high-performance work teams are becoming common in the world's leading companies. Each person will add unique insights, approaches, and methods to sell the suppliers on your issues. A typical team roster would include the following people:

▼ Director of Purchasing

▼ A member of upper management, the President, the Chief Operating Officer (COO), the CEO, or the Vice President of Operations, who can represent the interests of the company as a whole

▼ A commodity expert, who uses the commodity or service (typically a department head or engineer)

▼ A financial representative, such as the Chief Financial Officer (CFO) or Controller, who can talk about the stability of your company and discuss financial issues

▼ Other experts as the commodity area dictates, based on an individual's knowledge or experience.

As this team roster suggests, you will have a different team for most negotiations. For example, a pharmaceutical company might have one group who implements partnerships with its raw material suppliers and a different group for high-tech chemical testing equipment. The most effective way to train these teams is to identify all the people who will be on any team up front, at the beginning of the project. In this way, you can include everyone in the basic training and initial development of the issues to negotiate and then divide into teams to address different areas. This method will give you the most flexibility and efficiency throughout the process.

Empowerment

If the highest level executives are not involved, the negotiating teams need the power to accept or reject supplier offers on each specific issue and ultimately make the contract. There will always be situations in which new options develop, and the lack of authority to accept or reject these options will make the negotiations useless. Empowerment is a prerequisite for a successful completion of this program.

To receive empowerment from top executives, you must do two things:

1. Demonstrate your competence. By interviewing the people in your company, by thinking of all the negotiable issues, and by showing the level of detail you are going into with the suppliers, you will convince top executives that you will do a first-class job with the supplier partnership negotiations.

2. Include top management in your decision-making process. Although you are looking for the authority to negotiate on behalf of your company, if you

keep top executives involved enough to understand what is going on and to provide their insights into the process, they will feel much more comfortable with letting you commit the resources of your company.

Information Management

Early in this program, explain your goals to someone in the MIS department. An ally who will help you produce reports, summarize data, and support your project's data needs will be invaluable. One of the necessary steps is to provide a detailed summary of your annual purchases to your suppliers. The MIS department is one source for this information as well as for other data requests pertaining to other tasks. For this reason, you can save a lot of time if you explain the partnership process to the MIS department up front and solicit its assistance from the beginning. This can especially be true if the MIS department will have to gather additional data to meet your requests.

HOW TO OVERCOME THE SUPPLIER'S ANXIETIES
▼

For thousands of years, philosophers have taught the golden rule: "Do unto others as you would have them do onto you." These words are the foundation of your success in this project. As Benjamin Franklin once said, "A man convinced against his will is of the same opinion still." If you do not convince the supplier that your requests are for your mutual benefit, he or she will not accept your offers except by force. If the supplier is forced into a contract, he or she will not honor it in spirit. You are trying to implement a partnership in which both parties seek to work together. The suppliers might acquiesce in some instances, but they will not truly become your partner unless they think it is in their best interest. When the supplier arrives at the bargaining table, he or she is negotiating for more than your order—the supplier is negotiating for his or her job. The supplier feels as much pressure to win the business and not be taken advantage of in the process as you do to find a good partner.

As we will discuss in depth throughout this book, the underpinning of successfully negotiated partnerships is empathy for the supplier in each issue. It helps to walk a mile in the supplier's shoes, at least mentally. An open, empathetic attitude will maximize your chances to sell or convince the supplier your requests are in his or her best interests. To overcome suppliers' anxieties, you should do the following:

  ▼ Anticipate their interests.

  ▼ Anticipate their anxieties.

  ▼ Know your interests.

  ▼ Know your anxieties.

  ▼ Quantify your interests and anxieties into the minimums and maximums you are willing to accept.

  ▼ Develop tactics and evidence to address suppliers' anxieties.

  ▼ For each issue, list and explain the suppliers' interests and tie those interests to your requests.

Notice that the last two items, which relate to the supplier's anxieties and interests, are the only topics you talk about during negotiations.

CASE EXAMPLE

Which of the following hardware salespeople do you think is most likely to make a sale?

Salesperson A: "Thanks for letting me show you our hardware product line. I am very proud of our line and I know you will not find a better line in the market. We use only reinforced steel for our tools, and they last longer than other companies. Also, we have very competitive rates. How many may I order for you today?"

Salesperson B: "Thanks for coming. Based on our previous conversation at the office, I picked these tools to show you. You mentioned that you work with computer components, which cannot be subjected to magnetic fields. Based on that, I called around and found this set of tools made with a new steel alloy that never magnetizes, reducing any risk you might have of damaging your work. Also, these tools have a damage warranty, wherein the manufacturer will pay for any damage to your products that is caused by its tools. Since you are ready to buy some tools anyway, this set seems to match your needs better than any others in the market. How many may I order for you today?"

Salesperson B is most likely to make the sale, because he took the time to find out what was most important to the buyer, found a suitable set of tools, and pointed out the benefits as the buyer would see them. Salesperson A only mentioned generally that he believed it was a good deal.

One of the most important words in negotiations is *graciousness.* Graciousness is an outward sign of your desire to make the best contract for your supplier as well as your company. As a disagreement becomes apparent, remember that you never need be rude or insulting. You are trying to entice a supplier to offer his or her best possible deal and set up a long-term partnership. Concessions won by volume or rudeness will not last in the long term. Remember that the suppliers are your guests as they arrive to negotiate with you. Treat them with respect, and you will reap the benefits.

SUMMARY
▼

As you review the steps required to implement a successful long-term partnership, remember the importance of managing change. Often a good contract has been negotiated with a supplier but is never used because few people know about the contract and because few people were involved in negotiating it. The process discussed in this book is sensitive to the importance of change management.

At the most basic level, implementing a supplier partnership requires you to do the following:

1. Gather the data necessary to understand the service, quality, and pricing needs of your company.

2. Communicate your intentions of a true long-term partnership to current and alternate suppliers.

3. Develop a comprehensive historical summary of your purchasing needs to allow suppliers to bid specifically on your business.

4. Prepare the issues necessary to achieve the needs and goals of your company, and practice negotiating them.

5. Conduct your negotiations.

6. Select your partners.

7. Convert your business to your new partners.

8. Develop systems to monitor and evaluate the performance of your new partnership.

In addition to understanding the steps required to implement supplier partnerships, you should approach your top management and other executives to win their support for your project. You can win company-wide support by including as many people in the process as possible, preparing a presentation based on the thoughts and needs of people in every department, providing your company with evidence of other successful partnerships, and posturing your partnership goals in relation to the strategic plans of your company.

Even with the support of your company, you still require some basic tools to implement the project successfully. Through training and practice, you can continue to involve your co-workers in the process while you prepare the specific issues for negotiating with suppliers. In addition, the experiences and knowledge of your co-workers will be invaluable in developing specific requests for your new partners. This teamwork will be your most valuable change management tool.

Although you will be asking a lot of your new partners, it is vital that you remain sympathetic to their needs. If you lack this understanding, you will miss opportunities to save the suppliers time and money, and they will not be able to pass those savings on to you. In this process, you are a salesperson. By anticipating the needs and concerns of suppliers, you will be much more successful in selling the benefit of the partnership you are implementing.

Chapter 3 will take you through the first, and most important, step of the partnership process: identifying your needs and the needs of each department in your company.

CONDUCTING COMPANY AND SUPPLIER INTERVIEWS

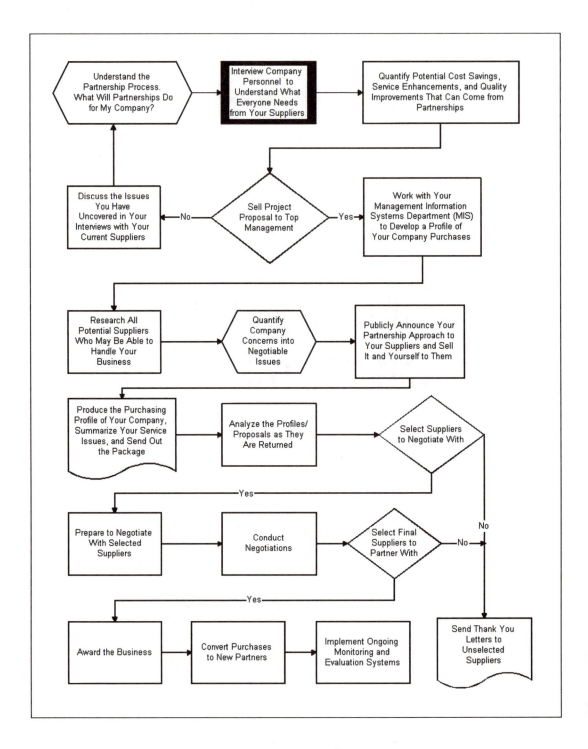

An effective manager tries to make decisions based on as much data as possible—to a degree. If you don't gather any data, you make spontaneous, capricious decisions. If you wait until you have gathered 100% of the available or potential data, your decisions will be untimely and of limited effect. The happy medium is to gather as much data as possible in a reasonable time frame (e.g., 75% to 80% of the possible data). The interviewing process satisfies this guideline. Although you could document every step your company labors through to produce your products and get them to customers, creating hundreds of pages of detail in the process, you don't need to.

Supplier partnerships are among the most efficient and effective ways to purchase goods from suppliers. However, if you do not buy the right products with the right services from your suppliers, you have not accomplished anything of real value. Interviewing helps you avoid this pitfall. In short, your goal is to define and understand the issues you can negotiate to minimize any risks in using a supplier, maximize the supplier's ability to support your manufacturing and other departments, and enhance your company's ability to service the customer.

Interviewing your company's personnel will help you understand your company's purchasing needs. Through these interviews, you can document the service and quality concerns of each department in your company. In addition, by listening to the needs and concerns of the people in your company, you will begin the process of winning their support in implementing the supplier partnerships. If they feel they have a say in the partnerships and that you are addressing their concerns, they will feel comfortable with you as a leader in this process.

In addition to drawing knowledge and participation from your co-workers, you can also obtain information from your suppliers. Your suppliers can help you understand what issues are important to them as well as what they can do for you. Many of your suppliers will have some expertise, some service enhancement, a quality perspective, or a cost-cutting idea that they would like to propose to you. Through a supplier interview, you can uncover some of these opportunities and include them in your negotiations. In addition, you want the suppliers to feel as comfortable with this process as your co-workers do, and this is best accomplished by listening to their concerns and questions.

MEASURING YOUR SERVICE NEEDS
▼

To implement effective partnerships, you need to understand and measure the service needs of your company. The best way I have found to do this is to ask the experts. Interviews afford you the opportunity to uncover, in a half-hour to two-hour session, the important concerns. As you interview your co-workers, you are documenting their service concerns—the first step in quantifying service needs.

Measuring and Quantifying Issues

There is a saying, "If you can't measure it, you can't negotiate it." There was a time when a handshake was all that was needed to initiate a long-term agreement. At that time, however, *service* may have meant nothing more than on-time delivery, a good product, and an annual Christmas card. Today, *service* can include up to 50 issues, each affecting your company and your customers. How do you negotiate good service? *Service* can mean different things to different people. You must determine specifically what you mean by *service* and how much of that service you need. Notice the progression in the following statements from a "blue sky" statement to a detailed and quantified negotiable issue.

A Blue Sky Statement

The company might say, "We have to provide good service to our customers, so we need good service from our suppliers." The supplier might respond, "I am glad to hear that, friend. We are on the same team. For us, service is king. You have my company's commitment and my personal commitment that we will provide the highest levels of service." In this exchange, what have you gotten from the supplier? Nothing! The supplier has no idea what services are important to you, and no actual levels have been set. All you got was a verbal sales brochure pitch.

To move away from a lack of specific service requirements, the first step is to divide the term *service* into smaller, digestible parts. Interviewing key personnel in your company and your customers will lead you to the vital service components you need to pursue. For example, on-time delivery, precertification of delivered goods, reduced lead times, or consignment inventory may significantly reduce costs or increase efficiency at your location.

Partial Quantification

The company might say, "Mr. Supplier, based on our relationship with our clients and the systems we currently use, on-time delivery is critical to our operations. In addition, it will save everybody money and time if defective parts are uncovered before the products leave your plant, so please precertify and inspect your shipments. Also, reduce your lead times for our orders and let us keep some inventory on consignment." A likely supplier response might be, "Obviously, you are prepared; you sure know what you want. Fortunately, we are committed to the same quality standards as you. We will deliver on time, minimize our lead times, and I will personally check your orders before they leave. And if you need consigned inventory, we can look into it as needed. No problem."

In this example, what have you accomplished? Very little. If you have a good salesperson calling on you, he or she may pass along your concerns to his or her operational people, but you do not have any specific promises from the supplier that you can verify on an ongoing basis. Consider the points one by one:

1. *On-time delivery:* Although you may think 100% on time is what you negotiated, the salesperson may assume that 70% is good enough.

2. *Reduced lead times:* You may think in days or weeks, whereas the supplier thinks in months.

3. *Prequality inspection/certification:* All you have is the supplier salesperson's promise to look at your products before shipment. This is not exactly a comforting thought; an engineer or quality inspector should be involved.

4. *Consignment inventory:* Basically, all you have is a promise to give you inventory when you ask for it. Whether a supplier will charge you, how much inventory it will provide, and how it will bill you has not been negotiated.

FULL QUANTIFICATION

The company might say, "Mr. Supplier, I think we all agree that if we together provide outstanding service to our collective customers, we will both grow our companies and be more profitable. In talking with our customers and our employees who serve them, we have uncovered four issues critical to our mutual success. The first is on-time delivery. For us to maintain the production schedules we promise our customers, we need to be able to count on your deliveries. Can we expect 98% or better on-time delivery to each of our locations, and at least 24-hour notification if you expect to be late for any reason? Second, our competitors offer faster turnaround to the market. We can, as a partner team, combat that with shorter lead times; specifically, 36-hour delivery on stock items and 72-hour delivery for special orders. Can you service us on this time schedule? Third, both your company and mine have spent time and money returning and processing defective products. To solve this, your quality engineer, or equivalent, should inspect every shipment before it leaves your facility and document compliance with the specifications we have provided you on an ongoing basis. It is important that no more than 1/2% of the products we receive be defective. Finally, we can avoid expensive emergency shipments if we maintain a consignment inventory of seven days of products on our location. On a monthly basis, your salesperson can review our usage and bill us appropriately for the inventory used."

In this example, the supplier can agree with your requests or not, but your requests cannot be avoided with slick sales quips. You have asked for specific and measurable services, black and white. In short, you have defined and quantified that elusive and broad term, *service*.

Defining Critical Issues

As you interview your co-workers and uncover and define the specific issues critical to your company, answer the following questions:

1. What services will the supplier provide?

2. Who is required to perform the service?

3. How will the supplier perform the service?

4. When will the supplier perform the service and how often?

5. Where will the supplier provide the service?

6. What will happen if the supplier does not provide the service?

7. What charges, if any, will be paid for the services?

CONDUCTING SERVICE ISSUE INTERVIEWS
▼

As with any meeting you conduct, it is important that you are prepared and organized. Your goal is to avoid jeopardizing the implementation process by careless mistakes and oversights. Before discussing some of the questions you can ask your co-workers, here are some tips on preparing for and conducting an interview.

Setting Up the Interview

At this point, try not to appear overly eager. Avoid discussing your ultimate plan of developing partnerships with suppliers. You have not yet gathered enough information or experience with this project to overcome the objections and obstacles that others will likely raise. Your goal is simply to ask your co-worker or supplier to let you ask some questions so that your department can better serve his or hers in the future. If you begin by explaining your intentions for a five-year partnership, your interviewees will flood you with horror stories about single sourcing and problems that cannot be overcome by suppliers outside the current supplier base. You need a solid foundation of information before you address these concerns. However, it is a good idea to ask for brief statements of concerns, new ideas, and desired procedural changes.

Preparing for the Interview

Write all of your questions on paper. Take some of the questions suggested in this book, develop additional questions based on your experience, and organize them in one place. By doing so, you will appear professional, prepared, and organized. Your co-workers and suppliers will appreciate your respect for their time, and your effort will be appreciated as you unveil your full program and ask for the support of the rest of your company.

Compiling Results

Take copious notes. At the beginning of your interview, ask if you can take notes so you don't forget any ideas or points discussed. Immediately after your interview, organize the most important notes according to the issues that were raised. In Chapter 4, we will discover how to compile these notes into a formal sales tool to use with top management.

Using a Service Issue Questionnaire

The following questionnaire will help you get specific answers from your co-workers, but the most important tool you can bring to an interview is your ears and your empathy.

- ▼ Who are your favorite suppliers?
- ▼ Why are these your favorite suppliers?
- ▼ Is the basic quality of their product superior?
- ▼ What services do they offer that other suppliers do not offer?
- ▼ Which suppliers would you rather not use in the future?
- ▼ Why don't you like these suppliers?
- ▼ How is their product of inferior quality compared to others, or compared to what you need?
- ▼ What services don't they provide that you need to accomplish your tasks efficiently?

▼ What are the most important services that you receive from the suppliers that affect your daily tasks?

▼ Is there a better product on the market in any area that you know of that you would rather use? Do you not use it because of price? Would you like to switch if the other variables could be worked out?

▼ Are there other methods or services that other companies use that we may try to incorporate? Please describe them.

▼ Is there anything else that you would consider important to enhancing the service your department is capable of providing to the customer?

These questions can be used with virtually all departments and across all levels and will provide a safety net for any ideas or questions that you do not think of during the interview. The following questionnaires target specific departments.

THE ENGINEERING QUESTIONNAIRE

Talk to actual design engineers as well as the department head. These are the people who design your products and the systems that create your products. The best answers to quality problems or opportunities are developed in the design and manufacturing of the product, *not* in the inspection of the product. Your goal is to find out if there are any changes that could be made, current practices that could be improved, or vital services that must remain in place unchanged from their status quo. Here are some topics and questions to lead into after you ask the basic questions:

▼ Are there any quality issues that can be addressed by supplier quality, service levels, or service enhancements? (Be sure to stress that this is a brainstorming session and any ideas are OK, regardless of their view of the chances of a supplier offering the service.)

▼ Is there any step in our manufacturing process that could be accomplished by the supplier who provides the part or service?

▼ If you were commissioned to develop a zero-defects quality program at this company, what are the top five ideas you would implement first?

▼ Would it help you improve the quality of the product, reduce the cost to manufacture or distribute the product, or streamline the process if you had a supplier engineer work with you (at no charge) in the conceptualization, design, or review stages?

The Manufacturing Questionnaire

Talk to the plant manager, a foreman, and two or three line workers. As the department that actually produces your goods, this department may have some of the best detailed suggestions. Talk especially to the line workers; any consultant will tell you that they are often a vital information source. Tom Peters, a well-known management consultant, has described his job as adding credibility to the line workers in the view of top management. He would interview the line workers, combine their ideas, dress them up, and present them to top management. Ask the line workers questions like these:

▼ Are there steps you perform that you think don't make sense?

▼ Please describe these steps. What do you do, what do you think you should do, and why hasn't your boss allowed you to make this change? What would be required to solve this problem?

▼ Are any of the materials you are given unsuitable for your tasks?

▼ Could any of the materials be modified that you use to make your job easier or your product better?

▼ Do you think your job could be changed so you could be more efficient?

▼ If you design new tools or components, do the supplier relationships we have assist you in improvements, or do they incorporate your changes but offer no advice?

▼ Could the supplier engineers offer sound advice and help minimize additional changes in the process?

▼ Have you seen any tasks in other parts of the plant that don't make sense to you?

▼ Assuming that I could effect any change to make your job easier, what five things would you ask me to do?

Ask the plant manager the following questions:

▼ Have any suppliers been able to make your plant run smoother?

▼ What have they done?

▼ Is there anything you see the purchasing department struggle with that you think could be made easier?

THE SALES AND MARKETING QUESTIONNAIRE

Talk to two or three salespeople, the Vice President (VP) of Sales and the VP of Marketing. As main links to the customer, sales and marketing personnel may have some creative ideas that internally focused personnel would not offer. In your introduction to sales-focused interviewees, tell them that you recognize that some customers complain to them about quality or service failures that have not been corrected. You are ready to hear those concerns and complaints and attempt to translate that understanding into a solution. Half the battle is won by simply accepting that a problem exists and identifying it.

▼ Have there been any repetitive service or quality complaints from any of your customers?

▼ If you could design any change in our products or services, what five things, in priority, would you change?

▼ Could we perform any service that our customers do not today expect that would make their processes easier? (Remember, this is a brainstorming session; all ideas are considered.)

▼ What is more important to our customers—our price, our services, or our quality? Rank them in importance.

▼ If service is most important, which services are most important?

▼ What are the worst ways we could mess up an order in the customer's view?

▼ Are there any other customer-related issues that we have not identified so far?

THE TRANSPORTATION QUESTIONNAIRE

Talk to the transportation manager, a shipping clerk, and the Vice President or Director of Logistics. The transportation department is the last department to touch a product before the customer receives it, and in many cases it can seriously affect customers' overall perception of the service and quality that your company offers. Any issues that can help the transportation department send products on time and with fewer damages will greatly enhance your customers' perception of your company. These questions may help uncover opportunities to raise the overall image of your company:

▼ Have there been any recurring damage problems for any of our products?

▼ What ideas do you have to correct or minimize these problems?

▼ For supplier to customer direct drop-shipments, are there any shipping issues that we should pursue to make our company look more professional to our customers?

▼ Have any suppliers affected your ability to ship on time or damage free?

▼ Are there any procedures that you perform that could be eradicated by paperwork by the supplier?

THE FINANCE AND ACCOUNTING QUESTIONNAIRE

Talk to the controller, an Accounts Payable (A/P) clerk, and the Director of Finance. Although the Accounting and Finance department may not have many insights into pure service issues, it has a deep commitment to pricing issues. Although many of us think of discounts as the main pricing concern, other issues do affect the cost of products and services.

A pricing issue defines how much, when, to whom, and in what form you will pay for the goods and services you will receive from the supplier. Traditionally, the cost of the product has been viewed as the unit price charged by the supplier. Experience has shown that this view is too simplistic, and other factors affect our costs. Ask the following questions:

▼ Which of the following are important to our company? What are our current levels, and where would you like to see them?

- Unit price
- Payment terms—discount percentages, days to pay with discount, and net days to pay
- Who pays for freight?
- At what point does title pass? (Important for damage in route and theft)
- Price increases and caps over the life of the contract
- Inventory stocking/consignment
- Return and restock charges
- Discounts and allowances

▼ Do any suppliers require less paperwork than others? What changes in procedures would you like to see?

▼ Would you welcome the use of electronic funds transfer and computerized invoice matching systems?

CHAPTER 3

THE PURCHASING QUESTIONNAIRE

Talk to at least one other buyer, the Purchasing Manager (even if you are that manager), and the Vice President of Purchasing. Now that you have gained some detailed knowledge about how your department affects the rest of the company, brainstorm among your co-buyers and manager about issues you would like to raise with your suppliers. Some of the questions you will ask refer to electronic data interchange, or EDI. EDI provides an alternative to processing manual paperwork with a supplier. Instead of paper, EDI allows two or more companies to share information directly through computer hookups. Although it is not important that you understand how this works, it is important that you understand that EDI can streamline paperwork, speed up communications, and reduce processing costs. EDI as an issue will be discussed in Chapter 6 and in the Appendix.

▼ Are there any paperwork decisions that we could eliminate through EDI?

▼ How many suppliers do we use for each commodity?

▼ What could we do to make our supplier's job easier?

▼ How have our payment terms been maintained?

▼ How much two-way communication have we had with our suppliers lately?

▼ What issues are most critical to our success?

- Insurance on inbound freight
- Delivery lead times
- Late changes in our specifications or orders
- Price
- Discounts on payment terms
- Time of day of delivery times
- Emergency stock
- Reduction of engineering changes

▼ Would EDI hookups be useful if the suppliers had the technology to hook into our systems?

▼ Do we currently work with any suppliers who have billing accuracy problems? If so, what steps would you like to see to minimize these errors?

▼ Describe the system of invoicing and payment in effect with the best supplier you know of.

CONDUCTING SUPPLIER INTERVIEWS
▼

You can gather information about service and pricing opportunities for your company by talking to your most important suppliers and prospective suppliers. These companies produce their parts and provide their services for many companies, not just yours. Because of this, they have a unique insight into new and innovative methods, procedures, processes, materials sourcing, and other areas that could reduce your costs and make you more competitive. As with your other interviews, you should downplay the importance of the partnership program for which you are laying the foundation. But do not lie; interviewees will find out eventually. So tell them your main interest is to explore new service enhancements and avenues that will lead to lower overall company cost for both you and them. In general, these visits should be four to five hours long. As you might expect, the best suppliers to see are the ones you spend the most money with or that are most critical to your manufacturing process.

Planning Your Visit

You should be well prepared for your visit. The following questions and activities will help you plan your visit. Of course, you can add or delete steps based on the circumstances of a particular supplier.

SUPPLIER VISIT AGENDA

▼ Introduce all participants and give their backgrounds.

▼ State the purpose of the meeting:

- – High-level overview of service enhancement and cost-cutting opportunities
- – Impact of future strategic plans on products we buy and services we use
- – Cost reduction and quality programs in place or planned
- – Specific service issues and concerns

▼ Have the supplier give a summary of the company's history, specifically addressing the following:

- – Current ownership
- – Growth percentages
- – Profit percentages

- Major customers
- Other programs with key customers
- Competition
- Changes in business
- Financing
- Capital expenditures
- Our company's impact as a customer (i.e., How important are we?)

▼ Take a tour of the supplier's operations. This will help you think of additional specific questions to follow up with that supplier.

▼ Discuss opportunities and specific service concerns.

GENERAL QUESTIONS TO ASK

▼ Do you see additional opportunities for our companies to work together in terms of

- Implementing EDI between companies?
- Additional interaction between the top management of our two companies?
- What we could do to take cost out of your organization?
- Information on our company that you track inside your own organization?
- Quality or cost issues unaddressed in our organization?

▼ Rate our company as a customer.

- List our three top strengths.
- List our three top weaknesses.

▼ How is your personal relationship with our people in the following areas:

- Top management?
- Purchasing?
- Engineering?
- Manufacturing?
- Accounting?
- Other key players?

ENGINEERING QUESTIONS TO ASK

▼ Are there any opportunities with your company in terms of the following:

- – Cooperative upfront engineering involvement?
- – Internships at our company for your design/product/process/packaging engineers?
- – New approaches to product or process design that we have not taken advantage of ?

PURCHASING QUESTIONS TO ASK

▼ How are we as a customer in the following areas:

- – Purchasing personnel skills?
- – Supplier product knowledge?
- – Inventory management—your product areas?
- – Ordering lead times?
- – Providing appropriate specs/drawings?
- – Calculating pricing?
- – Calculating inbound freight costs?

▼ How would a long-term contract for our business affect your operations?

ACCOUNTING QUESTIONS TO ASK

▼ Have we been a good customer in terms of invoice payment?

▼ Are we accurate in how we pay your invoices?

▼ Are there any opportunities for paperwork reductions between our companies?

MANUFACTURING QUESTIONS TO ASK

▼ How are we as a customer in the following areas:

- – Quality applications of the products you provide to us?
- – Knowledge of your products and how to use them in our manufacturing process?
- – Accepting new ideas?
- – Inventory management, especially in terms of your product areas?
- – Packaging issues?

Concluding the Visit

After you have asked the aforementioned questions and any other questions you customized your script with, it is important to end the meeting on a positive note, summarizing the achievements of the day. To accomplish this, do the following:

▼ Ask open-ended questions to make sure you cover any additional areas the supplier deems important, such as the following:

– Are there any other issues you would like to discuss?

– As you know, some of your competitors offer lower prices than you. If you were in my position, whom would you buy from and why?

– What are the most pressing issues facing your industry in the future?

– What else can we do as a customer to help you cut our mutual costs of doing business?

– Is there anything else we should look at before we conclude our meeting?

▼ Thank the supplier for his or her time and effort. Let the supplier know how much you got out of this meeting.

▼ Express your excitement at the prospect of implementing some of the supplier's suggestions.

▼ Ask one final question: Is there anything else we have not discussed that you feel might be important to either you or us as we go forward?

▼ Thank the supplier for his or her hospitality one more time.

WRITING UP YOUR SUPPLIER VISIT
▼

As with your internal company interviews, it is important to take many notes so you do not forget any important points. You may find it helpful to bring an assistant or secretary to help you take notes. It is likely that some specific points will be made during the meeting that will be important to your company as you develop your supplier partnerships. It is not likely, however, that you will be able to remember them all. The notes you take during these supplier visits will be a vital part of the foundation for what you negotiate later in the project.

Summary
▼

In this chapter, we have reviewed the importance of conducting interviews with your co-workers and suppliers to help you understand your company's service needs and opportunities. The questions included in this chapter cover many areas that may prove important to your company. As you add other questions specific to your company or industry, you will develop a foundation of knowledge for negotiating a supplier partnership that addresses the specific service needs of your company. To do so, you must complete the following tasks:

▼ Measure your service needs.

▼ Define your critical issues.

▼ Set up your interviews.

▼ Prepare for the interviews.

▼ Conduct service issue interviews with

- The engineering department

- The manufacturing department

- The sales and marketing department

- The transportation department

- The finance and accounting department

- The purchasing department

▼ Compile the results of your interviews

In addition to conducting interviews within your company, you also can gain valuable data and insights by interviewing your suppliers. In addition to gathering general information on their company and taking a plant tour, during your visit with the supplier you can address the following issues:

▼ Service enhancement and cost-cutting opportunities

▼ Future strategic plans that could affect your company

▼ Cost reduction and quality programs in place or planned

▼ Specific service and quality issues important to your company.

As with your internal interviews, you can address these types of questions to different departments, including

▼ Engineering

▼ Purchasing

▼ Accounting

▼ Manufacturing.

We also reviewed the process of defining a set of detailed critical issues. More than just asking for good service, having a set of detailed issues allows you to set up a partnership with measurable performance standards—a partnership that can be evaluated and monitored.

Once you have collected the thoughts of your co-workers and suppliers, you have the information to develop specific and detailed issues for supplier negotiation (see Chapter 6). Chapter 4 will walk you through the process of taking the notes you have from these interviews and developing them into a sales effort aimed at winning company-wide support for supplier partnerships.

If you did nothing but uncover the needs of each department in your company, your time would be well spent. Lack of communication can cause companies to miss opportunities for better serving themselves and their customers. By following the steps in this chapter, you will accomplish more than most do in a career, but greater things lie ahead if you forge on.

CHAPTER 4

WINNING COMPANY-WIDE SUPPORT

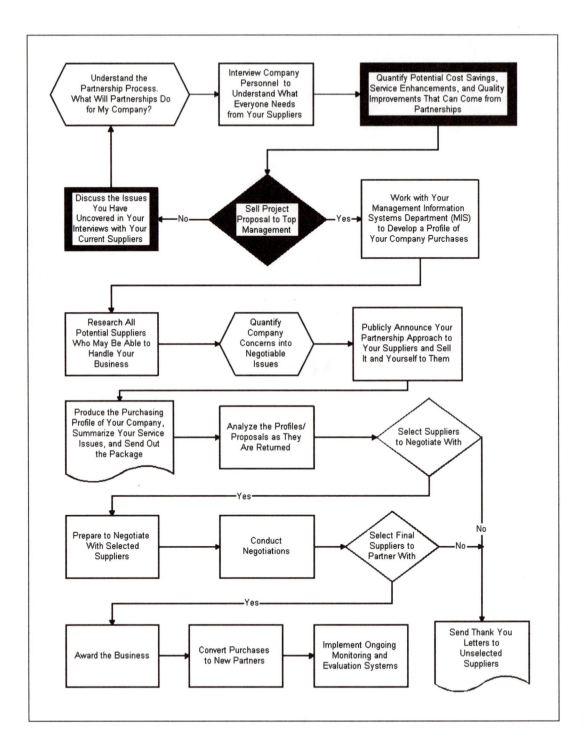

You are now ready to sell your project to your boss or to the president of the company, and ultimately to your co-workers and peers. As we have stressed, preparing for this sale is critical. Through the interviews you held (see Chapter 3), you have gathered the raw data to make a persuasive call for company-wide support in your partnership program; what is left is the final organization and presentation of your findings. Clearly, your goal is to help your company management feel comfortable departing from business as usual and expending company resources to develop controversial long-term partnerships. This is a difficult task, but you can complete it successfully if you follow this approach to sales:

1. Study and know your audience.

2. Show your audience why they would be better off doing your project; that is, what is in it for them.

3. Anticipate what objections the audience may have.

4. Prepare your sales materials.

5. Plan your meeting and prepare your agenda.

6. Outline and practice your speech.

7. Answer those objections in your presentation.

8. Ask for support.

9. Provide clear next steps.

STUDY AND KNOW YOUR AUDIENCE
▼

The statement "Know your audience" is such a foundation for anyone who speaks, acts, sells, or communicates with an audience that it has become a cliché. Listeners are best persuaded to action by communicators who tailor their message to their listeners' concerns, likes, and biases. It would be impossible to do this if you did not understand the audience first. The first step in listener-focused communication is to evaluate the people to whom you are communicating.

Begin by writing a thorough description of your listener(s). If you are communicating to a small group, describe each individual. If your listener group is large, describe a few, key decision makers. Describe your listeners in terms of the following:

- ▼ Age and sex
- ▼ Past experience or time with company
- ▼ Educational background
- ▼ Hot points, negative biases
- ▼ Pertinent personal information
- ▼ Political influences
- ▼ Conservative or progressive tendencies
- ▼ Style of management
- ▼ Creative, analytical, or emotional disposition
- ▼ Perceived biases regarding your idea.

To win company-wide support of your partnership program, you don't need to answer all of these questions about your audience. However, the more you know, the better positioned you will be to respond to their individual, specific needs.

DEVELOPING THE BENEFITS
▼

The best way to sell your project is to start by explaining its benefits. In the space provided, write the benefits of your project *as the buyer or buyers will perceive them:*

_____   _____

_____   _____

_____   _____

_____   _____

_____   _____

_____   _____

_____   _____

_____   _____

Compare your list to the following list. Does your list contain these points?

1. This is the state-of-the-art purchasing method.

2. The project will provide training for all participants.

3. We will negotiate over 50 service issues with the suppliers.

4. We will incorporate input from all departments.

5. Multidepartment cooperation and teamwork will be developed and utilized.

Are these benefits? No; they are attributes. They describe the process, not the benefits of the process. While these attributes might be very important to your company, they do not answer the question "What is in it for me?" Most ineffective presentations neglect to answer this key question for their audience. Attributes and features are things like red color, fast engine, and leather seats. Benefits of owning a car with these features include a sexy image, a rush of excitement while driving on an open road, and a luxury atmosphere while inside the vehicle.

In terms of supplier partnerships, some common benefits to top management include the following:

1. Going through this partnership process will guarantee that we, as a company, will have the best possible deal from our suppliers—the lowest cost balanced with the best service and quality.

2. Each department in this company has identified critical services and desired services that would maintain or enhance our competitive advantages as they are provided by our new supplier partners.

3. Through the partnership process, many steps and processes that we complete today will be performed by our suppliers.

4. Although we are talking about reducing costs through better relationships with our suppliers, streamlined processes, and enhanced quality, the primary reduction of costs will come directly from lower rates.

5. Other companies have experienced internal rates of return of over 400%, one-week payback periods (prorated over the initial year of the contracts), and net project cash flows ranging from 30 to 40 times the cost of the project. Although we may or may not reach those lofty goals, this project will provide us the best tool we have to accomplish these goals with our suppliers.

6. One of the competitive advantages we can exploit with our suppliers is EDI. Because of the value of developing this technology with them, they will be

willing to underwrite much of the costs of implementing computer communications and linkages, including hardware costs. This will position us
to minimize paperwork, shorten lead times, and offer the same conve-
niences to our customers as appropriate.

7. Although top management will be involved in some critical stages of this
    project, they will not be burdened with most of the work and effort. In
    short, if top management approves this project, I will review our goals and
    strategies with them, ask for some help in supplier relationships, and
    obtain their authorization for negotiating specific issues. From there, I
    (with a team of our people) will implement the rest of the project within
    nine months.

In addition to listing the benefits of supplier partnerships, you need to be prepared to answer any questions about the process.

ANTICIPATING OBJECTIONS
▼

Although you will provide ample reasons to implement supplier partnerships by
listing their benefits, you will inevitably run into objections. By anticipating what
those objections might be, you can collect any evidence and form your response
before the actual meeting. This will give you the best chance to make the rest of
the company feel comfortable with supplier partnerships.

Consider the six greatest objections that your listeners will have to your
idea. Write the objections in the space provided in the form of questions. Rank
the questions in order of priority from the listener's point of view.

_____

_____

_____

_____

_____

_____

Some objections people have encountered in the past include the following:

▼ Members of the audience might question the cost of implementing supplier partnerships.

▼ Members of the audience misunderstand the specifics of the service, quality, and pricing concerns you have outlined.

▼ Topics that the audience views as a necessary part of supplier relationships are not specifically covered.

▼ Some view the risk of supplier consolidations as too high.

▼ Some might not see the benefit of a formal partnership when favorite or powerful suppliers currently handle your business.

ANSWERING OBJECTIONS
▼

Evidence provides the teeth of your proposal. After you have hooked your audience with benefits and anticipated their objections and fears, it is time to answer those objections with evidence. For each objection, you can do the following:

▼ Provide a statistic that will ease their fears. For example, if you anticipate that they may feel that you cannot negotiate because there are few alternative suppliers for a specific commodity, research alternative suppliers in the *Thomas Registry* and provide the total number of applicable suppliers to the audience.

▼ Give examples. Give an example of another company that experienced the same dilemma or problem and how the company overcame it. If you have never implemented a supplier partnership, you might find it helpful to research the topic at the library. Scores of articles have been written that provide detailed accounts of how companies have implemented supplier partnerships in the face of many obstacles.

▼ Quote an expert. Dr. W. Edwards Deming, Phillip Crosby, Tom Peters, Wes Gibson, Peter Drucker, or an industry expert known to your top management will provide credibility to your argument. This approach takes effort. After you anticipate an objection, you must go to the library and search for articles or books that relate to your subject.

In addition, here are some common objections and options for handling them.

The Cost Is Too High

Whenever company resources need to be tapped to implement a project, the costs and benefits will be weighed before work begins. You have two primary methods for handling this:

1. Reiterate the service and quality issues that you intend to attack as part of this partnership. In many circles, *service* and *quality* are sacred terms, and any program that addresses them is given widespread support. If you would like to implement just-in-time delivery systems, electronic data interchange, or higher customer satisfaction, or if the supplier can help reduce paperwork, supplier partnerships are the road to take.

2. Emphasize that by negotiating partnerships as described in this book, your company will save money. In my experience, the ratio of the costs of implementing supplier partnerships to the cash savings produced by the efforts range from 3 to 1 to as high as 40 to 1 on an annual basis. This translates to a two-week payback period on the high end and a four-month payback period on the low end.

The following example highlights the difference between projects that enhance revenue and projects that reduce cost.

COST SAVINGS ESTIMATE VERSUS ADDITIONAL SALES PROFIT ANALYSIS

Since cost reductions increase profits by $1 for every dollar saved and new sales only bring additional profits at the net income (before taxes) percentage of the sales rate, sales would have to increase significantly more to achieve the same level of profits achieved through cost savings. Here is the formula:

$$\frac{\text{Purchasing project estimated savings}}{\text{Net income percentage of sales}} = \text{Required increase in sales to achieve similar results.}$$

For example, if your company has $10 million in sales and $500,000 in net income before taxes, with $6,000,000 in purchases, you would compute the analysis as follows (assuming that you could reduce the cost of purchased goods by 1% through a supplier partnership project):

$$\frac{\$6,000,000 \times .01}{(\$500,000/\$10,000,000)} = \frac{60,000}{.05}$$

$$= \$1,200,000 \text{ or a } 12\% \text{ increase in sales.}$$

This example shows the power of cost reductions. Although you can spend additional resources to increase sales, it is clear that partnerships can affect the bottom line through cost savings. This is a powerful argument for the financial prudence of implementing supplier partnerships.

The Misunderstood Issue

To prepare for this type of objection, you need to become intimately familiar with each issue and its underlying interests and concerns, as communicated by the company personnel during interviews. Often, when you describe a specific issue, individuals will disagree with your conclusions. If your peer disagrees with an issue, do not ignore him or her but instead work with that person to find out what is incorrect. Do not abandon the issue until you have worded it to the person's satisfaction. The disagreement probably stems from a simple misunderstanding. Regardless of how unreasonable the disagreement may seem, maintain a "we can work this out" attitude, which will win you respect. Your willingness to deal with disagreements in an open-minded manner will demonstrate that you are sincerely interested in your audience's concerns.

The Unincorporated Issue

Some audience members may have additional insights regarding service or pricing issues that need to be addressed with any potential partners. Once again, work with the person to word a description of the issue as he or she sees it. Be sure to point to your audience the iterative nature of this process: You are *always* looking for new ideas to incorporate into any partnerships you develop with suppliers. As with misunderstood issues, you deal with this objection through dialogue with your audience.

Aversion to Supplier Consolidation

If a person expresses reluctance to work more closely with suppliers, discuss his or her objections openly. For example, ask the person if a supplier

- ▼ was financially stable,
- ▼ provided the best quality product available,
- ▼ offered services unmatched by its competition, and
- ▼ charged prices well below the competition

would the person be willing to consolidate volume to that supplier? If the answer is no, assure the person that the goal of this project is not to consolidate suppliers but to find the best supplier or group of suppliers to handle your company's business. Emphasize that if the risks are too high to consolidate, you will not consolidate but will find the best suppliers to work with on a daily basis.

The Favored Supplier

Often, buyers, department managers, or other company personnel have suppliers that they protect. Sometimes this is for good solid business reasons. For example, one of my clients makes airline seats for American Airlines. Due to American's strict manufacturing schedule, if one shipment was one day late arriving to American's plant, American would charge my client a $50,000-per-day penalty. Consequently, my client required that its freight carrier assume that risk, which the carrier had done for the past 18 years. As we began to implement our purchasing project, most people at my client's company assumed that no other supplier could or would provide that service and beat the current supplier in overall service or price. However, we implemented the partnership process discussed in this book, and another carrier, who was approximately 15% cheaper and offered better service, agreed to be responsible for the penalty because it already did business with American and needed inbound freight. What we did not know going into the process was that another quality carrier had strategic reasons for wanting that business. However, if the process did not uncover another supplier capable of providing the service and protection, my client would have stayed with the current carrier. The point of this process is to develop the best group of suppliers, not necessarily new suppliers or fewer suppliers.

With these benefits and objections in mind, you are ready to prepare the materials for your meeting.

PREPARING YOUR HANDOUT
▼

In a presentation, handout materials serve two functions. First, a handout makes it easier for the group to follow along in the meeting—it provides a discussion outline. Second, a handout can provide notes that will help people prepare for the meeting as well as recall the contents of the meeting. The contents of your handout should include the following components:

1. *Executive summary.* In this section, you summarize your idea, list the benefits for your company, and summarize the detailed sections of the profile. This is your chance to encapsulate the entire project in one or two pages.

2. *Service issue summary.* Although some people might resist some aspects of a supplier partnership, everyone will agree that service and quality are critical issues for your company. By attaching these service and quality issues to your project, you will assure your audience that implementing supplier partnerships will satisfy these issues.

3. *Cost analysis.* Regardless of the service and quality aspects of a project, it must make fiscal sense. In this section, you can show the effects of supplier partnerships on the bottom line as well as explain the power of cost reduction versus sales enhancement projects.

4. *Project budget.* In addition to the savings available through this project, you need to summarize the personnel and out-of-pocket costs that will accompany this project. It is better to explain these costs up front than to explain them every time you request a resource or money.

5. *Next steps.* Now that you have your audience's attention, go for the sale. To accomplish this, you need to present the next steps that are required to implement a supplier partnership.

Figure 4.1, on page 56, is a sample handout. It is important to review this example because it is specifically written to give you a blueprint for every detail of the handout, including the wording. As you add specific stories from your interviews and experiences, you can tailor this example to meet your needs.

Your aim in using this handout is to show the service concerns that you wish to address in your project, the enhancements you intend to secure from suppliers, the amount you look to save the company in cost reductions, a preliminary budget for the complete project, and a project calendar of the required next steps.

PREPARING YOUR AGENDA
▼

In developing your agenda, remember that your basic goal is to present your idea and its benefits, answer any audience concerns, and then gain the audience's consent to commit resources. The following is a sample agenda that you can customize for your meeting.

OPPORTUNITIES IN PURCHASING MEETING: AGENDA

1. Introduction and executive overview

2. Opportunity summary

3. Service and quality issues review and discussion

4. Cost analysis

5. Next steps

6. Closing

Before you hold your final sales meeting, it is in your best interest to review your agenda and findings with each person, both those who will attend the meeting and those whom you have interviewed. When talking to your interviewees, explain that you have listed their service concerns and the concerns of their peers and are planning a project that will encourage suppliers to provide those services. This will give your peers a chance to provide feedback before the meeting, which will allow you to incorporate those suggestions and avoid embarrassing clashes in the meeting. In addition, reviewing your agenda and findings with each of your peers will help you win their support.

In the course of each personal review, you can go over the project summary, but do not give people a copy at this point. Since you will be incorporating changes, you will avoid confusion by handing out only the finalized version.

Figure 4.2, on page 65, provides a sample script to use as a starting point for preparing your agenda.

FOLLOWING UP AFTER THE MEETING
▼

Regardless of how the meeting turns out, it is important that you stop by and discuss the meeting with the people who attended it and the people whom you interviewed. In these discussions, thank participants for their support and ask if they have further ideas about implementing partnerships. This is a courteous step and will help you manage the change process by keeping people involved in the process of partnerships.

WHAT TO DO IF YOUR MEETING FAILS
▼

There is always a chance that you will not receive the support you need to implement supplier partnerships. Hidden agendas, political risks, business climate uncertainty, and other factors might prevent your company from pursuing supplier partnerships. If this does occur, you can still salvage some benefits for your company. Take your service and quality issue summary and your interview write-ups and develop a list of concerns you would like to review with your suppliers. In this way, you can obtain some of the service and quality enhancements that your company needs.

SUMMARY
▼

In this chapter, we reviewed the methods you can use to maximize company-wide support for supplier partnerships. Fundamental points include the following:

- ▼ Study and know your audience so you can tailor your presentation to audience interests.

- ▼ Focus your communications on the benefits that the company will receive.

- ▼ Anticipate and develop answers to likely objections.

- ▼ Prepare a handout that will walk the reader through the benefits of supplier partnerships and provide a summary of service and quality issues that your company faces.

- ▼ Prepare your agenda for the meeting. Be sure to provide for discussions of the next steps required to implement supplier partnerships.

- ▼ Prepare yourself for the discussion that will take place in the meeting, always focusing on the benefits of supplier partnerships and on the overall goal of securing the service and quality levels your company needs.

- ▼ Follow up with the key players after your meeting to maintain their involvement and participation in the process.

Before moving on to the next steps in implementing supplier partnerships, recommit yourself to managing change. The worst step would be to issue a mandate about which suppliers must be used. Instead, if you continue to involve other people in your company who are affected by the supplier, you will be able to gain consensus before you choose a supplier. People in your company will feel that they are part of the decision process. If you continue to maintain this focus in each step of the implementation process, you will be successful.

— Figure 4.1 —

Sample Handout

ACME Company Purchasing Project Summary

To: President
From: {Your Name Here}
RE: Strategic Purchasing Project

Dear President:

I have interviewed each of our department heads, many of the line workers, and a sample of our customers, and I have reviewed our purchasing data. Based on this work, I have found some opportunities to improve how we purchase goods and services. One common thread from all of my discussions is the importance of servi ce and product quality, innovations and supplier flexibility, and cost reductions to every department in our company.

The following summary provides an action plan that leads directly to significant cost savings, enhanced customer service, and improved product quality. I am proposing that we address each of these service and pricing issues with both current and alternative suppliers to provide better service and quality at the same or lower cost to our customers. In addition, if these same goals are important to you, I have provided an executive project overview, an explanation of the primary service and quality issues, a summary of potential estimated cost savings, an estimated project budget, and a list of the next steps to be taken in obtaining these benefits from our suppliers.

Executive Project Overview

The goal of this project is simple: to enhance the product quality and services we purchase from suppliers while reducing our out-of-pocket costs.

The vehicle we can use to accomplish this goal is supplier partnerships. Supplier partnerships offer us the opportunity to negotiate with our suppliers in detail about the many service and quality issues that affect our company and our customers, to construct new networks of communication with our suppliers (allowing them to tailor their services and products to meet our needs), and to offer our suppliers longer term contracts with our company that will enable them to redirect their sales efforts to other accounts. Although we will benefit from lower costs, streamlined processes, enhanced and tailored services, and better product quality, our suppliers will also benefit from reduced mutual costs, commitment of supply (not a guarantee of volume), and the resulting freedom of their sales force to sell to new customers. Because we are looking to negotiate a longer term contract, the supplier will have our business (subject to honoring our service and quality levels) and will not have to compete continually with other suppliers for our company's business. These mutual benefits will make it desirable and worthwhile for the supplier to negotiate with us on many issues and provide services and pricing levels which they do not afford to other "nonpartner" customers, regardless of their size and purchasing volume. One common concern in discussing partnerships is the risk associated with supplier consolidation. When possible and prudent, it may be in our best interest to consolidate the suppliers of some commodities, simplifying paperwork and increasing the volume discounts available to us. However, we can implement effective partnerships without consolidating suppliers when the risks are too high. The answer will have to be determined on a commodity-by-commodity basis. If there are other risks that you see in implementing supplier partnerships, please let us discuss them together to arrive at a viable conclusion for our company and our supplier partners.

The backbone of any supplier partnership are our service and quality needs and the respective needs of our customers. The following section details some of the vital issues discussed in the individual interviews I have held over the past month.

Service and Quality Issues

As a purchasing manager, my first instinct is to go for the lowest price. It is clear, however, that our unique business needs require us to look deeper into the true costs of doing business with different suppliers who have different cost structures. I have found that the services we receive and pass onto our customers are at least as valuable as shaving a few percentage points off our invoices. Specifically, the following service and quality issues have been identified by each department in our company and have been communicated to me in our one-on-one interviews. Each of these issues is geared toward providing higher quality products to our customers, with better service and at lower costs. These goals can be achieved primarily by working with our suppliers in what is called a supplier partnership. These issues are categorized by the department that is most affected by the issue.

ENGINEERING

Proactive Engineering Involvement

As we develop a new product or improve a current product, we would like to have the supplier who will ultimately tool and produce the product get involved at the conceptual design stage. This would minimize engineering changes, incorporate innovations and product expertise of the supplier, and ultimately reduce the cost of the product for both our company and the supplier.

Engineering Support

Since the supplier is the expert in what he or she makes, we would like the supplier's engineers to work with us on our product designs through internships with our company. Specifically, our supplier's engineers can help develop innovations in raw material usage, tooling, insert molding, alternative processes, and other areas. This 6- to 12-month internship program will provide a design or product engineer who will work exclusively at our plant locations and design facilities and study our processes, design capabilities, material uses, and other factors. Ultimately, this service will provide us with expertise in areas other than our own and will reduce costs for both our company and our suppliers.

SALES AND MARKETING

Lead Times

Any support, innovations, system change, or other effort that could be used to speed up the lead times we can offer to our customers will help us sell more products. How long does it take to get products from different suppliers for stock and specialty items; how long does it take for us to process and ship an order to our customers; how long does it take to process a purchase order? By working with our suppliers and available technologies, we may be able to reduce stock lead times one half to one full day, or more. Nonstock items can be streamlined in many cases, but no standard applies.

Innovations

Each improvement in product quality, product strength, product flexibility, and product features will also help us sell more products. Related to the engineering issues listed earlier, we will negotiate with our supplier to gain early availability of innovations and to be a test site for selected products. This issue will ensure that we are always on the cutting edge, leading our competitors.

On-time Delivery

Another component of a strong competitive advantage is the consistent production and delivery of product when promised to the customer. Although this is a mundane issue, it is also one of the most important. We need to be given first priority for on-time deliveries (receiving not less than 98% of all shipments when promised). This will enable us to schedule our manufacturing process better and to assure our customers that their orders will be on time (without having to increase inventory).

MANUFACTURING

Training

Line workers and plant management alike will benefit from detailed training that focuses on incorporating the supplier's product into our final product. This could reduce quality exceptions, lead to innovative production changes, and increase safety on the job. In addition, because this training will be provided by our suppliers, we will avoid the costs that accompany outside training and gain the benefits of being trained by a company that is intimately familiar with our products.

Process Review

The supplier, as an expert in his or her component of our product, should work on and with our line for a week at the beginning of our partnership to understand how his or her company fits into the whole picture. This should be redone annually. The benefits of doing so include quality improvements, system cost reductions, production enhancements, and overall better communication with our supplier. (This issue primarily relates to companies that do not need full-blown engineering support.)

Just-in-Time Delivery

We need the supplier to stock inventory on his or her site, provide shorter lead times on standard products, and reduce inventory at our locations. This will allow us to reduce dramatically our investment in inventory without having to compromise commitments to our customers. This issue is related to the electronic data interchange issue, discussed next.

PURCHASING

Electronic Data Interchange

Each order placed with our suppliers costs, on average, $32 for the supplier and for us. Electronic data interchange (EDI) will allow us to send orders; check delivery status; receive, match, and pay invoices; and receive management reports automatically. This simplification of our purchasing function will save both us and the supplier money. In addition, we need the supplier to provide the hardware necessary to implement EDI. One of the key benefits for our company is that we will be better positioned to reduce our inventory levels without endangering customer orders (due to reduced lead times). Implementing EDI with our suppliers will help us use JIT principles.

Order Quantities

Many suppliers reserve the right to add or subtract 10% of the ordered quantity on a purchase order. This complicates the purchasing function, forcing us to incorporate these changes when we calculate the quantity to order. Therefore, we will negotiate for the supplier to supply the exact quantity we order.

Pricing

This partnership process will be attractive to our suppliers because they will no longer have to sell our account. Because we are looking for longer term (up to five or seven years) partnerships, our business will be theirs to lose. As long as they honor the terms we negotiate in our contracting process and maintain service and quality levels, we will continue to buy their products as needed. In addition, many of the service issues listed in this summary will not only reduce our costs but will reduce our suppliers' costs as well. Because of these factors, we will also look to reduce our current pricing levels. Typically, these pricing reductions can run from 1% to 20%, depending on our historical purchasing methods and our strategic fit with the supplier.

ACCOUNTING/FINANCE

Caps

To plan for future costs and to limit our risk of increasing prices, we need the supplier to guarantee caps on the increases he or she will seek over a five-year period. In years of inflation, this issue can save as much money as increased discounts. [Good evidence for this issue would be an index of price increases you have been charged over the years.]

Terms

Based on our ability to pay, we will negotiate a 2% discount off the invoice if we pay within 10 days, with an allowable period to pay the actual invoice amount within 30 days (known in accounting terms as 2/10 net 30). This would allow us to take advantage of additional discounts for paying quickly and would enable us to take up to a full month to pay if cash is tight. [This is only an example; your company might look for a longer term to pay or a higher discount for early payment.]

Financial Stability

If we are going to enter into a five-year agreement with a supplier (or group of suppliers) to provide products and services to us, we must be certain of the supplier's financial stability. We are looking for more than just the ability to survive—we seek the desire and power to grow, innovate, research and develop new products, and provide uninterrupted service in times of repression or depression. By reviewing suppliers' financial statements and annual reports, we hope to gain a reasonable understanding of their financial foundation.

TOP MANAGEMENT

Strategic Plan

We want to be on the cutting edge. To help make this happen, we would like to be included in the supplier's strategic planning process in the capacity of a client-advisor. This will allow us to incorporate the supplier's achievements, innovations, research and development (R&D), mergers or acquisitions, or other factors in our product designs. Since this is to be a partnership, we also seek to open our strategic planning to selected supplier partners as appropriate.

Company Stability

More than just the balance sheet, we are interested in the overall stability of a prospective supplier. We ask to be notified of any occurrences or plans that may affect the supplier's ability to service our needs and our customers. For example, if the head R&D engineer is leaving, the CEO resigns, or a competitor is trying to buy the supplier out, we want to know before the general public has time to act and put us at a disadvantage. As we work toward consolidating our volume into a supplier or group of suppliers, our risks associated could rise geometrically, and we must know of any threats to our flow of supply.

SERVICE AND QUALITY ISSUE SUMMARY

These issues are designed not only to mitigate the risks of working with fewer suppliers but to exploit every possible benefit of committing business to a supplier. In some cases, we have purchased many of our commodities from one or a few suppliers, without gaining any special services, cost concessions, or top-level involvement. This project is our chance to remove the supplier's cost of repeatedly selling to us or competing for individual orders and to replace those costs with the opportunity to work shoulder to shoulder with us in developing better processes, products, services, and prices. In short, these issues and this project are all about gaining competitive advantages.

Cost Analysis

Cost savings will come in two forms through this project. First, many of the service issues we will discuss with the suppliers will relegate to the supplier tasks that we currently do in-house. This will happen because, in some cases, the supplier will be better prepared and will have the infrastructure in place to accomplish these tasks better and cheaper than we can. In addition, some of the service issues will request monetary support from suppliers for specific programs, including marketing and advertising, customer surveys, and employee training. Furthermore, this project will foster streamlining and paperwork reduction. EDI, computer hookups, blanket orders, and evaluation and performance reporting are just some of the issues that will help us and our suppliers reduce our mutual costs of doing business. These service-related cost savings will not only reduce some of our out-of-pocket costs but will also reduce our lead times and enable us to respond to customer orders and requests more quickly.

The second type of cost reduction will come in the form of outright price reductions. Based on our commitment to buy any of a specific commodity we need from a specific supplier for a five-year period, and based on some of the cost savings issues we will have negotiated, we will negotiate with suppliers who will increase our discounts. Although this reduction could be as little as 1% of the current cost of purchases, it would nonetheless be significant. The following analysis compares any cost reductions we may win in the supplier partnering process to sales-enhancing processes we could undertake as an alternative:

COST SAVINGS ESTIMATE VERSUS ADDITIONAL SALES PROFIT ANALYSIS

Cost reductions increase profits by $1 for every dollar saved. Conversely, new sales bring additional profits at the net income (before taxes) percentage of the sales rate. Consequently, sales would have to increase significantly more to achieve the same level of profits achieved through cost savings. Here is the formula:

$$\frac{\text{Purchasing project estimated savings}}{\text{Net income percentage of sales}} = \text{Required increase in sales to achieve similar results.}$$

For example, if our company has $10 million in sales and $500,000 in net income before taxes, with $6,000,000 in purchases, we would compute the analysis as follows (assuming that we could reduce the cost of purchased goods by 1% through a supplier partnership project):

$$\frac{\$6,000,000 \times .01}{(\$500,000/\$10,000,000)} = \frac{60,000}{.05}$$

$$= \$1,200,000 \text{ or a 12\% increase in sales.}$$

This example shows the power of cost reductions. Although we can spend additional resources to increase sales, we see that we can affect the bottom line through cost savings efficiently. Of course, the added benefit of supplier partnership projects is that through our service and quality enhancements, we will give our company additional competitive advantages with which to increase sales in addition to any cost savings that we negotiate.

These cost savings could be dramatic for our company, but they are secondary to the quality and service issues discussed earlier. These service and quality issues will increase customer satisfaction, reduce our cost of doing business, and enhance or maintain our competitive advantages. These are the changes that will keep our customers coming back and that will attract new customers. To accomplish these changes, we need to implement our proposed supplier partnerships.

Project Budget

Depending on a number of variables, this project could be completed within 6 to 12 months and will require some top management support, including the following:

▼ Assistance in my current day-to-day duties to allow me to interact with our suppliers, customers, and project team members as needed.

▼ The authority to hire additional temporary help to assist with various project duties.

▼ Permission to work with the MIS department in developing our company's historical shipping profile.

▼ Permission and support in gathering a team to complete the supplier negotiations. This team will be involved in the supplier presentation, issues development, actual negotiations, contract award, and conversion issues.

▼ The budget required to host the supplier presentation and to print our request for proposals.

▼ Permission to apply resources for the aforementioned requirements based on the following estimates:

TYPICAL PARTNERSHIP PROJECT EXPENSE SUMMARY
(assumes 100 potential suppliers)

Description	Dollar Level
Printing	
Letters and correspondence	$ 200
Profiles (depending on binding, could range from $2 to $15 each)	$ 1,500
Take-away package (at the presentation)	$ 500
Postage	
Letters and correspondence	$ 200
Profiles	$ 500
Take-away package (hand out at the presentation)	$ –
Presentation	
Banquet room for 100 people	$ 1,000
Lunch for 100 people	$ 2,000
Audiovisual equipment	$ 300

Conducting Negotiations

Banquet rooms for 15 negotiating sessions	$	1,500
Lunch for 8 people at 15 negotiating sessions	$	1,200

Awarding the Business

Assuming 5 banquets with 15 people attending	$	1,500
Total Estimated Expenses	$	10,400

<u>Note</u>: This summary is only an estimate, assuming some general statistics. Please note the relationship between the expenses and the number of suppliers participating. The numbers increase proportionally for each additional supplier. In addition, you might have other expenses based on the specific tasks you perform based on your company's circumstances.

Next Steps

The following major tasks will be required to implement the best supplier partnerships available to us. These steps are designed to maximize the service and quality we receive from our suppliers and to minimize the respective costs to our company:

1. Compile purchasing data.

2. Prepare supplier request for proposal.

3. Research all potential suppliers for each commodity area.

4. Invite each current and alternative supplier to a company presentation to suppliers.

5. Present our company and partnership project to our population of suppliers.

6. Prepare and send out supplier request for proposal with historical purchasing profile and service issue sections.

7. Analyze returned proposal for service capabilities and pricing levels.

8. Prepare each of our service issues and quantify specific negotiating points.

9. Invite selected suppliers for each commodity group for negotiations.

10. Negotiate service and pricing issues with selected suppliers.

11. Select suppliers to partner with based on service capabilities, pricing levels, and financial stability.

12. Award business to selected suppliers.

13. Proactively manage conversion to any new suppliers.

14. Set up ongoing monitoring and evaluation systems.

15. Perform periodic reviews to fine-tune relationships with our partners.

Summary

I have expressed the benefits and requirements of implementing supplier partnerships. With your support, we can have partnerships contracted and converted in our major commodity groups within 6 to 12 months. If you need any additional analysis, please let me know. Thank you for your time and consideration. I will follow up with a visit to discuss any ideas or concerns you may have.

Sincerely,

Your Name
Your Title

— FIGURE 4.2 —

SAMPLE PRESENTATION SCRIPT

The following document is a sample script for your sales meeting. In addition to the basic agenda discussed in the text, this is an example of what you might say at different points in the meeting. It may seem like overkill, but the wording you choose can make or break the success of your meeting. The word choice and messages provided here are intended to maximize the buy-in of your company by focusing on benefits and the work of others (so they feel included). Of course, this is only an example; you will need to modify it to your needs.

OPPORTUNITIES IN PURCHASING MEETING:
Sample Script

Introduction and Executive Overview

"Thank you for coming to this supplier service enhancement and cost containment meeting. Many of you have provided the foundation for this meeting with the time you spent explaining your service issues and concerns. Today, we can strategize how we can best work together with our suppliers to provide better products, at lower costs to us and our customers, and provide faster and friendlier service than we can today. We can accomplish these goals through supplier partnerships. This morning, we will discuss the partnerships, what they must contain for us and for our customers, and the steps we must take to implement these partnerships."

Opportunity Summary

"The first step in this process is detailed interviews of people from each department of this company. In a minute, we can review the services identified as critical to our company and our customers. Regardless of the vehicle we use to achieve these customer service objectives, our ultimate goal is competitive advantages through service: supplier service and customer service.

"Although the interviews with our personnel revealed many important quality and service enhancement opportunities, there is another reason to concentrate on solidifying our supplier relationships: cost. We are not going to compromise cost to gain service and quality improvements; in fact, we are positioned to save significant dollars on an annual basis."

Service and Quality Issues

"At this point, I would like to share some of your critical service issues. The summary report describes what the issue is about and why we are interested. In the interest of time, starting with myself, we can take turns reading each of the issues. Please feel free to add any comments or ask any questions."

At this point, review the service and quality issue summary handout with the group. This should take the majority of the meeting, giving you ample time to demonstrate your commitment to satisfying everyone's concerns. Remember, implementing supplier partnerships is only a means to an end. Your most fundamental goal is to understand and address every need of your company. At the same time, supplier partnerships have proven to be the best means to achieve your needs. With that in mind, concentrate the discussion on what must be accomplished for the company, but do not let the uniqueness of your company's needs dilute the benefits of supplier partnerships. Before the meeting, review the discussion of common objections presented in this chapter and anticipate any other objections you might encounter.

"Although the main goal of this meeting is to support each of you and your departments through the service and quality issues we just discussed, we also have the opportunity to reduce the price we are paying for our products.

Some of the indicators show that we can negotiate away 1% to 5% of cost through supplier partnerships. Some of the factors I analyzed include our overall number of suppliers, the range of prices we pay for similar items, and industry averages. In addition, I would like to share with you the power of our position. If we are only able to reduce costs by 1%, which is clearly achievable, we would have to increase sales by _____ to drop the same dollars from the bottom line. Please refer to the cost analysis section of the handout for a demonstration of this relationship.

"In short, in addition to obtaining better service for our customers, we have the opportunity to save between $_____ [at 1% of your cost of purchased goods] and $_____ [at 5% of your cost of purchased goods]. The handout contains a budget for the costs of implementing supplier partnerships. Based on that budget, we would save an estimated ___ to ___ times our costs on an annual basis [fill in the ratio of savings you expect (low end and high end) from the supplier partnerships to the cost to implement them]."

Next Steps

"In your handout is a list of the steps we need to take to begin implementing our supplier partnerships. As we review these together, it is important to note that we face no risks by going through the implementation process. If we go through the process and find that our current suppliers are the best equipped to handle our business, we can keep our current suppliers. If we do find, however, that a mix of our current and alternative suppliers are interested in working intimately with our company, our rewards could be dramatic and could provide significant competitive advantages."

At this point, review the purchasing project steps summary. Each step is crucial in achieving the best possible supplier relationship. It may be a good idea to review the first two chapters of this book to refamiliarize yourself with the steps of the process.

Conclusion

"Now that we have reviewed the benefits of implementing supplier partnerships, are there any questions that you have?"

After you answer questions, conclude the meeting.

"Ladies and gentlemen, thank you for your time and attention today. We have reviewed the state-of-the-art method for achieving service, quality, and pricing benefits available to us. I am ready to begin compiling our data and researching alternative suppliers. Before I do this, are there any other concerns we need to address?"

If there are concerns, you can continue to discuss them, but your final goal is to end by receiving permission to begin the process.

CHAPTER 5

GATHERING PROFILE DATA AND RESEARCHING SUPPLIERS

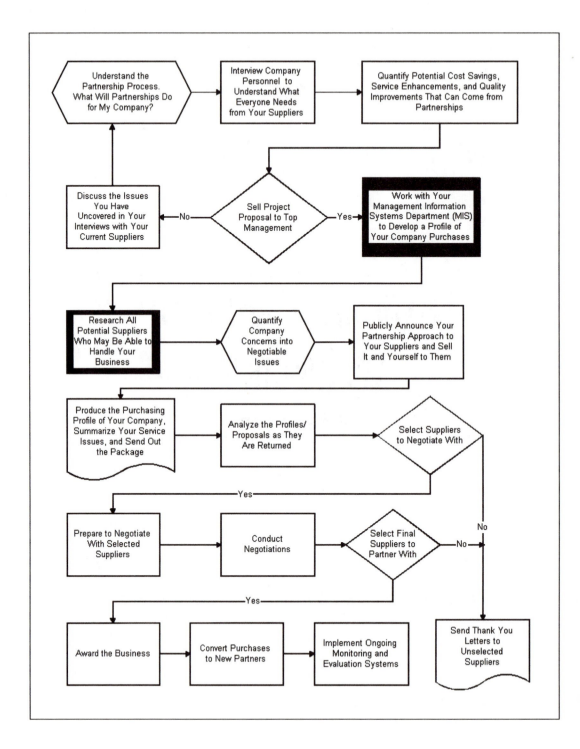

In this chapter, we discuss two main topics. The first topic is compiling the purchasing data that you would use in your profile (also known as a request for proposal). The purchasing data in the profile will show the supplier as much detail as possible about the products and services in question. The second topic is developing the list of suppliers that will receive the profile. At this point, you need to research and identify all the suppliers that will be part of this partnership process. You are looking for suppliers who currently sell to you and for as many alternative suppliers as available. These new suppliers could, as an alternative to your current suppliers, provide services or products. This step will help you understand and anticipate the competitive environment in each of your commodity areas. These two steps should be done simultaneously because you need the results of both tasks before you can send out any profiles.

PREPARING THE PROFILE DATA
▼

Through this partnership process, you will make important and significant decisions. Your goal, of course, is to make the best decision for your company, and you want the suppliers to make good decisions for themselves. This is the only way your partnerships will work in the long run and provide the benefits you want for your company. For a long-term partnership, both parties must make a decision based on valid assumptions, clear logic, and, to some extent, emotional factors. You need to understand all the issues that affect your decision. This understanding can only come from knowledge of what the supplier is offering you. Likewise, the supplier needs to know what he or she is bidding on.

You are trying to provide your company with the information you will need to make your final decisions. To compare different suppliers against each other on a fair and equal basis, you need to understand in detail how much suppliers are proposing that you pay for the services and product you wish to buy. The best way to do this is to provide the supplier with a full year's purchasing history. In turn, the supplier will be able to determine exactly what your needs are and how he or she can fulfill them. If you fail to provide the supplier with this information, you risk partnering with a supplier who cannot handle your business.

In this chapter, we will list the specific data required to document and quantify your purchasing history, discuss how to organize and download this information, and discuss the effects of multiple company locations and decentralized purchasing management.

How Your MIS Department Can Help You
▼

Before you can discuss how to gather and organize data, you need to establish a relationship with your computer or management information systems (MIS) department. The key word is *leverage*. If you lack a good relationship at this point with your MIS department head, this would be a good time to sit down with him or her and explain the supplier partnership project. Go through the project write-up and summary, the detailed interviews you have conducted, and the sales presentation you put together for the top brass. Explain what benefits you see for the company and, potentially, for the MIS department as well. Refer to Chapter 4 and the documents you have prepared so far to help you in working with the MIS department.

Establishing a Database

After you have explained the project to the MIS representative, you can submit your first request for a database report. For the partnership profile, organizing the following data elements into a database will give you and your suppliers a knowledge foundation.

THE PRODUCT DATABASE

Each data element is listed and explained next.

1. *Product code:* The internal code your company attaches to each purchase or inventory item.

2. *Product description:* Although the product code is important, the product description will help most people understand what the actual product is. Be sure to include any specifications or additional description fields that exist.

3. *Industry codes:* If there is an industry standard code for the product, then you can provide that code to third parties and they will be able to identify the specific product you are discussing.

4. *Quantity:* How many of the products did you buy over the past year? (If you do not have a full year's history, use as much data as available.)

5. *Unit of measure:* The unit of measure (UOM) is critical to understand how much of the product you purchased (examples include feet, inches, cases, yards, liters, gallons, miles, tons, etc.).

6. *Supplier name:* Although you may purchase the product from different suppliers, it is important to document which supplier supplied each of your purchases.

7. *Supplier number:* In addition to supplier name, this will help you match with other databases that may have detailed information about each supplier.

8. *Commodity code:* In what general category does each purchase fit? This field may not be available in the system, in which case you must input which commodity each purchase relates to. Examples include raw materials; maintenance, repair, and operations (MRO); packaging materials/corrugated; hardware; and molded products. If this field is not available in your system, review your options with MIS regarding the best way to input the information.

9. *Buyer:* Who is currently responsible for buying this product?

10. *Division:* If you work for a multidivisional company, be sure to capture which division/location is responsible for a given purchase.

DEVELOPING ADDITIONAL MANAGEMENT REPORTS

The following are basic management reports you can program based on the aforementioned data fields:

Buyer summary: This report summarizes the dollar amount purchased in each commodity area by buyer. Specifically, for each buyer list every commodity purchased, summarizing the amount spent in each commodity. This will serve as a test of the reasonability of the data. Each buyer can then review his or her statistics to see if the data are reasonable. You can use these purchasing data to provide detailed information to your suppliers regarding how many of what products you buy. The Securities and Exchange Commission (SEC) or the Internal Revenue Service (IRS) will not use or audit these data. Therefore, the data need to be reasonably accurate, not 100% accurate.

Division summary: Similar to the buyer summary, this report provides a summary of dollars spent for each commodity by each division. This report can also be used to audit the numbers. Compare the total purchases for each department to your financial statements or general ledger numbers. Each department should contain substantially the same amount of purchases in the summary report as contained in the financial statements. When these numbers do not match, discuss the possible problems with the

MIS representative and, if necessary, with a representative from accounting who can reconcile the two numbers.

Commodity summary: This report summarizes the dollars spent for each major commodity you purchase. This will help you review for errors in the data. Review this report, the division summary report, and the buyer summary report with your buyers and have them assess the reasonability of the data.

Profile: This is your final product for the suppliers. After you have completed your reasonability reviews and have had the MIS department update the data as needed, it is time for you to produce the purchasing profile of your company. This profile will summarize how much you purchase of each of the products for a given commodity. Specifically, for each commodity group, summarize the quantity purchased, the unit of measure, and the average purchase amount for each product.

These descriptions should help you to understand the direction of each report. If you cannot replicate the report exactly, you can work with your MIS department to achieve the same goal in another way.

COLLECTING DATA WITHIN MULTIDIVISIONAL COMPANIES
▼

Do supplier partnerships make sense for companies with multiple divisions or locations? No two locations are alike, and different issues are important to different locations. On the other hand, although each location or division has unique needs, many needs are common across divisional lines. The challenge this presents in gathering purchasing data can seem intimidating. If your corporation has a centralized computer system that tracks the purchases for all divisions and locations, you can access those files directly, as described in the previous section, through your MIS contact. If your corporation is more decentralized, then you will have to work with the MIS department of each division or location to download information. This approach demands more work and coordination on your part, but it can be done. Remember, however, that you do not have to gather 100% of the data. If you have trouble getting information from a division or group of divisions, focus only on their top commodities in terms of dollars or importance to their business. The more information you can gather, the better off you are—but only to the extent that you do not stall the process. If you are not able to get a download from a specific location or division, consider the following alternate approaches:

▼ Work with the buyers of the division to estimate their purchases in their major commodity groups.

▼ Call the division's major suppliers and see if they can provide a download file or management report summarizing the division's purchases for a given year.

▼ Consider raising the volume of other division purchases to include the estimated amounts of similar products purchased by the division that lacks information.

▼ Work from available division reports to estimate purchases as best you can.

Multidivisional companies are not at a disadvantage in partnership negotiations. If the rates currently paid by a multidivisional company were not negotiated in cooperation, there may be even more opportunities to reduce costs through a company-wide partnership process (due to economies of scale that accompany increased volume).

In addition, supplier partnerships do not centralize currently decentralized companies. The supplier partnership process helps the divisions cooperate in negotiating rates and services but leaves the day-to-day operations and decisions to the remote locations. Each division will enjoy the full benefits of belonging to a larger whole while continuing to enjoy the benefits of a decentralized/entrepreneurial atmosphere.

RESEARCHING SUPPLIERS
▼

After you have discussed collection of purchasing data with the MIS department and their efforts are underway, you can begin to build your list of suppliers that will be included in the partnership process. Each supplier will eventually receive a copy of the information your MIS team is gathering.

Although one of your goals may be to reduce the number of suppliers from whom you buy, you want to give the greatest number of suppliers the chance to win your business. One of the common threads I have noticed in partnership programs is the power of a strategic fit. Your business is unique. Your locations, mix of products, quality level, marketing plans, customer base, and other factors distinguish you from other companies. Because of this uniqueness and due to each supplier's knowledge of his or her own business, you cannot predict which suppliers will win your business. You are looking for a partner who has a strategic reason to want your business. For example, a supplier might be considering opening a facility near you and would welcome as much volume as possible to cover fixed costs.

Here are some techniques for developing an exhaustive list of suppliers.

1. Obtain a download of all current suppliers from your MIS department.

2. Review your notes from the employee interviews and extract the names of alternate suppliers mentioned during your discussions.

3. Review the *Thomas Registry,* which lists companies by industry and product line. Most public libraries have a copy of the *Thomas Registry*. Because the *Registry* is sorted by commodity, you can skip directly to the commodity you are researching.

4. For some of your larger commodity areas, you can read through trade publications and industry magazines for advertisements, articles, or press releases. Although there are too many trade publications to list here, many public libraries have a copy of the *Standard Periodical Directory,* a reference book that lists every magazine published in America by subject matter, along with information on how to obtain or review copies of the magazines.

5. You can search through various online databases, such as Compuserve, the Dow Jones, Internet, and others. In addition, various CD-ROMs provide listings of every business in the United States by subject and address. For example, the Phone Disc USA©, by Digital Directory Assistance, Inc., contains over 9,000,000 business listings on one CD-ROM. With this type of CD-ROM, you can request a download of every business that works in a specific commodity type.

6. Ask current or alternative suppliers if they know of other suppliers who they would recommend for areas other than those they service. Suppliers often belong to associations and are knowledgeable about their industry. If they do not provide a product or service you require, they can often provide you with some leads.

7. You can request leads for the commodity groups you are researching from one of the following purchasing associations. (If these associations do not provide the help you need, many libraries have a copy of the *Encyclopedia of Associations* or the *NTPA's National Trade and Professional Associations of the United States,* reference books that list the trade associations in the United States by subject matter.)

    ▼ Council of Logistics Management (708) 574-0985

    ▼ American Production and Inventory Control Society (800) 444-2742

- ▼ National Association of Purchasing Managers (602) 752-6276
- ▼ National Association of Black Procurement Professionals (202) 223-1273
- ▼ National Association of State Purchasing Officials (606) 231-1906
- ▼ National Association of Education Buyers (516) 273-2600
- ▼ American Purchasing Society. (813) 862-7998
- ▼ Coalition for Government Procurement (202) 331-0975
- ▼ National Purchasing Institute (301) 951-0108

ESTABLISHING A SUPPLIER DATABASE
▼

The database you develop of your list of suppliers will be used in many steps as you implement supplier partnerships. To prepare for each of these tasks, it is important that you capture the following information for each supplier that you research.

- ▼ Supplier name
- ▼ Commodity group
- ▼ Specific products sold
- ▼ Current annual volume actually purchased from the supplier (if any)
- ▼ President's name and specific title
- ▼ Phone number
- ▼ Address
- ▼ Vice President of Operations name and specific title
- ▼ Vice President of Sales and Marketing name and specific title

If you have access to a staff assistant, this would be an ideal task to delegate. Regardless of who does the research and enters the data into your database, gathering this information will provide one of the best tools to enhance your negotiating leverage. There is nothing like competition to motivate suppliers to offer their best deal.

SUMMARY
▼

In this chapter, we discussed developing your purchasing history database as well as researching the suppliers you will eventually send this history to. Although collecting your historical data may be time consuming, it is important to do so for three main reasons:

- ▼ These data will enable the supplier to bid on your business based on detailed knowledge of what you will require as a customer.

- ▼ These data will minimize the risk that a supplier who becomes your partner will be unable to handle your business due to unanticipated circumstances.

- ▼ These data will provide you with a strong negotiating tool, allowing you to compare different suppliers on a fair and detailed basis. Calculating the actual amount you would have to pay a supplier over a given year to purchase your materials will allow you to determine the costs of different suppliers.

With this in mind, your interest is to get the MIS department involved as soon as possible. The MIS department can either provide you with a download of the information you need or can point you in the right direction. In conjunction with the MIS department, the basic reports you need to create include the following:

- ▼ Detailed product history

- ▼ Buyer summary

- ▼ Division/company summary

- ▼ Commodity summary.

Although these data are critical to your success, you must balance the benefits of additional information versus progress. On the one hand, you want to provide suppliers with enough information to make sound, informed decisions about your business while providing enough quantification to help you decide between suppliers who offer good service. On the other hand, the longer it takes you to implement the partnership, the longer you have to wait for the benefits. By working with your MIS department you will maximize your ability to keep progressing in your project without compromising the quality and thoroughness of your data. In addition, working with multidivisions provides you with unique challenges in collecting data and coordinating efforts. Although this can be time consuming, consolidating volume purchases across divisional lines can provide significant purchasing power for your negotiations.

As your MIS department begins to collect these data, you can also begin to research alternative suppliers. In this chapter, we provided some ideas on collecting these data. Remember, you can never know which supplier is right for you until you give each supplier a chance to bid on your business in detail. The last supplier that you find might be the one that provides the best mix of service, quality, and competitive pricing.

After you begin the process of collecting the purchasing data and researching alternative suppliers, you are ready to develop the issues you want to negotiate with suppliers. In Chapter 6, we will discuss different tools you can use to accomplish this task.

CHAPTER 6

HOW TO DEVELOP NEGOTIABLE ISSUES

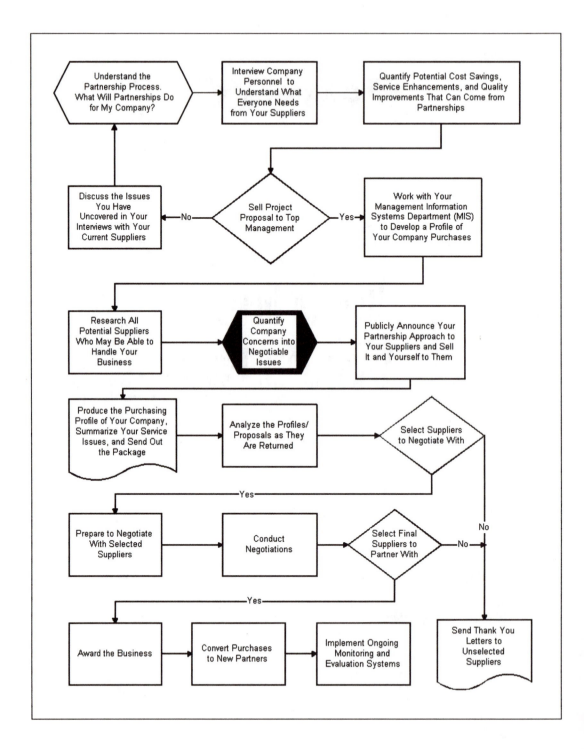

This chapter provides the structure for your negotiations. Based on your interviews with your company personnel and some of the ideas presented in this book, you have the building blocks for a successful negotiating session. We can take the ideas you have gathered in your interviews and develop them into defined issues that can be negotiated. Specifically, in this chapter we will talk about issues—how to present them, how to develop them, how to sell them, how to order them, and how to quantify them. We will see what roles people play in negotiating these issues, and we will develop the list of issues that you will use to conduct your negotiations.

IDENTIFYING TYPES OF ISSUES
▼

Before we begin to develop your company's issues, we will review the basic types of issues. There are three main types of issues that you can negotiate: the deal breaker, the issue that is open to supplier performance, and the giveaway issue.

The Deal Breaker Issue

This issue is critical to your company's operations and cannot be compromised during negotiations. If the supplier cannot meet your expectations on a deal breaker issue, then a partnership with that supplier is impossible. For example, if you guarantee your customers delivery within two weeks of their order, then the lead time of raw materials becomes a critical issue to your business. If, in your production planning, you build a five-day lead time for raw materials, a supplier could not offer you a seven-day lead time and become your partner. If a supplier did respond to your request for a lead time shorter than five days with an offer for seven days, you would need to respond as follows:

> We currently receive our materials within five days of ordering our products. We guarantee our customers shipment within 14 days of their order. It would be impossible for us to accept a lead time over five days. To continue our negotiations, you need to find a way to reduce the lead time to less than five days. What ideas do you have?

The Issue That Is Open to Supplier Performance

This issue is important to you and your company. However, a supplier who is not able to meet your basic interests may still become a long-term partner, depending on other issues. For example, one of the issues that is discussed in the Appendix is having a customer service representative dedicated to your account. This issue would be open to the supplier's capabilities because there are many ways to satisfy your interest. If your desire is that the company install voice mail, it is not critical that the supplier agree (other solutions might be pagers or car phones). What you are really seeking are timely, expert, and efficient responses to your customer service requests and questions. The equipment you desire is simply one way to satisfy that interest.

The Giveaway Issue

This issue is designed to provide some benefit to the supplier but is not critical to your company. Payment terms are an example. If a supplier is normally paid in 45 days, and you can pay in 30 days, payment terms might be a giveaway issue. You would have the chance to sell this issue to the supplier by saying, "We told you when we started this process that we were interested in a true partnership: a two-way partnership, in which we use communication, innovation, and effort to do what is in our mutual best interest. We understand from industry publications that on average people pay you in 45 days. Because of our financial strength, we are able to pay you in 30 days. We would like to offer that to you in the spirit of this partnership." You have sold the supplier a benefit, and you can ask for a more meaningful concession in return.

Another form of a giveaway issue is an issue that interests you but that you do not expect the supplier to agree to (e.g., a joint advertising program). You may ask the supplier to put together an advertisement that would go into magazines and trade publications, or even on a radio spot that would feature your company in some way. Although some companies that have the resources and opportunity would do this, there are other companies that may not. If the supplier cannot agree to your request, you can move on to another issue, you can "give it away."

DEFINING POSITION VERSUS INTEREST
▼

Now that we have defined the different types of issues, we need to understand what is important in an issue and what your real interest is. Many people begin negotiation with the disadvantage of being locked into a specific position. To maximize your effectiveness, you need to determine your real interests for each negotiable issue. In the context of negotiations the definitions of *interest* and *position* are as follows:

Interest is the basic goal, opportunity, risk, or problem you would like to address.

Position is your initial best estimate of how the supplier can address your interests.

You develop a position based on your interests. For example, one of my clients asked a supplier to install a voice mail system to facilitate communication with the supplier's customer service representative. The supplier thought about installing voice mail but eventually declined, explaining his position as follows:

> It's a very expensive notion that you're talking about, not to mention the fact that we don't want people calling our company and getting hold of a machine. We always want our customers to talk to a person when they call us. We realize that passing messages through our secretary can be slow and does not allow you to leave detailed technical messages. So, here is what we are willing to do. We will give your customer service representative a pager and a car phone. What do you think?

My client's first reaction was to continue to insist that the supplier install a voice mail system. That is what he asked for; that was his position. After thinking it over, my client realized that although his position had been to ask the supplier to install voice mail, his real interest was that the customer service agent be accessible to him at all times, and with a short response time. As he thought about it, he realized that the supplier's offer did satisfy his interest, although not his position. Consequently, after discussing with me his real interest in this issue, he decided to accept the supplier's offer. It was not a concession. Providing a car phone and pager to the representative satisfied my client's interests. The supplier's approach would allow my client to contact the representative quickly. By not being locked into a predetermined position, my client achieved a mutually beneficial outcome for that negotiable issue.

The lesson is to understand and work to satisfy your interest in every negotiable issue, and be prepared to adapt your position to the circumstance. Although it is important to develop specific positions that satisfy your interests, never lose sight of what is really important. Negotiate creatively and propose innovative approaches to solve problems. Specifically, in the aforementioned case, my client realized that what is important was contact with the customer service representative, not voice mail.

A Case Example Using Training

You may decide that some people in your company could benefit from continued professional training. This training can range from your suppliers' inter-

nal training programs, to courses taught by outside professionals, to classes custom designed for you by suppliers. Your position may be to have the supplier pay
for your course and related travel costs. (As skeptical as you may be, this type of
arrangement is becoming increasingly common.) Outside training can be as
important and beneficial to the supplier as it would be to you. Many suppliers
recognize the costs that can stem from customers who do not understand the
products they are buying. Customers who are not current in industry trends and
technology may therefore be more expensive as customers.

Although your position is for the supplier to send you to outside training at
no out-of-pocket cost to your company, your interests might include the following:

▼ Ensure that your buyers and purchasing executives are educated about
   what they are buying so that they can make intelligent decisions about the
   style, quality, pricing, and specifications of the products they purchase.

▼ Ensure that your employees are familiar with the trends in the industry and
   effectively apply these concepts to your company.

▼ Teach employees cost-cutting and quality-enhancing techniques that have
   been successful at other companies.

▼ Provide opportunities for employees to network with other companies,
   learning from them and building corporate goodwill.

▼ Ensure that your supplier partners, who will share in some of the benefits
   of the training your buyers receive, also share in the cost of the training.

For example, you may negotiate with a large supplier like 3M, NCR, or IBM,
or any company that has its own training facilities or that can provide certified
training directly to you. Although your initial position may be that you want the
supplier to sponsor your people for a specific course offered by a local university, it may satisfy your interest to accept the supplier's internal training course
instead. If the supplier counters your request for outside training with an offer of
internal training, ask the following questions to ensure that the offer meets your
interests.

TRAINING QUESTIONS TO ASK THE SUPPLIER

▼ How many of your people will you put through your courses?

▼ What courses do you offer?

▼ What if there is a course offered by an outside party that you do not offer?

▼ What costs will you pick up for your people who attend your training?

▼ Will you pick up the travel and lodging costs associated with your classes?

▼ Will you provide onsite training?

▼ How often do you offer your training courses?

▼ What other companies will be involved in the training sessions that our people would attend?

▼ Which of your courses will provide continuing professional education (CPE) credits to our buyers?

▼ Many of the courses taught by universities discuss current trends in quality control, customer satisfaction, cost reduction, and salability. How do your courses approach such topics?

The answers to these and other questions will help you determine how well the counteroffer satisfies your interests.

INVESTIGATING AN ISSUE IN DEPTH
▼

In preparing an issue, getting past the obvious and superficial concerns will help determine how successful your negotiations will be as well as how much renegotiation you will need after the partnership is in place. If you work toward anticipating every facet of an issue and negotiate it with the supplier, you will rarely be surprised by what happens during the partnership. Before we explore specific issues, we will review the best method for investigating a supplier's ability to accept your initial positions or satisfy your interests.

Questions You Should Ask during Negotiations

You can ask a supplier the following generic questions during negotiations. These questions, if asked politely, will aid your negotiations and help you and the supplier arrive at an innovative and appropriate agreement.

▼ What are your capabilities?

▼ What plans do you have to change or add capabilities?

▼ What is the best way for us to capitalize on your capabilities and investments in this area?

▼ How much have you invested in this area?

▼ If we needed this specific thing (state your position), how could this work given your capabilities?

▼ What alternatives do you see that will still help us accomplish our interests (explain your current situation and your related interests)?

▼ Given that we are committing our business to you for at least five years through this partnership arrangement, what additional investments do you think would provide benefits to you, our company, and our mutual customers?

▼ Are there any alternatives that do not require investment and will help us arrive at our interests?

▼ What have you done with other customers to solve this problem or opportunity?

▼ What have some of your competitors done to solve this problem or opportunity?

▼ Is there anything we can do as your customer to help solve this problem or opportunity?

These questions will only be fruitful if you are negotiating with the supplier's executive level. Sales representatives, regional managers, district managers, and service representatives will not be able to respond with authority to your inquiries. Only the president, CEO, COO, and some vice presidents will be able to work with you to solve a problem, authorize solutions, and implement them. This topic, and methods to attract top-level executives to the negotiating table, will be discussed in Chapter 10.

CREATING YOUR ISSUES LIST
▼

Before you can quantify issues, you must define what the issues are. Enlist the efforts of everyone involved in the process and brainstorm to identify all issues that are important to your company, across functional areas, relative to dealing with your suppliers. Use the following tools:

▼ An agenda that summarizes the relevant issues for supplier negotiations

▼ Your notes from the employee interviews

▼ Your presentation materials and purchasing program summaries

▼ The Appendix of this book, which lists and defines many common negotiable issues.

Developing an Agenda

The following agenda can be used to organize a brainstorming meeting about the issues your company needs to negotiate. This meeting can be an effective team exercise if you organize it well.

▼ Develop a list of all possible issues and concerns to discuss with suppliers.

▼ Consolidate all similar or related issues after the list is developed.

▼ Delete inappropriate issues.

▼ Discuss the next steps.

During the brainstorming session, it is OK to repeat similar issues. In other words, if two issues are related and eventually might be consolidated into one, you can list each issue so you preserve the nuance of each. One way to keep track of the ideas generated in this session is to use flip charts. Write down every issue on the chart so you will have a visual and written record of ideas. The Appendix contains a list of issues. Supplemented by the notes that you have taken during your interviews of your peers, these should be the foundation of your brainstorming. Include every idea generated by the personal interviews you conducted earlier.

Knowledge of the negotiable issues is important, but it no more prepares you to negotiate than knowing the menu at a restaurant prepares you to cook the food. Each issue must be quantified and planned thoroughly, including the specific goals, acceptable ranges, tactics to be used, and benefits to the supplier. This level of detail will help you maximize the negotiated offer; but, more importantly, it sets the foundation for a successful partnership. From the beginning, this preparation will establish a high performance standard for the supplier.

DEVELOPING AN ISSUES DIAGRAM
▼

An issues worksheet or diagram is one of the most effective means to organize the information you need for negotiation. It is helpful to dissect each negotiable issue into several modules that can be studied independently and combined to form a complete plan for negotiations. The following are the definitions of each module or section of the negotiable issue (see also Figure 6.1).

— FIGURE 6.1 —

ISSUES DIAGRAM

Issue: Payment terms	
Interest: To minimize company cash flow burdens	

Evidence:	**Discussion Outline:**
Review our payment history with the supplier.	
Disclose the number of days it takes for our customers to pay us.	
Show our cost of capital.	
Demonstrate the cost to the supplier to provide us with the payment terms we are requesting.	
Position:	**Supplier Benefits:**
2%/10, net 60	Reliable payment schedule
Ability to pay through electronic funds transfer	Streamlined payment process
	Ability to plan and manage cash flow
Lowest Acceptable:	
Net 30 days paid through electronic funds transfer	

Lead negotiator:	Storyteller:	Note taker:
Estimated time:	Observer:	Issue Type:

Issue:

A succinct explanation of the issue. You will quantify the specifics of the issue in the other sections. In many cases, a one-word topic is enough to give the participants a good understanding of the issue. *Example:* Payment terms.

Interest:

Many people confuse this section with position. Describe your most basic interest in this issue. This section is near the top of the page because it is so critical to your negotiations. If you keep your interest in mind, you will be better able to negotiate creatively with innovative suppliers. *Example:* Minimize the cash flow burden on your company (payment terms).

Supplier Benefits:

Although it is critical to know what you are interested in, it is crucial that you keep the needs and desires of the suppliers in mind. In this section, outline the benefits the supplier is likely to receive if he or she agrees to the issue. *Example:* Reliable payment schedule, streamlined payment process, ability to plan and manage cash flows (payment terms).

Position:

Based on what you are interested in, your position quantifies the best offer you would like from the supplier. Do not hold back based on preconceived notions about what the supplier has offered in the past. *Example:* 2% net 60 days through electronic funds transfer (payment terms).

Lowest Acceptable:

Although you state the optimal solution as you see it in the position section, this section is where you list any items that are required as a minimum. *Example:* Net 30 days through electronic funds transfer (payment terms).

Evidence:

Many facts, statistics, quotations, and other pieces of evidence will help you support your position but may not fall into any of the other sections of this worksheet. This is the information catchall section. Example: Review payment history with the supplier, your receivables with your customers, disclose the number of days it takes for our customers to pay us, show your cost of capital, demonstrate the cost of the supplier to provide us the payment terms we are requesting (payment terms).

Discussion Outline:

Each of the other sections lists important points for each issue. In this section, you outline the discussion of the issue as a whole. Whereas the interest section provides the strategy for each issue, this section provides the tactics. A sample basic issue outline is provided in Figure 6.2.

Lead Negotiator:

Each issue will require different roles. The lead negotiator presents the issue, directs the discussion, and speaks for your team on a given issue.

Storyteller:

An assistant to the lead negotiator, the storyteller provides examples, evidence, and insights to support the issue.

Note Taker:

This role is extremely important. During each issue, specific agreements and concessions will be made. You can use these concessions only if you remember them in detail. The note taker will take notes during each issue and, before you move on to the next issue, will summarize the agreed conclusion to the issue.

Observer:

As we discussed in Chapter 4, knowing your audience is critical to effective communications. The observer is responsible for watching the reactions of the supplier negotiators during each issue. Often the observer may see extreme hostility, anxiety, or other cues that will require action, such as a caucus or a break from the negotiations.

Issue Type:

Indicate whether the issue is a deal breaker issue, an issue that is open to supplier performance, or a giveaway issue.

— FIGURE 6.2 —
BASIC ISSUE DISCUSSION OUTLINE

---

1. Identify the issue.

2. Sell the issue, summarizing the supplier benefits.

3. Ask for your position.

4. Be silent. (Let the supplier respond!)

5. If the supplier accepts, summarize the issue and the points of agreement.

6. If the supplier does not accept, discuss evidence, supplier benefits, current situations, and their objections.

7. Make a counteroffer.

8. Return to Step 2.

9. Upon agreement, summarize the issue.

HOW YOUR ISSUES DIAGRAM WILL HELP YOU NEGOTIATE
▼

Although it requires effort and time to complete this diagram for every issue you wish to negotiate, having all the quantified facts and information on one page is critical to ensure the following:

▼ You do not overlook any part of your position or interest during negotiations.

▼ You will have a list of supplier benefits in front of you, which will help you keep in mind the supplier's needs and desires during the negotiations and persuade him or her to meet your requests.

▼ You have a guide that will keep you on track if the negotiations get out of control.

▼ You have a detailed summary of each of your negotiable issues that can be reviewed by different executives at your company.

As we discussed earlier, the basic skeleton of an issue includes the following: interests, minimum and maximum positions, issue outline, evidence, supplier benefits and administrative facts. The best way to develop any issue is with your negotiating team. It is helpful to get input from everyone who will be involved; groups tend to increase the options available and form goals that more closely match the interests of the company.

QUANTIFYING AN ISSUE USING EDI
▼

The following example demonstrates the use of EDI, which is increasingly common in American businesses.

Defining the Issue

EDI is a computerized link between companies. EDI links allow companies to transmit data (which may currently be mailed or faxed) directly between each company's computers. For example, instead of sending an invoice to a company for payment, an EDI link would allow a supplier to send the invoice directly to a customer's computer for processing and payment. This method of communication saves paper, time, and money for all companies involved. Other EDI capabilities include shipment tracking, order placement, management reporting, and information trading in general. In short, the issue definition for this issue is simply "EDI and related supplier support." How well this issue is negotiated helps determine the success of the implementation and eventual realization of potential benefits.

Defining Your Interest

In EDI, what is important? Is it important that we have computers that can talk to each other?—not in itself. Is it important in itself that we communicate faster?—not necessarily. Is it important in itself that we have computers?—no. It is important that you take cost out of the system and provide better, faster information with which to make decisions. In other words, you want it to cost less to order products and communicate with the supplier. You do not want any more paperwork than necessary because paperwork costs money, time, and environmental resources. In short, your interest is to take advantage of technological advances and the capabilities of suppliers to reduce paperwork, increase information flow, shrink lead times, and reduce manual processes related to ordering, invoice payment, invoice auditing, and any other repetitive purchasing task.

Defining Your Position

In determining your position (or, specifically, what you are going to ask the supplier for), you need to answer the following questions:

- ▼ What do you want done?
- ▼ How will it be accomplished?
- ▼ Who will do it?
- ▼ Who will pay for it?
- ▼ When will it be done?
- ▼ Where will it be done?

You can develop your position by anticipating what must be done to implement EDI with a capable supplier. Of course, this depends on what the supplier can do, as in the following example:

- ▼ We need access to and support for all of your EDI capabilities, including online invoicing, ordering, shipment tracking and tracing, performance reporting, and other modules you may support.
- ▼ We would also like you to offer us access to any new modules that you add to your EDI capacity.

If the supplier has some degree of EDI capability, you need to negotiate how the supplier can implement it with your company. You might discuss your specific requirements beforehand with your MIS department (e.g., hardware purchases, system programming, system conversion, system testing, user training, and system monitoring).

Based on your specific needs, the following points could be part of your position:

▼ A computer workstation, including a 486-based computer, printer, color monitor, and modem powerful enough to allow our purchasing department to access supplier computer files. These items must be delivered within 30 days of the contract.

▼ A system engineer or programmer to install the EDI applications and to work with our MIS department to link those applications to your mainframe accounts payable, ordering, and inventory systems.

▼ A system engineer or EDI expert to train your employees on site on the actual applications we will use.

▼ A system engineer to work with our MIS department to test the applications and audit their ability to work accurately and precisely.

▼ A system engineer to audit the system annually or when requested.

After you have defined how the EDI applications should be installed, develop a schedule for installation and who will own (and pay for) any equipment purchased. For example,

▼ The system engineer will begin working with our MIS department within 30 days of the contract, all required hardware will be ordered and installed within 60 days of the contract, and all applications will be installed and tested within six months of the contract.

▼ Based on the supplier's preference, the hardware provided for this contract can remain the property of the supplier, returnable upon completion of the contract.

Other points include who will maintain the computers and how many hours of system engineering support the supplier will provide.

Avoiding Piracy

The concept of piracy applies in negotiations. If you are negotiating EDI and you need three computer systems to handle and manage ordering from that supplier, but you ask for five because you think the supplier will comply, that is piracy. The most crude form of piracy is to increase your demand after the supplier has agreed to a lesser request. If you indulge in piracy, the supplier might give in to you but will realize quickly that you are going after everything you can get and are not interested in a true partnership.

One word of caution: In developing your position, avoid tempering your requests according to current trade practices. Just because a supplier does not do something for most customers in the normal course of business does not mean that you should not ask for it. The supplier partnership approach to purchasing is itself a departure from business as usual. This brings us to the Second Law of Partnerships (the first law of partnerships is on page 6):

> Every issue should be developed and quantified based on the best solutions to business problems and should not be limited by current industry practices.

Developing Your Minimum Position

Some suppliers will not be able to comply with your reasonable requests, and others may be unwilling. What is your minimum? At what point do you say, "If you cannot meet this request, we get the strong sense that you are not interested in working with us as a true partner"? This is a powerful statement and is only effective if used rarely. Here is a sample minimum position statement:

▼ You will provide to us every module that you have available for EDI at no charge within 30 days of the contract.

▼ Your EDI experts will train our people on all EDI applications we install within six months of the contract.

▼ Your EDI expert will work with our MIS department to make sure that we are correctly hooked up with your company and that we are not missing any capabilities of the system.

▼ You will provide any modules you develop or support in the future to us at no charge, including training and systems support.

You have quantified what you want in an issue. Now you must work on selling the issue to the suppliers.

Developing Your Evidence

In this section of the issues diagram, include any facts, quotations, statistics, or other pieces of evidence that may be useful in a negotiating session. Examples include the following:

▼ How many orders you place per year

▼ How often you trace or track orders

▼ How many loss or damage claims you file per year

▼ The cost of processing an order

Many companies have studied the costs of processing an order for a typical man-ufacturer or distributor. My most recent clients and I have studied the cost of the paper forms that are used, how much time people spend filling out those forms, and any other directly related costs. Based on this review, we have found that companies spend at least $30 (and sometimes as high as $75) to process each order. The key is that EDI can significantly reduce the cost of processing orders for both supplier and buyer. Here is an example:

> EDI potential cost savings: _____ annual orders × $30 = _____ (for example, if your company places 500 orders per year for a given commodity group, this number would be 500 × $30 = $15,000 per year).

Developing the Supplier Benefits

A supplier benefits from agreeing to provide the computers, software, and training to implement EDI with your company. In addition, supplier benefits include the following:

▼ The first benefit would be the $30 per order reduced by EDI. EDI tends to encourage a paperless and efficient ordering system that will significantly reduce the supplier's cost of doing business with your company.

▼ Because it will be easier for you to order from the supplier who has imple-mented EDI with you, you will be more likely to increase your orders from that supplier.

▼ Because of the shorter lead times, lower paperwork costs, and streamlined process, you and the supplier will become more competitive as a group and reap increased mutual sales. In many cases, you can turn this into a mar-keting advantage to your end customers.

▼ By integrating its EDI system with your computer system, the supplier has cemented a long-term relationship with you. It will be difficult to sever this relationship after the initial five-year contract.

Developing the Tactics

At this point, we have defined all the pieces of the puzzle. The discussion outline section will help you put the puzzle together by giving you the overall pic-ture. Following is an outline for discussing EDI with the supplier. In the negotia-tion, you can follow this outline, or you can deviate from it based on the suppli-er's answers to some of your questions. You can include specific stories you wish to tell, benefits you wish to drive home, facts you want to quote, or key phrases you find meaningful.

EDI ISSUE OUTLINE

1. Introduce EDI as an issue.
2. Ask the supplier what EDI capabilities he or she has.
3. Discuss the benefits of EDI for both companies.
4. Specifically discuss the $30 per order example, including your order volume.
5. Ask for your position.
6. Wait for the supplier to respond.
7. Upon agreement, summarize the issue.
8. If your first offer is not accepted, discuss the supplier's alternatives to your offer.

Administrative Section

The administrative section is at the bottom of the diagram in Figure 6.1. For each issue, list the lead negotiator, the storyteller, the note taker, and the active observer. In addition, you can list the issue type to help keep it in perspective during the negotiations (i.e., you will not fight as hard for a giveaway issue as you will for a deal breaker issue).

Issue Order

Imagine a baseball team manager who randomly decided the batting order for each game. Even the youngest little leaguers would agree that the team's offensive effectiveness would be hampered by not strategically organizing the batters to take advantage of strengths and minimize the exposure of weaknesses. In addition, the smart manager will take the other team's strengths and weaknesses into account when structuring the line-up. Think of negotiations in the same way. By carefully considering the impact of the agenda order, you can leverage your strengths to your advantage and protect your risks and weaknesses.

First, always start with an easy issue, like a giveaway issue. If you get a supplier in the habit of saying yes, he or she will be more likely to agree with you on some of the tougher issues. In other words, build momentum. If the supplier is in the habit of saying no, he or she will continue to say no. If the supplier is in the habit of agreeing with you, and a feeling of cooperation is evident, he or she will tend to continue to say yes.

Second, when considering issue order, you can use personal investment to your advantage. That is, it's a good idea to negotiate pricing issues late in the process, because the supplier will have a heightened personal interest in winning the business. If a supplier has been negotiating for four or five hours and has made many concessions and much progress toward a final agreement, he or she will want to win the business. In fact, many suppliers have commented to my clients that when they arrived at the pricing issue, because they had invested so much in the process up to that point, they felt that they had to be flexible about pricing because they would have lost so much time and effort if they were not.

One additional word of caution: Although these two tactics seem to work well in actual negotiations, remember their place. The most important thing you can bring to a negotiation is a sincere desire to get the best answer for both companies. Dishonorable tactics will not help. But you will have to fight hard for some issues, such as pricing. Using prudent methods to decide issue order is not a dishonorable tactic in itself, but be careful not to resort to base tactics to win concessions. If you do, the result will be a long, five-year "partnership" filled with anger, frustration, and distrust.

SUMMARY
▼

In this chapter, we walked through the process of developing an issue. To prepare yourself to negotiate individual issues effectively, you need to do the following:

- ▼ Create your issues list.

- ▼ Categorize the issue by type.

- ▼ Develop your interest for each issue.

- ▼ Develop your position in regard to each issue based on your interest and your investigations.

- ▼ Develop the benefits that would accrue to the supplier if he or she satisfied your position and interest.

- ▼ Develop the outline for discussing the issue with the supplier.

- ▼ Determine who will lead the negotiation of that issue with the supplier.

- ▼ Determine who will act as the storyteller, providing insights throughout the negotiations.

▼ Determine who will take notes based on what is agreed to in the negotiation.

▼ Complete the issues diagram as you complete these steps.

As you worked through the EDI issue case example and reviewed the issues diagram, you studied the structure of negotiations. No amount of negotiating prowess will make up for requests that are not well defined. No matter how smooth you are, you cannot negotiate good service. The steps provided in this chapter will help you define your issues and empower you to negotiate specific concessions from your suppliers.

In addition, team involvement throughout the company is vital in this step. If you work alone to develop the issues, you will overlook details and good ideas from your co-workers, and you will put yourself in a difficult position. The issues you negotiate will become "your issues," and the negotiations will become "your negotiations." If a partnership is to work and if you are to keep your sanity during the partnership, you need everyone who would be affected by the supplier relationship to feel that it is their partnership, not just yours. In many circles this is referred to as change management. Your best tool for managing change and winning the long-term support of your company is to include the rest of your company in the negotiating process.

Now that you have defined your needs within your company, you are ready to announce your partnership goals to the public. In Chapter 7, we will review different approaches to this task.

CHAPTER 7

How to Develop a Supplier Presentation to Encourage Partnerships

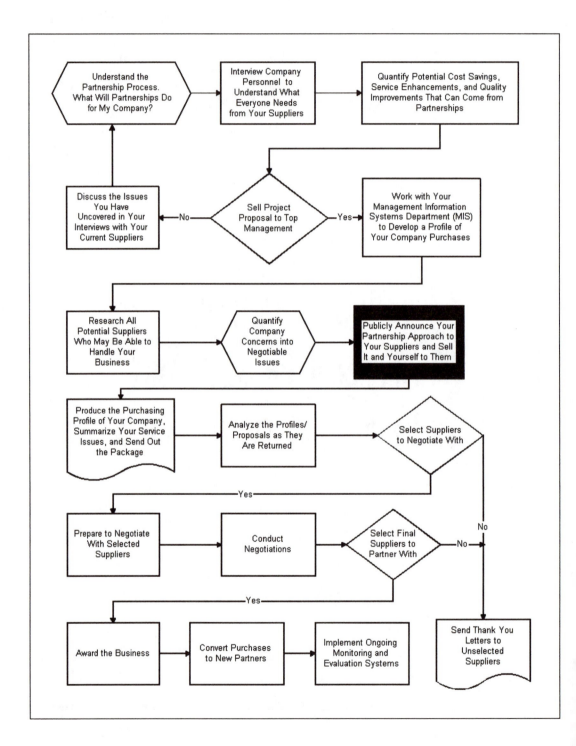

Understand the Partnership Process. What Will Partnerships Do for My Company? → Interview Company Personnel to Understand What Everyone Needs from Your Suppliers → Quantify Potential Cost Savings, Service Enhancements, and Quality Improvements That Can Come from Partnerships

Discuss the Issues You Have Uncovered in Your Interviews with Your Current Suppliers ←No— Sell Project Proposal to Top Management —Yes→ Work with Your Management Information Systems Department (MIS) to Develop a Profile of Your Company Purchases

Research All Potential Suppliers Who May Be Able to Handle Your Business → Quantify Company Concerns into Negotiable Issues → Publicly Announce Your Partnership Approach to Your Suppliers and Sell It and Yourself to Them

Produce the Purchasing Profile of Your Company, Summarize Your Service Issues, and Send Out the Package → Analyze the Profiles/ Proposals as They Are Returned → Select Suppliers to Negotiate With

Prepare to Negotiate With Selected Suppliers → Conduct Negotiations → Select Final Suppliers to Partner With —No→ No

Award the Business → Convert Purchases to New Partners → Implement Ongoing Monitoring and Evaluation Systems

Send Thank You Letters to Unselected Suppliers

In this chapter, we will discuss what a supplier presentation is, why to hold a supplier presentation, which people from your company you should include in it, where you should hold it, how to prepare for it, whom to invite, what a sample agenda looks like, and how to manage the details.

DEFINING A SUPPLIER PRESENTATION
▼

A supplier presentation is your official public kickoff of your strategic purchasing partnership or alliance program. During this presentation, you will present your company and your intentions for supplier partnerships. It is helpful to think of this presentation as one you would give if you were trying to sell the business. You need to sell the audience that you are an attractive customer who will provide the supplier with long-term value. Topics for this presentation include the following:

▼ What you are trying to accomplish with this new purchasing program or vision.

▼ Explanation of how you understand partnerships. The terms *partnerships* and *alliances* have been well used and misused in the past, and you need to explain exactly what you mean by them so you do not scare away suppliers who have had bad experiences with other partners.

▼ The specific steps of the process, and what will be required of the suppliers who participate.

▼ Current service and quality issues that you intend to address through these partnerships.

▼ Your company's background and future. Specifically, here you discuss your financial strength, your anticipated growth, how you plan to grow, and how the suppliers that partner with you will benefit.

▼ Common concerns. Often, suppliers will be nervous about your program. Smaller suppliers will fear that you will consolidate them out of your purchasing cycle, and current suppliers will fear that you will replace them with new competitors. Although you do not provide any guarantees about these concerns, you can address the issues to let suppliers know that your intention is not necessarily to replace current suppliers. Your interest is to find the best mix of suppliers to serve your customers.

Why You Should Host a Supplier Presentation

Some companies believe that, because they control the purse strings with suppliers, it is not cost effective to spend time and money courting vendors, especially with a large-scale presentation such as we recommend. Let's examine some of the benefits of such a presentation:

▼ By inviting your suppliers' top executives, you have the attention of strategic decision makers. Truly effective supplier alliances are always highly customized programs, tailored to the needs of the buyer. You will need upper management involved to make strategic decisions that go beyond normal policy for the suppliers. The better you are at presenting your company as an attractive customer, the more successful you will be in negotiating the agreements.

▼ You are giving more information than ever before to the suppliers so they can make a wise decision about how much money, time, and effort they should invest into becoming your partner.

▼ When you invite all of the suppliers that can handle some or all of your purchases in various product areas, there will be suppliers in the room that compete with one another. This is an ideal way to set a competitive tone before asking suppliers to submit proposals.

▼ During this presentation, you will present your intentions for long-term agreements. If suppliers are allowed to get information through the grapevine, or if their concerns are not mitigated by a letter, they may be less inclined to participate in the program. If suppliers think that you are interested only in consolidating suppliers or cutting prices, they may implement a counterstrategy that would undermine your intentions. This could range from dropping out of the program to making price the focus of their proposals. The best way to handle these potential problems is to communicate directly to the suppliers so they all hear the same message and have the chance to ask you questions about the process.

The presentation is the most thorough approach to initiating your partnership program publicly, but there are other approaches that will accomplish some of the same goals. These approaches will be discussed later in this chapter.

Selecting Your Company's Participants

A great Hollywood film starts with a good screenplay. Yet if it is not cast well, the result is a mediocre movie. Similarly, assembling an appropriate roster of speakers for your supplier presentation is essential to communicating your message successfully. Although the best mix of people will depend largely on your company's organizational structure, there are several basic precepts that will guide your decision.

First, you need top management. Supplier partnerships are a sourcing strategy, and that strategic direction will be communicated more credibly if your top management are present. Later in this chapter, we discuss the merits of having senior supplier executives in your audience. For courtesy and protocol, your company should be prepared to give suppliers access to your company's top management as well.

Second, one or more key buyers who have responsibility for purchasing and maintaining supplier relationships should be among your speakers. The presentation is an early step in developing personal relationships with supplier executives. Those with buying responsibilities will gain the most from these relationships as the long-term agreements are executed, and they should not miss this opportunity to interface with suppliers. By talking with the suppliers at the presentation, these buyers will get a chance to begin the communications that will make the partnerships a long-term success.

Finally, if you have a particularly strong communicator, find a way to utilize his or her skills by building a role into the presentation. For example, a director of information systems may not have an obvious role but could talk about the potential benefits of linking technology and sharing information. Be careful not to focus only on the strongest presenters. We all know that an all-star cast cannot guarantee a quality production when packaged with a poor screenplay and faulty direction.

We recommend the following mix of speakers for a typical manufacturing company's supplier presentation:

▼ The company President

▼ The Chief Financial Officer

▼ The Vice President of Operations

▼ The Director of Purchasing/Program Leader

▼ One or two buyers (of your choice)

▼ Another strong speaker from another part of your organization.

If you have trouble scheduling each of these people to be a part of the presentation, you can make an effective presentation without one or two of them. For example, if the Chief Financial Officer is unavailable, you can cover the financial stability and future growth of your company in another speech by the President, who has overall responsibility. In addition, if there are any other executives who would be working closely with the suppliers and would have relevant thoughts about the process, you may want to include them as well. (For example, an engineer, plant manager, sales executive, or co-user of the suppliers' products.)

Deciding Whom to Invite to Your Presentation

The biggest mistake a company can make in developing the invitation list is to let personal biases affect decisions. In a certain product category, you may "know" that a certain supplier is going to gain the business—either he or she is a current and excellent supplier or the only player in the marketplace. However, there may be other suppliers that can better meet your company's needs. It is also important to examine carefully the urge to omit suppliers that you believe have no chance at becoming viable suppliers due to past service or quality problems, poor industry reputation, lack of experience in your market, or lack of competitiveness on previous quotations.

Unfortunately, both types of narrow thinking seldom lead to the best suppliers or the best negotiated agreements. Reducing your supplier options automatically reduces the level of competition. Any supplier who thinks he or she has a lock on your business will behave more competitively if he or she knows you are seriously considering other sources.

Furthermore, companies that limit themselves to known and comfortable options run a dangerous risk of missing unique opportunities. Past performance problems do not preclude a supplier from making a comeback. Moreover, new entrants to markets often add innovation and value. Avoid the perils of conventional wisdom and let the detailed partnering process described in this book guide you through the supplier evaluation process.

PREPARING FOR YOUR PRESENTATION
▼

Select a date for your presentation, and clear it with your company. Check that there are no general conflicts in the industry with the date that you have chosen. For example, check that there are no major conferences, trade shows, or seminars scheduled on the same day or even in the same week of your presentation. This would reduce the number of people who attend your presentation.

Selecting a Site for Your Presentation

Before you send off the invitations, you need to decide where you're going to hold your presentation. Typically, it's a good idea to hold your presentation in hotels near the airport for the convenience of out-of-town guests. Make it as easy as possible for them to attend. If you are located in a small town, consider traveling to the nearest major metropolitan area and hold your presentation there.

Sending Invitations

The invitation letter is the supplier's first contact with your program, so it's important to set the proper tone. Two things are critical in the letter. First, let the suppliers know that this is not just another supplier partnership program—it is an entirely new way of dealing with your suppliers and it calls for a bold and creative approach from both sides. Second, you want to maximize the attendance of your target audience (top executives). Be enthusiastic and emphasize the potential benefits to suppliers. A sample letter of invitation is shown in Figure 7.1.

— FIGURE 7.1 —

SAMPLE SUPPLIER INVITATION LETTER

Contact's Name
Title
Company Name
Company Address
Company City, State, Zip Code

Dear Supplier:

I would like to take this opportunity to introduce myself and my company to you. We are _____, a manufacturer of widgets located in the Midwest, with customers spread throughout North America. Annually, we spend $26,000,000 in purchasing products and services in the course of producing and distributing our products. We have always been an innovator in our market, and we now look to maintain that status by changing how we work with our suppliers. We are engaging in a program to develop long-term strategic alliances with a select group of suppliers who share our vision.

Toward that end, we are holding a supplier presentation to explain in detail how both of our companies might benefit in this program. Although the benefits to us are clear, here are some examples of what you may look forward to as one of our partner suppliers:

▼ You will have the opportunity to participate in as much of our $105,000,000 in product and services spending over the next five years as your company can handle.

▼ For our current suppliers, this new approach to purchasing represents an opportunity to secure the business you now have with our company for at least the next five years, in addition to gaining the business that we may now give to various competitors of yours.

▼ For new suppliers, this approach by our company offers the opportunity to win new business for your company with at least five years of secured sales.

▼ Our selected suppliers will have the opportunity to develop a close working relationship with our company's purchasing, engineering, sales, operations, MIS, transportation, manufacturing, and accounting departments. Most important, top management involvement will ensure strong ties between your company and our company in the agreement.

▼ Our company has continually grown in sales since our inception, with sales averaging $50 million for the past few years. With sales increasing through market share and acquisitions each year, you will have a golden opportunity to grow with us.

▼ Finally, you will benefit from working closely with a progressive company—our company.

If these types of benefits are important to you and your company, please join us at our presentation on Friday, September 22, 1995 at the Chicago O'Hare Hilton from 8 A.M. until noon. Shortly after the presentation, we will send you a detailed profile (and request for proposal) of our forecasted material needs as well as every service and quality issue important to our mutual success.

Once again, I want to emphasize our enthusiasm about the potential benefits of establishing long-term agreements. You will have a unique opportunity to enjoy a wide range of quality and performance benefits by working closely with us over the next several years. I look forward to seeing you and your management team on September 22, and I hope that you will make every effort to attend.

Sincerely,

I. M. President
President, Our Company

FOLLOW-UP PHONE CALLS TO INVITEES

About 7 to 10 days after you mail the invitations to the suppliers, follow up by phone. A phone call can be beneficial at this point for a number of reasons:

1. It will give you a chance to solidify the number of attendees you are expecting for the presentation. This will help you plan the day and make arrangements for lunch and snacks.

2. Many people will have questions or concerns about the invitation and the partnership process as a whole. The phone call affords you the opportunity to address any concerns and to sell the concept as a whole to the suppliers—but not in as much detail as your presentation would provide.

3. Based on the questions and concerns you receive from the supplier phone calls, you will be able to incorporate your responses in your presentation. This will help you address supplier concerns and demonstrate your sincerity.

Setting the Agenda for Your Presentation

Ask this basic question about each part of your presentation: Why is this important to my audience? By focusing on the interests of your audience, you will maximize the effectiveness of your message.

The best way to start is by putting yourself in the supplier's shoes. If you had received an invitation to propose on a company's business for three or five years, and if you knew that this long-term contract would be based on a competitive negotiation process, what topics would you need to understand before you would feel comfortable about participating in the process? Figure 7.2 shows a sample agenda of information that may be relevant to your audience.

MAKING YOUR PRESENTATION
▼

Effectively conducting a major presentation with multiple speakers requires that you execute a number of steps well. Based on experience in both delivering public speeches and helping clients prepare for them, I have compiled some helpful information about making your speech, having a dress rehearsal, using graphics and visual aids, and handling a question and answer session.

— FIGURE 7.2 —

SAMPLE AGENDA

8:00–8:30	Chief Executive Officer Jane Doe will discuss company history, structure, and strategic plan. (This will show the suppliers how they will fit in with your company's future.)
8:30–8:45	Chief Financial Officer John Smith will discuss sales history, financial stability, and supplier payment issues. (All suppliers want to be assured that you will be around for many years.)
8:45–9:00	Purchasing Manager Richard Roe will describe the products and services your company purchases and summarize its purchasing profile.
9:00–9:20	Plant Manager Susan Smith will discuss specific service issues, current operational practices, and expectations for the future.
9:20–9:35	Vice President of Sales William Jones will outline your company's sales future, product developments, marketplace pressures, and R&D.
9:35–10:05	Sourcing Program Manager James Cotton will provide detailed descriptions of the partnership process, next steps, expectations of suppliers, key dates, fairness of the process, and administrative information.
10:05–10:30	Question and answer session.

Hints, Tips, and Information

One communication training industry rule of thumb is to practice your presentation up to 20 times before you give it for real. This may seem excessive, but remember what is at stake. The risk of not practicing is that your style of presentation (or lack thereof) could diminish the power of your message.

USING A VIDEOCAMERA

One of the tactics I have used to teach public speaking is to have each participant deliver an impromptu speech in front of a videocamera. The next videotaped exercise involves a prepared speech. The videotape consistently shows a significantly more polished and professional presentation the second time around. Few people can look good if they are unprepared, and even the best are better with preparation.

Review the videotape for eye contact: The rule is never to talk unless you are looking at the audience. It is OK to look down at your notes or at the ceiling. It is *not* OK to talk while you do that. People tend to assume that if you cannot look at them while you talk, you are being dishonest. It's acceptable to regroup or find your place—as long as you pause while doing so.

Avoid nonwords such as *uh* and *um.* These are a common reflection of nervous energy and relay that you are not sure of your intended message. Watch and listen to yourself on the videotape, and then practice filling the gaps between words with silence. This will help the audience see you as a professional speaker and focus on your message.

Slides or graphics support can add immensely to a speech, but they can be distracting if you talk directly to the screen. Try looking at the screen, gathering your thoughts, and then turning back to the audience to begin speaking.

USING BODY LANGUAGE

People are convinced about a subject as much by how something is presented as by what is presented. Enthusiasm can be communicated in a number of ways—most effectively by varying your volume, pace, and pitch and using gestures to emphasize points.

Purposeful movement helps you make your point, whereas random movement distracts your audience. Try to avoid pacing, hand holding, pencil twirling, shifting, and directionless walking. Instead, walk toward people while making a point, move with confidence, and use pointers only to point at a visual aid.

By focusing on these points, you will be well on your way to delivering a solid, professional presentation. Of course, books have been written and schools established to teach public speaking, so any additional assistance or resources that you can corral to help you be a better speaker will be invaluable.

Holding a Dress Rehearsal

It is difficult to overemphasize the importance of the dress rehearsal. No matter how many times you may have practiced, going through the motions one last time as close to the live setting as possible—at the podium, with the microphone, etc.—is essential. You do not want the actual presentation to be the first time you practice handing over the microphone or stepping up on the risers. Some people may not have worked with a microphone before, and a dress rehearsal is the optimum time to try one out.

Finally, consider staying the night before in the hotel where you are holding the presentation so you will not have to worry about cars that don't start, commutes, and normal household responsibilities. Instead you can sleep a little later, eat breakfast, and be ready to greet your guests as they arrive.

Recommendations for Presentation Day

Relax. You have prepared long and hard for this day. Now it is time to execute. Although you have addressed the major tasks that need to be accomplished for this presentation, the following recommendations can maximize the effects of the day:

▼ Try this energy expansion exercise. Before you begin the presentation, practice by running through the first two minutes of your speech at double your normal energy rate. This will help you prime yourself for the actual presentation.

▼ Greet the guests. Beginning after your energy expansion exercise, open the doors to the meeting room and mingle. This is an optimum time to gather intelligence about specific suppliers and to begin gauging the overall level of interest in the program.

▼ Debrief your team. After everyone leaves, get together with the rest of your team and discuss the major points different suppliers brought up in informal conversations or at lunch. Note any concerns or objections that you will need to address, and then make sure someone addresses them.

▼ At lunch, make sure you and your executives don't sit together. Scatter among the different tables and suppliers. The conversations you will have over lunch may help you identify hungry suppliers as well as allow you to answer questions and address concerns.

▼ Make sure that the meeting room is easy to find. If necessary, work with hotel management to put up signs directing the suppliers to your meeting room.

▼ Check the facilities:

   – Have coffee, juice, and rolls available to the guests as they arrive. This sounds basic, but it is important to show your gratitude for your guests' time and efforts by being a gracious and attentive host.

   – Keep the room temperature between 70 and 75 degrees. If it becomes too hot or too cold, people will be more concerned with their comfort than with your speech.

- Check your audiovisual equipment. Test the microphone, slide projector, podium light, and any other equipment the night before the presentation. Forcing the hotel to set up the night before and test the equipment ensures that you will not have an emergency minutes or hours before the presentation.

- Confirm that everyone has a pencil and paper in case they wish to take notes.

- Confirm that the reservation desk is aware of any deals you work out with the hotel for room rates for your guests.

Using Graphics and Visual Aids

Effective visual aids will enhance your presentation. Multimedia technology has advanced to a point that most companies can develop highly creative, engaging graphics and sound effects to complement presentations. If you do not have this capability, I recommend researching local graphics companies that might be able to help you.

Guidelines for Answering Questions

A skillfully handled question and answer session will achieve several benefits for your company. In addition to giving the impression that you are a courteous and gracious host, this session will give you a chance to listen to suppliers' concerns and fine-tune your overall strategy for your sourcing program.

There are several techniques that the best public speakers consistently use in effectively handling questions. You can use the ones listed here to perform like a seasoned professional.

1. Repeat the question. Often, part of the audience is unable to hear the question that is asked. Repeating the question will give everyone the benefit of understanding your answer. In addition, repeating the question will give you a few moments to think about your answer. Finally, doing so gives control of the discussion back to you if you want to paraphrase or slightly rephrase the question. Politicians are masters of this "spin" control.

2. Never be confrontational. If someone is rude or asks an inappropriate question, do not lose your composure. Respond with "I understand your question, but I think we should cover that in person. Please stop by to see me at lunch. Thank you."

3. If you do not know the answer, say so. One thing that is worse than telling an audience that you do not know an answer is to give a wrong answer.

Take a moment to reflect on the question and explain that you will be glad to follow up, but you need to do additional research to answer the question properly. Make sure someone from your company writes down the question for future action.

4. Feel free to deflect questions. If someone asks a question that is better answered by someone else in your company, refer the question to that person. Be careful to warn the person by saying something like, "I understand your question, but I think Bob is better qualified to answer. Bob will you please answer ..." and then repeat the question for Bob to hear.

5. Explain that the suppliers will have the chance to ask questions on a one-to-one basis over lunch or on the phone.

Preparing a Take-Away Packet

Although the presentation itself and all the wonderful things you say will leave an impression on the audience, it is a good idea to summarize your presentation in the form of a booklet or take-away packet. Not only will this help the suppliers remember the key points of your presentation, but it will also do the following:

▼ It will help suppliers remember your words and ideas as they prepare their sales presentations.

▼ It will allow the attendees to share your presentation with other people in their company who were unable to attend.

▼ It will show your dedication to the partnership process and goals because you took the time to put your ideas in writing in a professional manner.

Your packet could include the following items:

▼ A letter from the president. Have the president of your company write a letter to the suppliers that sells the strategic alliance process, explains your excitement and dedication to working closer with them to reduce mutual costs and enhance customer service, thanks them for their efforts, and formally empowers the project leader and his or her team to negotiate for the company.

▼ Speech outlines. If you developed 35-mm or computer-generated slides for the presentation, you may want to reproduce them in this section to provide a visual summary of your presentation and its ideas. However, be sure to exclude any slides that you do not want the reader to have in writing, such as financial information or competitive analysis.

▼ Company brochures. Include product pictures, marketing brochures, research and development press releases, newspaper articles, customer testimonies, or other documents that will help the suppliers understand your business.

▼ Articles. Many magazines and periodicals have published articles that unveil, discuss, and explain the benefits and approach of supplier partnerships and strategic alliances. Including reprints of some articles in your take-away packet will further explain your approach to strategic alliances and will lend credibility from an outside source.

HANDLING ALTERNATIVE APPROACHES
▼

Although the presentation discussed in this chapter has proven effective in selling suppliers on the concept of supplier partnerships, there are times when you should take an alternative approach. Remember, having a presentation is not your interest. Rather, it is your position that the presentation will help persuade suppliers to take a strategic interest in your company and partnership approach. Your interest, however, can be satisfied in other, although less effective, ways.

Each of the following sections describes an alternative approach to announcing your supplier partnership process to suppliers. To make your decision regarding which approach to take, ask yourself the following questions:

▼ Will your company benefit if the CEO or President of a supplier company hears firsthand how you plan to implement long-term mutually beneficial partnerships?

▼ Will your company be able and willing to invest the resources in allowing you to present your message to suppliers in a professional atmosphere? Anything less could hurt your process.

▼ Are there any circumstances related to your company or any of your suppliers that might make it vital to communicate, face to face, the concepts that are driving your partnership process?

▼ How many suppliers do you need to communicate with? (If there are too many for individual phone calls and meetings, a presentation may be the best way to communicate face to face.)

Based on your answers to these questions and based on the desires of your co-workers and company management, you might consider the following alternatives to a supplier presentation:

Written Presentations

Even though you don't hold a presentation, you can still prepare the take-away packet. Include the same items discussed earlier. The benefit of this approach is that with considerably less expense and effort, you are able to communicate the basic ideas and concepts that you would in a full presentation. The main risks of this approach include the following.

▼ losing the competitive spirit that goes with having suppliers in the same field observe each other at the presentation

▼ losing the verbal presentation of the material.

Informal Presentations

In addition to producing a take-away packet, you might consider informal discussions with key or strategic suppliers. This discussion would be similar to the supplier visits discussed in Chapter 3, but could include alternate suppliers as well. The main benefit of this approach is that you can address directly any concerns of specific suppliers without the costs and efforts that accompany a supplier presentation. The glaring risk in this scenario is that you might not communicate with the "right" supplier. Part of the power of the supplier partnership process is the search for alternative suppliers. If you preselect suppliers to meet with before giving them a chance to hear your presentation, you might disqualify a supplier that could have been a powerful partner.

Using Letters and Phone Calls

You could implement an extended letter campaign followed up by phone calls. This method involves incorporating the same ideas communicated in the presentation in a letter format. This approach is the easiest and the least effective. The benefit of this approach is its low cost in terms of dollars and effort. The risk is that your letter will be given the same treatment much mail receives—none, and that your phone call will not go any further than a voice mail or written message that receives little attention. Although your cost is low, the likelihood is high that you will not be able to communicate your ideas effectively.

SUMMARY
▼

Regardless of how well you document and quantify your issues, you need the support of your suppliers and the cooperation of their top management to formulate an effective strategic alliance. The supplier presentation is the most effective and thorough method to win that support and top-level collaboration.

When planning the content of your speeches, your overriding concern should be "Why is this important to the listener?" The next most important ingredient for success is preparation. You must craft your message carefully and videotape your rehearsals of it. You must also plan the administrative details, such as invitation letters and venue.

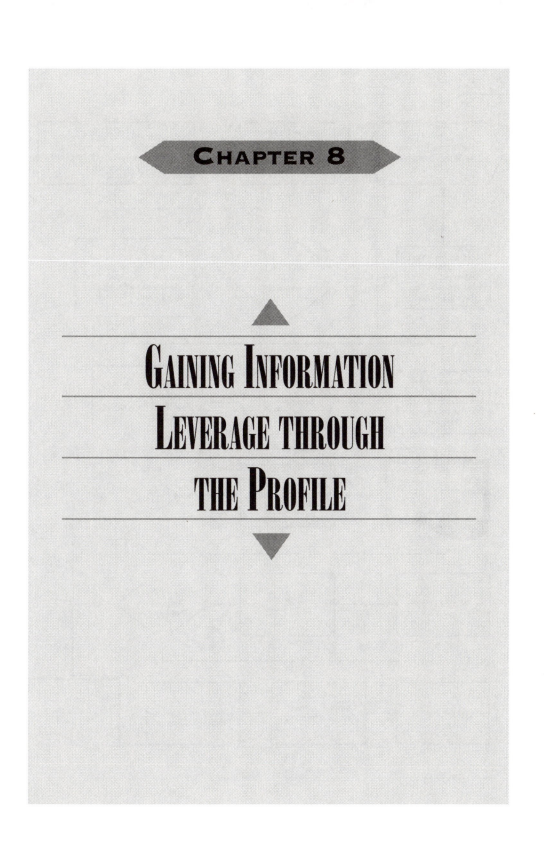

GAINING INFORMATION LEVERAGE THROUGH THE PROFILE

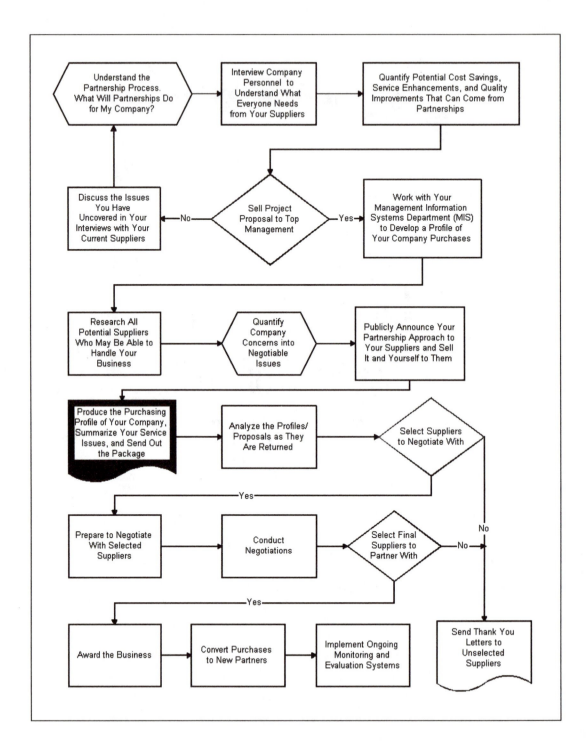

Ideally, as you have been preparing for the supplier presentation, practicing your speeches, calling up suppliers, writing them letters, and inviting them to the presentation, the MIS department has been working on your profile. The product area profiles are highly detailed requests for proposals: They contain detailed summaries of your purchases over the last year as well as questions and requirements regarding key organizational, operational, and strategic issues. Through the presentation, you have primed the suppliers to receive a summary of exactly what you buy in their product areas and what you are asking them to provide. The profile shows the suppliers exactly what you expect to buy annually and gives them the opportunity to make an intelligent, informed business decision about how much of your business they can handle.

In some circles, the profile is referred to as a request for proposal. It is an invitation to a supplier to bid, or propose, on supporting and supplying your business product and service needs. The profile is divided into two main sections. The first section details your expected future purchases, and the second section asks the supplier about the service and pricing issues you have identified in your interviews and issue development (Chapters 3 and 6). In this chapter, we will consider the importance of the profile, outline the specific contents of the profile, and provide examples of some of its key elements.

How the Profile Will Help You
▼

The supplier presentation explained your philosophy and approach to strategic alliances, proclaimed your commitment to your potential supplier partners, and motivated each supplier to be competitive in this process. In contrast, the profile is used to provide suppliers with a detailed picture of your business and serve as a common basis of comparison between suppliers. This is important for two reasons. First, in some ways, the profile is a stronger sales tool than the supplier presentation because it will give supplier executives actual data with which to make hard decisions. Most companies are hesitant to provide too much information to suppliers because they believe that this openness hurts their negotiating position. However, the process we are outlining provides a framework for increasing your leverage with suppliers by providing them with more information. By detailing every product purchase you make in the course of a normal year, you give suppliers everything they need to make informed business decisions regarding your account. Specifically, the profile can help you in the following ways:

▼ By showing the supplier all of your purchases, possibly in multiple commodity areas, you stand the best chance that a supplier executive will decide to invest strategically to get your business. This investment could come in the form of reduced profit margins and pricing levels, capital expenditures to expand the supplier's ability to service more of your business, and/or a commitment to react to your service issue requests with necessary top-level authorization.

▼ The profile can help you gain the suppliers' trust by giving them the chance to express their views, ideas, and concerns about the partnership process.

▼ It can help you gain a strong foundation for negotiation leverage by providing you initial offers from all competing suppliers in terms of pricing, service issue commitments, and quality levels—standards that all suppliers could be held to. My experience is that this is the most effective form of benchmarking.

▼ The profile will enable you to demonstrate to the suppliers that you are serious about developing a true alliance by showing them the multitude of service issues in which you are interested (i.e., it is not just a price negotiation). In addition, the amount of information you have provided to help the suppliers make a sound decision about your business will demonstrate your commitment.

Second, in the spirit of the strategic alliance or partnership you are implementing, providing accurate and sufficient information to the supplier is your single most important responsibility. This brings us to the Third Law of Partnerships:

> A partnership will ultimately be successful only to the degree that all vital information about your company and related purchases is communicated to suppliers during the negotiation process. Any significant factors omitted will surface in time and strain the relationship.

Providing Information in Your Profile

Traditionally, American manufacturers have been reluctant to share information with suppliers. The primary reason is mistrust—people know that suppliers also have relationships with their competitors and, intentionally or otherwise, shared information could end up in the wrong hands. Another common reason that companies can be reluctant to help suppliers understand their business is that suppliers are often viewed as opponents. The belief is that if a supplier wants some information, it must be for some subversive purpose. Finally, companies do not share valuable information with suppliers because the contacts occur at the purchasing agent/sales representative level. Senior executives are more likely to use this information to develop business opportunities or implement cost reductions.

The good news is that this attitude is changing. Successful manufacturers are finding ways to benefit by working more closely with suppliers. This book (and the profile, in particular) is an integral part of helping suppliers understand your business and allowing them to become informed partners.

You may want to include the following information in your profile:

▼ Seasonality of your demand

▼ Damage claim patterns

▼ Special orders

▼ Customer specifications

▼ Customizing or rework issues

▼ Marketing studies

▼ Sales forecast

▼ Long-range strategic plans

▼ Planned operations/manufacturing changes

▼ Environmental issues

▼ Computer files of engineering drawings

▼ Pending acquisitions or divestitures that you expect will change your purchasing habits (of course, leave out any confidential details as appropriate)

▼ Any special request you would make of a supplier who provides you products on an ongoing basis

▼ Any other information that will help suppliers make intelligent proposals.

ESTABLISHING THE CONTENTS OF YOUR PROFILE
▼

A profile is more than the typical request for proposal. You want to present detailed information about your company's interests and elicit the most valuable information possible from suppliers through their proposals. The following profile structure will help you achieve your goals.

1. *Letter from the president.* This is important because it underscores top management's commitment to the supplier relationship.

2. *Program timeline.* This will provide an overview of the major steps and how they are related in time.

3. *Instructions for completion.* This section will lay out each step, each section, and each action the supplier should take in filling out the profile. In addition, if this section is complete, it will reduce the number of further inquiries and delays.

4. *Supplier information.* In this section, request background information such as annual reports, financial statements, product brochures, quality manuals, etc.

5. *Strategic and philosophical issues.* It is critical to the success of a long-term relationship to align with suppliers that have common goals, strategies, and interests. In this section, you explain your commitment to supplier partnerships, what you hope to gain for you and the supplier, and your commitment to the process. Most important, you also ask the supplier about his or her views, commitments, and plans as they relate to this process. In addition, obtaining important information about the supplier's strategic plans will help you spot opportunities and formulate your negotiating strategy.

6. *Service and quality issues.* Although you will not define each issue in as much detail as you have quantified in Chapter 6, list the types of service issues that interest you. This will give suppliers a wide range in responding to you about their abilities, plans, and commitments.

7. *Pricing issues.* Although pricing is not the sole focus of your partnership, it is often the biggest single component of the lowest total cost equation. In this section, you want to gain general information and ask for specific proposals on price-related issues.

8. *Line item pricing.* In this section, you provide item-by-item details of purchases you expect to make in a one-year period. This will provide you with pricing information and will show the coverage that suppliers offer.

9. *Electronic summary explanation.* In addition to a hard copy version of your purchasing history, you may include an electronic version to allow the supplier to respond in a spreadsheet or other format online. This will allow you to analyze the supplier in greater detail. This is a fairly complicated procedure, however, and detailed instructions for suppliers are required.

10. *Proposal summary.* In this section, you give the supplier the opportunity to summarize the amount of business, by commodity, he or she is proposing to cover. This will help you prioritize the profiles as they return.

11. *Statement of confidentiality.* You will likely be providing sensitive information in the supplier profile. A statement of confidentiality is appropriate.

A Letter from the President

Your president's letter should do the following:

1. Sell the process to the suppliers.

2. List the main benefits to the suppliers in the partnership.

3. Re-emphasize top management's commitment to the process.

4. Give facts about the profile and the partnership process (i.e., next steps).

The Project Timeline

Many suppliers will be nervous about this process. Current suppliers will fear losing your business, whereas many new suppliers will be making the largest sales offer of their careers. They will be concerned about the timeframe of this process. For this reason, be conservative when estimating the calendar. If you think you will be ready to negotiate in one month, state two months in this timeline. If you think you will be ready to award the business in three months, state five months in this timeline. In addition, be careful to explain that the calendar may be changed based on conflicting schedules or unforeseen problems. Figure 8.1 shows a sample timeline.

— FIGURE 8.1 —

SAMPLE COMPANY SUPPLIER PARTNERSHIP PROGRAM TIMELINE

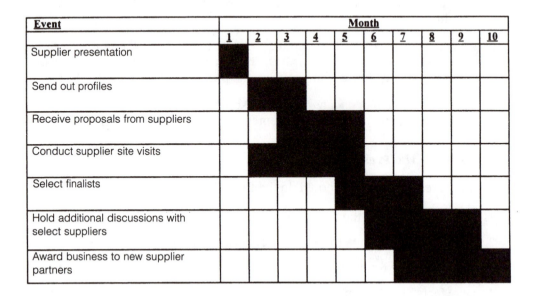

Instructions for Completing the Profile

Although this section will not provide any provocative ideas or thoughts, it will help you maintain a high level of similarity among the profiles you receive from the suppliers. If the profile is correctly developed, all responses should be in the same mode or format. This will minimize the number of phone calls you will receive while the suppliers attempt to fill out the profile. A sample of the instructions that you may include is shown in Figure 8.2.

— FIGURE 8.2 —

SAMPLE INSTRUCTIONS

We recognize that this profile is long and complex. Each of the issues presented in this profile is critical to us and our customers; therefore, we ask you to be as complete and thorough as possible. However, if a question is inappropriate for you and your company, skip that question and explain briefly your reason.

Please do the following in filling out this profile:

▼ Answer every question that applies to your business in as much detail as you can.

▼ Provide supporting materials when possible. Although written answers are helpful, brochures, reports, marketing materials, and annual reports will be of value to us.

▼ If you have any technical questions, please call _____ at our company at (XXX) XXX-XXXX for assistance.

▼ Please return your completed profile, along with four copies, to the following address no later than November 1, 1995:

> (Your name)
> (Your department)
> (Your company)
> (Your address)

▼ Since we are negotiating many commodity areas, it is possible that your proposal will be handled later in the process. For this reason, please do not interpret a delay in the process as a rejection of your offer.

Asking for Supplier Information

You should request key documents and information from the supplier. Although every supplier will not be able to provide every piece of information you request, it is important to ask for everything. Specific requested items include the following:

▼ Three years of audited financial statements (Public companies are required to publish annual reports.)

▼ Five customer references

▼ A list of customers with whom the supplier currently has similar partnerships

▼ Marketing brochures

▼ A copy of performance reports produced internally or provided to select customers

▼ Brochures or summaries of EDI capabilities

▼ Planned capital investments

▼ A copy of the quality control policy manual

▼ A copy of the environmental policy

Strategic and Philosophical Issues

In this part of the profile, you will provide the supplier with a summary of your intentions for the supplier partnership process. In addition, you will ask a number of questions that will give the supplier a chance to express his or her views. A sample introduction and a list of possible questions to include are shown in Figure 8.3.

— **FIGURE 8.3** —

SAMPLE INTRODUCTION AND QUESTIONS

Partnerships have been defined in many ways. Many companies have exploited partnerships as a way to achieve higher discounts from suppliers. This is in effect a one-sided partnership. We recognize that this view of partnerships is short sighted and of limited benefit. We look for partnerships that will help us and our suppliers face the competitive forces in today's marketplace. We are committed to continuously improving the service and quality we provide to our mutual customers. In addition, by working together, we can take cost out of the system through paperwork reductions, computerization, engineering cooperation, and other methods. Just as many American companies were left behind in the 1970s because they missed the opportunity to focus on quality, the companies that fail to unite and commit to their suppliers will fall behind in the 1990s.

This is our basic philosophy in terms of strategic alliances and supplier partnerships. The following questions are provided so you can express your philosophy as well as your strategic plans for the future. By answering these questions, we can determine the best fit and approach to working together in the future.

Questions: (In the actual document, leave plenty of space between questions for answers.)

1. What are your major strategic plans for the next 5 to 10 years?

2. How do strategic alliances and customer partnerships fit into your plans?

3. What benefits do you expect to reap as a result of partnering with our company?

4. Do you have any strategic alliances in place today?

5. What aspects of our company would make us your best customer?

6. What plans do you have for capital investments?

7. Would any of your capital investments be directed toward business you might do with us?

8. What plans do you have to introduce any new product lines?

9. What plans do you have to acquire any other companies in the future?

10. What concerns do you have as we enter into this strategic alliance process?

Service and Quality Issues

In this section, you provide the supplier the opportunity to communicate some of his or her specific abilities to meet your service needs. By presenting your issues and concerns in an open-ended format, you stand a better chance of receiving the supplier's unbiased approach. For example, if you are discussing quality certification, instead of presenting your position on how the supplier should certify shipments to you, simply ask the supplier to discuss his or her method and give you a copy of his or her policy manual. A sample service and quality issues section is shown in Figure 8.4.

— FIGURE 8.4 —

SAMPLE SERVICE AND QUALITY ISSUES SECTION

Service and quality are critical parts of our corporate strategy and are key to our competitive advantage in the marketplace. Below we have provided space for you to explain your approach to service and quality in a number of areas. Please describe your specific capabilities and proposal regarding our service and quality interests, as outlined in this profile. In addition, please include any brochures, manuals, or policies that might help us understand your operations.

Service Questions: (In the actual document, leave plenty of space between questions for answers.)

1. Describe your commitment to quality and service and how your top management and sales representatives will monitor and identify service opportunities.

2. Describe quality programs you have in place in your company. Are all of your employees active participants in these programs?

3. Do you have quality programs in place with your other customers? Indicate who these programs are with and how long they have been in place.

4. What types of management reporting programs, designed to enhance quality, do you have in place? Provide examples of these reports.

5. It is important to have a dedicated customer service representative available who can handle the day-to-day operations with our company. Over the years, we have learned that someone dedicated to the program develops a better understanding of our needs and those of our customers. Such individuals are willing to share their own thoughts and ideas to improve service and efficiencies. Provide the name(s) of a contact that will have direct responsibility for our company.

6. Quality issues cannot be one sided. To better understand your needs and those of your employees, provide us with ideas or improvements that we can examine to improve the quality of service to you and ultimately to our customers.

7. What certification methods and procedures do you use to ensure that products which leave your facility work and are of the highest quality?

8. Does your company adhere to ISO 9000 standards? Specifically, which standards have you been certified for?
   — ISO 9001
   — ISO 9002
   — ISO 9003
   — ISO 9004

9. If a substandard or broken product were shipped to us, how would you propose to rectify the situation?

10. In many cases, inferior quality is designed into the system. Describe your expertise and commitment to work with us to review processes, product designs, blueprints, engineering issues, and other technical issues to develop mutually beneficial solutions that increase quality and reduce costs.

11. What other quality issues do you think we should address as we enter into a long-term relationship?

12. For the years listed, what have been your absolute ontime performance ratios? (We use the term *absolute* to refer to the total number of late shipments divided by the total number of shipments without regard to early shipments.)

    1990 _____ %
    1991 _____ %
    1992 _____ %
    1993 _____ %
    1994 _____ %

13. Please describe how you calculated this percentage.

14. What ontime performance will you guarantee to our company over the next five years? _____ %

Inventory

One of the key areas we must manage is inventory. We continually try to balance the cost of carrying inventory with customer service and responsiveness. This is a key area we can focus on in our partnership to reduce our mutual costs as well as to address key customer service issues. Please answer the following related questions in as much detail as possible:

1. Stockouts and back orders can cause serious production problems and can lead us to buy more inventory at a given time because we are not able to trust that our supplier will have stock when we place an order. What programs or ideas do you have that could reduce this risk for us and our mutual customers?

2. We understand that regardless of how well each of our companies plan, shortages may occur for some products. How do you handle these situations? Specifically, do you allocate products to all customers, fulfill orders completely until stock runs out, take care of special customers only, or do you use another method?

3. How would you propose to handle stockouts or shortages under our strategic alliance or partnership?

4. Describe your warehousing capacity and how that could affect our ability to respond to our customers quickly.

5. What ideas do you have to optimize our inventory levels at our company locations to balance inventory carrying costs with customer service?

Communication

Communication is a vital link in strategic alliances. The better we communicate with each other, the better we can understand each other's business on an ongoing basis. This will help us continue to formulate ideas and innovations, thus improving efficiencies and reducing costs throughout our relationship. Please answer the following questions regarding communication.

1. What ideas or innovations do you have that will enhance the communication process?

2. Communications at all levels can improve mutual operations and strategic focus. What channels of communication do you think would be critical to keep open between our companies as we continue to work together?

3. Technology has provided innovative and efficient ways for companies and people to communicate. What technologies do you currently employ to enhance communication, and what technologies do you plan to implement?

4. Tracking orders and shipments is important in our planning and customer service. Please provide contact names and telephone number(s) of your customer service personnel. Are you willing to dedicate a customer service representative to our company for the day-to-day operations of our business?

5. To reduce the amount of time spent on the telephone tracking orders and shipments, we support the use of automatic telecommunications to keep us and our customers informed of the location of shipments. What suggestions do you have to develop this program further?

6. In addition to informal communications, we might benefit from periodic meetings with representatives from different levels, at which we can discuss performance, progress, additional opportunities, changes, and other topics. What ideas do you have in this area?

7. Are there any other topics in the area of communications that you would like to discuss?

Operations

There are many issues that determine your efficiency and profitability. We would like to understand more about your operations. We understand that a true alliance requires that each company study the other partner. In this way, we can better work together to reduce mutual costs and enhance mutual efficiencies. Please answer the following questions regarding your operations.

1. What is your company's unionization status?

2. What process do you use to plan production?

3. What types of automation do you employ at your company?

4. What plans do you have to improve the quality and efficiency of your production process and the speed and accuracy of your distribution process, or to minimize the paperwork and ordering lead times at your company?

5. What types of information could we provide to you that could help your company reduce costs? (forecasting, detailed product specifications, customer expectations, production plans, etc.)

6. Based on your knowledge of our company or our industry, what ideas do you have today that could be implemented as part of our alliance to reduce mutual costs, lead times, or quality problems?

7. Please discuss your current capacity and related peak/nonpeak issues. In addition, please list any steps we could take to optimize your operations in this regard.

8. Many processes have setup costs in addition to the variable costs of production. How does this apply to your company, and what efficiencies can we help you achieve?

9. What operational issues do you think we should address in addition to the ones already listed?

Claims/Returns

Clearly, one goal of our partnership is to minimize any need to return products. However, some quality problems will slip through the system, some shipments will be damaged by the supplier, and some random acts will continue to make this an important issue.

1. Please describe, in as much detail as possible, your current claims and returns handling procedures.

2. Please tell us what your returns and claims policy will be for our company.

3. To minimize the number of claims processed and to avoid the paperwork that is a part of these claims, up to what dollar level will you settle a claim of our company without requiring claim submission? $_____

4. For some products, it makes sense to return the shipment to you for rework, whereas for other products it may be more economical to dispose of the product. What are your policies and views on this issue?

5. For damaged products that do not need to be returned to you, how would you propose to handle disposal?

6. What programs have you instituted with other customers to handle returns and claims more effectively?

7. What ideas do you have to minimize returns and claims?

Training

Our company believes that a sustainable competitive advantage is to have employees who are empowered with training, knowledge, and a bias for change.

1. Describe your company's training philosophy.

2. Specifically, what training classes, facilities, videos, binders, books, or other items does your company offer to its employees or customers?

3. Describe the following:

   ▼ Training facilities
   ▼ Training classes
   ▼ Training video library
   ▼ Training library
   ▼ Charges you would apply to our company training services or materials

4. As we begin our alliance, what ideas do you have to train our engineers, line workers, top management, buyers, customer service representatives, and other personnel to use your services and products?

EDI

Through the use of electronic data interchange (EDI), both our company and our suppliers have the opportunity to reduce paperwork, increase access to tracking and stocking level data, conduct electronic ordering and invoicing, and streamline other areas. In answering the following questions, please indicate your abilities, strategic plans, and specific ideas for our company in regard to EDI.

1. Describe your current EDI capabilities.

2. What EDI programs are you currently ready to install at our company locations?

3. What technical assistance programs do you offer? How would you train our company personnel to maximize utilization of EDI?

4. Our company would ultimately like to have a paperless system, including ordering, invoicing, payment, on-hand inventory levels, etc. List customers for whom you implemented this type of system and describe how it works.

5. List customers for whom you have installed EDI, including the date of installation.

6. List any additional programs or procedures that we can implement to further minimize paperwork and other non-value-adding tasks. Some examples may include automatic preassigning of pro numbers or claims processing via EDI.

7. Some of our locations may not currently have the equipment to run all of your EDI applications. So that all our company locations can benefit from access to EDI, what ideas and recommendations do you have for providing this service to the unequipped user?

8. Provide any additional thoughts or literature you have concerning EDI.

Customer References

Our company industries can only become partners with suppliers who understand and actively pursue excellent service. Please describe your commitment to quality service and how top management and sales representatives will monitor and identify service opportunities. In addition, list five references that we could call to discuss your service history and commitment.

References:

Name: _____   Title: _____

Company: _____   Phone #: (   )_____

Name: _____   Title: _____

Company: _____   Phone #: (   )_____

Name: _____   Title: _____

Company: _____   Phone #: (   )_____

Name: _____   Title: _____

Company: _____   Phone #: (   )_____

Name: _____   Title: _____

Company: _____   Phone #: (   )_____

Pricing Issues

Although you should never focus exclusively on price, material pricing and price-related issues are often the biggest drivers of the total cost equation. Pricing issues can include payment terms, payment methods, price increases or decreases over the life of an agreement, pricing new parts not in a contract, and anything else that affects the final cost that you pay for materials.

The sample shown in Figure 8.5 will help you get started on an appropriate pricing section for your company.

— **FIGURE 8.5** —

SAMPLE PRICING SECTION

The ability to avoid unanticipated change in costs is critical for our company. Similarly, you can benefit by having clear and reliable projections of future business volume and revenue. Thus, our company and its preferred suppliers must develop agreements that allow for only planned changes in purchasing costs.

1. What is your proposal for ensuring a stable financial planning horizon for both our company and your own company?

2. Please indicate the maximum percentage increase you propose over each of the next five years. Please circle the respective percentage increase cap for each year.

Year 1	0 1 2 3 4 5
Year 2	0 1 2 3 4 5
Year 3	0 1 2 3 4 5
Year 4	0 1 2 3 4 5
Year 5	0 1 2 3 4 5

3. What have been your average price changes over the past five years? Have your prices risen or fallen?

4. What terms of payment are you willing to offer our company as a strategic partner?

5. Describe your overall pricing method. Include any part the following play in your pricing: percent off list prices, quantity discounts, cost plus, indexed formulas.

6. Exactly how have you determined our pricing? What were the five most important factors, in order of importance?

USING COMPUTER DISKETTES FOR PRICING PROFILES

Consider asking your suppliers to use computer diskettes for line item pricing. Doing so can offer many benefits to you and the supplier. The supplier will be able to manipulate data in a spreadsheet and thus understand the data better. The supplier may also be able to upload the data into the pricing system, thus saving time and increasing accuracy. Your company will receive information in a computer file that is ready for analysis through a database or spreadsheet software. Computer, as opposed to manual, analysis saves time and allows more complete financial analysis.

If you decide to pursue this option, there are several points to keep in mind:

▼ Write instructions carefully so that there is no confusion on the part of the user.

▼ Offer the files in a computer format that is widely used, such as Lotus 1-2-3® or an ASCII text file.

▼ Provide a hard copy for reference that is printed and sorted exactly as the computer file is viewed on screen.

▼ If your software allows, protect the cells or fields that contain the bidding information so that the supplier cannot inadvertently change the pricing specifications, quantities, etc.

▼ Have another person in your company attempt to follow your diskette instructions prior to sending the profile to suppliers. This extra review will help work any bugs out of your system.

▼ Think ahead about how you will be analyzing the data from suppliers. Plan a computer format that will allow you to perform this analysis repetitively with multiple suppliers.

Historical Purchasing Summary and the Request for Proposal

This is the meat of the profile. Work with your MIS support person and generate a report that contains the following information:

▼ Product code

▼ Product description

▼ Annual purchase quantity

▼ Average order size.

Provide field headings with blanks so the supplier can write in his or her proposal:

▼ Lead time offered

▼ Base price offered

▼ Discounted price offered

▼ Annual total dollars.

A sample introduction for this section is shown in Figure 8.6. In addition to the data report, you might include a number of other charts, graphs, or explanations to help the supplier anticipate your purchasing patterns and habits. Omission of any facts or patterns of your purchasing can seriously challenge your ability to negotiate a true and successful long-term partnership. You might include the following:

▼ Seasonality charts showing the volume purchased by month

▼ Descriptions of the commodities listed in your profile, including any specifications that relate to each of the individual line items

▼ Geographic maps showing the volume purchased by each of your locations, by commodity if appropriate

▼ Plant layouts that may help the supplier understand your business

▼ Product blueprints for specialty items.

— FIGURE 8.6 —

SAMPLE INTRODUCTION FOR HISTORICAL PURCHASING DETAIL AND
REQUEST FOR PROPOSAL SECTION

Beginning on the next page is a report detailing every purchase we have made in the past year for the listed products and services. Whether you respond electronically or by hand on the hard copy, please provide the following information for each product you propose to handle over the next five years or so with our company:

Lead time: Expressed in days, please quantify the elapsed time from the point that we place an order to the time we would receive the product at our dock.

Base price offered: Expressed in dollars, this would be the catalog or list price for the item.

Discounted price offered: Expressed in dollars, in the context of our long-term partnership, what is the street price you would offer to us?

Annual extended dollars: Expressed in dollars, and to avoid any misunderstandings, please extend the price for the total quantity listed on the report.

In addition, we have provided a graph showing the seasonality of our purchasing and a map showing our major locations. It is our intention to provide you with all the knowledge and data necessary to make an informed business decision about how to handle and price our business. If there is additional information we could provide to help you in this process, or if you have any questions, please call our technical support hot line number: (000) 000-0000; ask for Mr. Jones.

Proposal Summary

This section is included for *your* convenience. To help you prioritize the returned proposals, ask the supplier to total the number of your annual purchases he or she proposes to handle. In your profile, replace the #,### symbol with the actual total quantity of all products purchased in the commodity area(s) presented in the profile. Figure 8.7 is an example of a supplier proposal summary.

— **FIGURE 8.7** —

SAMPLE SUPPLIER PROPOSAL SUMMARY

The following section is designed to give our company a hard copy summary of your proposal in terms of the number of orders covered and the related total cost. Please complete the following table as a summary of your bids on purchasing history detailed in section 9. PLEASE NOTE THAT BY BIDDING ON A PRODUCT, WE WILL ASSUME THAT YOU CAN SERVICE IT 100%. THUS, FOR THIS SUMMARY, SIMPLY ADD ALL PURCHASE QUANTITIES AND THE EXTENDED DOLLAR BIDS FOR THE PRODUCTS THAT YOU PROPOSED. Please return this page with your other proposed materials.

(B)	(A)	(A)/(B)
Actual Number of Product Quantities for FY 1994–95	Total Quantity of Product Purchases Proposed On	Percent of FY 1992–93 Purchases Proposed
#,### _____	_____%	

Total Cost for Proposed Purchases: $_____

Statement of Confidentiality

Considering your company's sensitivity to competitors, you may decide to include a statement of confidentiality in your profile. This statement will bind the suppliers not to disclose any of the facts contained in the profile to other companies without your express and written approval. Most likely, your legal council will have a standard nondisclosure agreement or statement of confidentiality, but Figure 8.8 shows one example that you may customize for your company.

— **FIGURE 8.8** —

SAMPLE STATEMENT OF CONFIDENTIALITY

The documents, statements, facts, reports, graphs, questions, and other forms of communication included in this profile are presented to you so you can make an informed decision regarding our business. In the wrong hands, these documents could be used to our detriment. Based on that fact, please respect our request for confidentiality and do not allow anyone outside of your company to review or copy any of the materials contained within the profile. If you need to review some data items with another company in the course of proposing on our business, please call me directly to discuss the issue.

If this is not amenable to you, please return the profile to our company.

If you agree to act according to this nondisclosure statement, please sign the following and return this page with your proposal. Thank you for your understanding.

Understood and signed: _____

CUSTOMIZING YOUR PROFILE
▼

Now that we have seen an example of a purchasing profile, we can review additional items that could be incorporated into your profile as appropriate.

Targeting Commodity Groups

Although it may be easier to include every commodity you buy in all the profiles you send out, you may find the printing costs prohibitive. Many suppliers can support only one or two major commodities. For example, although Maintenance, Repair, and Operations (MRO) is provided by companies like W. W. Grainger, C&H Distributors, McMaster Carr, and Global, these companies do not provide raw materials for your products. Your task is to separate your purchases by commodity group. Examples of commodity groups include the following:

▼ MRO, Heating, Ventilation, and Air Conditioning (HVAC), lawn care and maintenance, building security

▼ Plastics, including plastic molders, vacuum injections, and injection molding

▼ Steel

▼ Electrical suppliers

▼ Engineered items

▼ Electronic equipment

▼ Engineered or manufactured parts

▼ Corrugated and packaging

▼ Shipping and transportation, including less than truckload, truckload, small package, rail, and international

▼ Forms and printed materials, office supplies, computer supplies, etc.

▼ Fabrics and sewing

▼ Subcontracted, premanufactured parts

▼ Metal fabricators

▼ Capital equipment and machinery

▼ Airline tickets and travel arrangements

▼ Temporary labor services.

This list is by no means exclusive or complete. It is provided only as the starting point. In addition, if you do have suppliers that provide more than one commodity, there is nothing wrong with combining multiple commodities into one profile. For example, you may include HVAC, lawn care, cleaning services, and security in the same profile because they have to do with MRO-type services, and some companies provide more than one of those individual services (e.g., a cleaning company that also does lawn care). Although you may wish to divide your purchasing data into different commodity groups, how far you go in that area is left to your best judgment.

Consolidating Part Descriptions

Another item to be aware of as you prepare your profile data is consistency. If the supplier is to understand exactly what you are asking for, you must provide consistent part numbers and part descriptions for what you purchase. In other words, if you buy brooms and in one line you call a broom *broom* and in the next line you call it *brooms,* and in the next *brm,* the supplier will not understand exactly how many brooms you buy. Split the database between all the buyers and have them consolidate as many of the part numbers and part descriptions as possible. This will give your suppliers the best understanding of what you buy.

Defining Units of Measure

One of the most significant misunderstandings in a purchasing project can occur due to poorly defined units of measure and inconsistent units of measure. Make sure that the unit of measure that is listed for every purchase is correct and is explained enough so the supplier will know what you are asking for.

Assuring Your Profile's Reasonability

When you have prepared your profile, consolidated the part descriptions, checked over the units of measure, and split the purchases between commodity groups, do a summary for your profile or ask your MIS department to help you with it. You need a summary so you can do reasonability checks of your database. For example, if you know that you buy about $7,000 worth of MRO per year but in your database summary you discern $6,590,000 worth of purchases annually, you know that there is a problem. The problem could pertain to units of measure, quantities, time period that the database includes, annualization factors, or other culprits. If you do find areas that are unreasonable, print out the details and review them with an MIS representative and the appropriate buyer to figure out how to correct the data. Most likely, you will find either a specific record that is out of line, a group of purchases that have an incorrect unit of measure, or some mathematical problem that can be fixed.

Benefiting from Your Company's Growth

If the history that you receive from MIS is not current—in other words, if you get last year's history—and you know what your expected growth is, incorporate that figure into your data and increase the quantity appropriately. Doing so is in your best interest and in the supplier's best interest. It doesn't do anybody any good to underestimate your purchases in growing areas or declining areas. Different products may have different profitability areas or different economies of scales for different suppliers, and the mix of what you buy could be crucial. As much as possible, ensure accuracy by including growth factors in your data.

Using Your Colleagues' Expertise

There is no reason why you need to become an expert in information systems and databases. Although this is a worthwhile area to study, it is not inherently useful to develop all of these information needs and reports on your own. Get an information expert involved early, especially if there is somebody who is enthusiastic and technically competent. Such experts do not have to be the best in terms of competency, but if they are excited, enthusiastic, and eager to help you, they will be great teammates. Invite this MIS person into your project early and ask him or her to help you out. Explain each of the informational needs that you will encounter (including the profile), the supplier presentation slides, the summarization and presentation of the results of your interviews (see Chapter 3), the savings analysis that you will provide to your top management after the project is finished, and ongoing monitoring systems to ensure that the suppliers are maintaining their performances, pricing, and service levels.

OTHER PROFILE TOPICS
▼

The following topics provide additional opportunities to customize your profile. Regardless of whether an issue relating to your company is addressed in this chapter, any item that a supplier would need to know about your company to make an informed decision about your business should be included.

Understanding Suppliers' Strategic Plans

One of the more important aspects of this process is to understand the investments that the supplier is making in its future and its customers. You need to understand whether the supplier is a cutting-edge company that will continue to develop state-of-the-art improvements in its product and services, or a company that has found a niche, is happy with where it is, and is not investing significantly in developing new products and services.

Questioning a Potential Supplier's Partnership Track Record

You can ask general questions about partnerships and how suppliers have approached them in the past, how they view them now, what they look forward to in a partnership with you, and what concerns they may have about how you are proceeding with your partnership. This is important because it will show the supplier's enthusiasm (or lack of it) to become a partner with your company as well as what the supplier is nervous about. Maybe the supplier is nervous about your request for a price cut; about the time commitment in a five-year contract; or about being consolidated out of your supplier group. Understanding what the supplier is concerned about will be an important negotiation tool.

You are now ready to send out your profile to suppliers. Review the following summary of the basic points to include in your profile.

SUMMARY
▼

In this chapter, we reviewed the development and promulgation of a profile of your company's purchasing and service needs. To maximize the benefits of the profile, keep the following points in mind:

▼ How the profile will help you

  – The most compelling reason to prepare a profile is summed up in the Third Law of Partnerships: A partnership will ultimately be successful only to the degree that all vital information about your company and related purchases is communicated to the suppliers during the negotiation process. Any significant factors omitted will surface in time and strain the relationship.

▼ Consider the following sections for your profile:

  – A letter from the president
  – Program timeline
  – Instructions for completion
  – Supplier information
  – Strategic and philosophical issues
  – Service and quality issues
  – Pricing issues
  – Line item pricing
  – Electronic summary explanation
  – Proposal summary
  – Statement of confidentiality.

▼ Another point to consider is having the supplier price your purchases on diskette. This will help you immensely in analyzing the proposals.

▼ To customize your profile to your company needs, consider the following:

- Develop customized profiles for each specific commodity group. By doing this, you can ask questions specific to that industry and avoid awkward questions that apply to other areas.

- Be sure to define correctly all units of measure for each purchase you summarize.

- After everything is put together, review the profile to make sure it is reasonable.

- Incorporate growth plans into your purchases. For example, if you expect to grow by 10% in the coming year, reflect that fact in your purchasing data.

▼ In addition to these customization ideas, additional points to keep in mind include the following:

- Include questions to help you understand the strategic direction of the supplier.

- Design a set of questions to address the supplier's past service records and how the supplier intends to improve in the future.

CHAPTER 9

EVALUATING SUPPLIER PROPOSALS

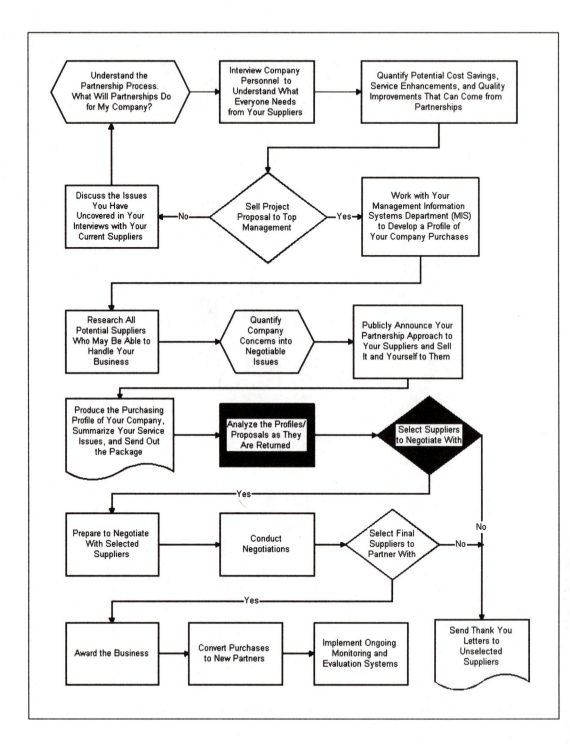

Within three weeks after you send out your profiles, you can expect initial returns from your suppliers. Although each person on your team could review and analyze each proposal you receive, in this chapter we will discuss methods to summarize the supplier proposals and thus streamline the process. Your goal is twofold. First, you want to pick the best suppliers to negotiate with. The only way to do this is to compare the suppliers in terms of quality, service, and pricing issues. Second, you want to manage this process to maximize support from the rest of your team. You can best accomplish this goal by including your team in the analysis process. Both of these goals are achieved by summarizing each supplier's proposal (which details the supplier's capabilities and offers pertaining to your service concerns), and comparing each supplier's pricing structure.

How to Decide Where to Begin
▼

Although it might be overwhelming to consider analyzing every profile you receive from suppliers, it is not so intimidating if you analyze the proposals one commodity area at a time. Use the following critical factors to determine which commodity areas to attack first:

- ▼ Areas with the most opportunity
- ▼ Areas with the greatest dollar volume
- ▼ Areas critical to your company
- ▼ Areas with contracts about to expire.

Identifying Areas with the Most Opportunity

There is nothing like success to motivate you and your team. For this reason, begin with an area that is likely to provide strong results for your company. Normally, dollar savings is the first characteristic that comes to mind when you want to display your success to the rest of your team and your company. Factors that can indicate significant opportunity for a specific area include the following:

- ▼ Multiple suppliers used when a core group of suppliers might be appropriate
- ▼ A large range of prices charged for similar products by different suppliers

151

▼ A new competitive atmosphere in the market

▼ A particular supplier that is hungry for your business.

Although dollar savings can be dramatic, there may be other issues that are more critical or conspicuous within your company. Choose the group of suppliers who will be able to address that area instead of price alone. For example, if there is a product that is difficult to purchase due to high demand or low supply, you might begin with that area to secure the products your company will need in the coming years.

A CASE EXAMPLE

One dramatic example is of a fertilizer company that ships 80% of its products in a two-month window every year. One of the products the company ships is anhydrous ammonia, which is considered a hazardous material by the United States Department of Transportation (DOT). To ship this product legally, a pressurized glass-lined bottle trailer is required. This is the same type of trailer used to haul petroleum. As you might expect, as the busy season approaches, the company's transportation department is forced to scramble to find carriers willing to stop hauling petroleum, clean their trailers, and ship anhydrous ammonia. At the beginning of the partnership process, this was perceived within the company as a reason not to enter into long-term agreements. The thought was, "We cannot rely on one or two carriers; we need to be able to source trailers wherever we can find them." As it turned out, by negotiating for long-term partnership relationships, the company was able to source all of its shipping needs during the off season, for the next three to five years. That one success set the stage for company-wide support of the rest of the partnership process. The transportation manager was relieved that he no longer had to spend the majority of his day sourcing trucks on a day-to-day basis. Instead, he was able to focus on managing load consolidations, conducting service enhancement projects, and supporting the rest of the company in negotiating for other commodity areas.

Reviewing Areas with the Greatest Dollar Volume

In the absence of areas that would provide "home runs," negotiate the areas early in the process that command the largest share of your company's annual purchasing volume. In Chapter 10, we will review factors to consider in inviting specific suppliers for negotiation.

Selecting Areas Critical to the Company

When you have a number of high-cost areas, consider choosing the commodity that is most critical to the product your company manufactures or distributes.

Examining Areas with Contracts about to Expire

Consider areas with contracts in place that will expire within the next year. Work to avoid last-minute negotiations whenever possible. The ability to plan, negotiate, convert to the new supplier, and set up a monitoring system depends on sufficient time.

GENERATING ANALYSIS REPORTS FROM YOUR SUPPLIER PROFILES
▼

Some suppliers may cover multiple commodity areas; to avoid duplication of work, prepare each supplier's complete proposal analysis when you come to the first commodity area he or she services. Then include a copy of the analysis in each commodity binder for that supplier.

The following reports will form the basis for your analysis. Each report will help you understand what each individual supplier is offering your company. As with the historical data, you might find that your MIS department can provide significant assistance in this process. As soon as you develop each report and have the information for a given supplier, distribute the reports to your negotiating team. This will give your team members as much time as possible to review supplier data.

Developing a Profile Control Log

The first report to develop in your analysis of the profiles is the profile control log. Although this report may not provide insight into the proposal of a specific supplier, it will help you organize your analysis and maintain a grasp of each commodity area addressed in the proposal.

Figure 9.1 is a sample profile control log report. The fields you might consider tracking for each proposal you receive include the following:

Field	Description
Code	A unique code that you can use to link computer database tables and to identify specific records.
Supplier company name	
Primary commodity area served	This will help you summarize the population of proposals received by commodity group, an important tool in gauging the coverage each group has received and which ones require additional follow-up with alternative suppliers.
Secondary commodity area served	The supplier may service more than one of your segregated commodity areas.
Supplier contact name	The person at the supplier who you should direct communications and questions through.
Supplier contact title	
Supplier contact phone number	
Supplier address	
Information not included in the proposal	Some proposals do not arrive complete. Document any items not included. Most often, items that are not submitted include company financial statements (for private companies), bids on diskette (for noncomputerized companies), and company brochures.

— FIGURE 9.1 —

YOUR COMPANY

PARTNERSHIP IMPLEMENTATION PROJECT

CORRUGATED PROFILE CONTROL

Control Number	Supplier Name	Date of Receipt	Contact	Contact Title	Contact Phone Number	Portion Not Received
5	AAA Boxes Company	9/13/94	JoAnna Van Amiga	President	(815) 555-4357	
3	American Box Inc.	9/01/94	John Sherman	Director of National Accounts	(800) 555-8923	
1	Boxes R Us	9/10/94	Dan Musielski	Plant Manager	(312) 555-1234	Did not include financial statements
2	Corrugated Manufacturers	9/07/94	Kevin Spengel	Vice President of Sales	(312) 555-0100	No company brochures
4	Packaging Systems	9/12/94	Mike Dobbs	Sales Representative	(312) 555-7500	Did not put pricing on diskette
6	Shipping Systems	9/13/94	"Honest Joe"	President	(708) 555-4321	

Creating the Executive Summary Report

The next report to develop is the executive summary of each supplier's proposal. Because it contains high-level quantitative information about the supplier and a qualitative summary of the supplier's service and quality issues, this report will give your team members a one-page synopsis of each proposal.

Figure 9.2 is a sample executive summary report. You might include the following information in this report. However, some of the items included may not be necessary for your company; therefore, you need to work with your group to develop an executive summary that addresses your needs and concerns.

Item to Summarize	Description
Code	By placing the code in this database table, you can link this table with the profile control table and avoid double input.
Company information	This information, captured in the profile control table, can be included in the report. The goal of this executive summary is to reiterate all the information regarding a supplier's proposal on one page.
Primary commodity area summary	You might go into more detail than in the profile regarding this information. Specifically, list the dollar amount and the percentage of line items covered by the supplier. In addition, you might include other indicators of supplier capacity, such as the number of locations the supplier has, what percentage of the supplier's total annual sales your company would represent, or total units produced annually.
Secondary commodity area summary	Same information as above, except for the second product type the supplier services.
Quantitative service commitments	In this section, you may summarize some key indicators of the supplier's past and promised performance, including

- Ontime delivery
- Back-order percentage
- Damaged goods and returns
- Damage claim resolution time frame
- Quality goals and rework percentage
- Specification adherence standards
- ISO 9000 or other quality standard certifications the supplier has qualified for.

Strategic plan summary	Summarize the supplier's response to your strategic plan questions in the profile. Specifically, include any intentions for capital investments, growth plans, specific mention of partnerships, commitments to quality, etc.

Partnership concerns and expectations

If the supplier lists any concerns about the partnership process in the profile, summarize them here. You should confront these concerns up front, thus demonstrating your commitment to a true "win/win" partnership, not just higher discounts. Typical concerns include

- Some companies use partnerships to achieve better pricing.
- Some companies have good ideas, but the people setting up the partnerships do not have the authority or support to implement a true partnership.

Supplier differentiation

What aspects of the supplier set it apart from its competitors?

EDI capabilities

List the supplier's capabilities in terms of specific EDI functions. In addition, summarize any plans for future development as well as any comments the supplier made in the profile about his or her willingness to help install EDI at your company.

Pricing summary	Although this is not a detailed list of supplier prices, you can summarize the supplier's pricing as a whole. For example, you can characterize the supplier's proposal as aggressive, high, competitive, or incomplete or explain some aspect of the supplier's pricing methodology.
Current supplier relationship	Summarize any dealings or relationships you have had in the past with the supplier. This may be important if the supplier has provided superior service in the past, if the supplier has detailed knowledge of your company, or if the supplier has failed in some areas.
Executive summary preparer comments	This is an open field in which you can document any feelings, biases, or conclusions you have in relation to the supplier or its proposal.

Issuing a Rate Summary

You can print a summary of each supplier's pricing proposal. Although some of the reports that compare each supplier's proposal will be helpful in choosing suppliers to negotiate with, a basic proposal summary is important. First, this type of report can be used to audit and test the supplier's proposal. If the supplier provided a printed copy of the proposal, you can compare your report with the information in that copy. This will ensure that you avoid misunderstandings during the negotiations. Second, by printing out the product-by-product rates proposed by current suppliers, you can compare their rates to what they have charged you in the past for similar items. This information can be used in negotiating rebate issues for overcharges and in benchmarking the supplier's proposal.

— FIGURE 9-2 —

IMPLEMENTING SUPPLIER PARTNERSHIPS
EXECUTIVE SUMMARY OF SUPPLIER PROPOSALS

CONTROL NUMBER: 1 *****Boxes R Us *****

Proposal Submitted By: Dan Musielski, Plant Manager (312) 555-1234

COMPANY INFORMATION:

Type:		1994 Revenues:	$40,199,353.00
Primary Commodity:	Corrugated	1994 Net Income:	$ 2,009,967.65
Primary Service Area:	Nationwide	Number of Locations:	3

PRIMARY COMMODITY SUMMARY:

Number of Products: 1,138,000
Percent of Products: 100.00%
Total Cost of Proposal: $299,910.00

SERVICE STATISTICS:

1993 Order Fill: 95.00% 100.00% of all claims will be resolved
in 30 days.

1994 Order Fill: 94.00%
Proposed Performance: 95.00%

CUSTOMER REFERENCES: **PRICING SUMMARY:**

John Doe:	312 555-1212	Discount off list:	10.00%
Jane Smith:	414 555-1212	Bar Code Label Charges:	0.00%
Bob Cloud:	312 555-1212	Emergency Order Charges:	0.00%
Joe Smith:	602 555-1212	Restock Charges:	20.00%
Dwayne Robinson:	717 555-1212	Other Charges:_____	0.00%

PRICING CAPS: (These are the maximum percentage increases the supplier will levy in the relative year)

Year 1: 1%   Year 2: 3%   Year 3: 2%   Year 4: 3%   Year 5: 2%

COMMENTS:

Expected Benefits/   Added volume, growth in customer base, become better known through-
Partnership Concerns: out the industry

Strategic Plans: We look to grow our business through customer partnerships and through
an increased focus on EDI to reduce paperwork costs.

Distinctions: Service oriented organization, has an intensive safety program

EDI: Has the ability to accept orders via EDI and can bill invoices over EDI

Pricing: Mild savings, with complete coverage of all of our needs

Overall Assessment: This company covers all of our products and offers EDI support.
We could choose this company if we can get some movement on their
pricing.

CONTROL NUMBER: 2   *****Corrugated Manufacturers**   *****

Proposal Submitted By: Kevin Spengel, Vice President of Sales   (312) 555-0100

COMPANY INFORMATION:

Type: 1994 Revenues: $25,000,000.00
Primary Commodity: Corrugated   1994 Net Income: $ 1,250,000.00
Primary Service Area: Southwest   Number of Locations: 1

PRIMARY COMMODITY SUMMARY:

Number of Products: 888,000
Percent of Products: 78.03%
Total Cost of Proposal: $257,610.00

SERVICE STATISTICS:

1993 Order Fill: 90.00%   100.00% of all claims will be resolved
                                                        in 30 days.

1994 Order Fill: 93.00%
Proposed Performance: 93.00%

CUSTOMER REFERENCES: **PRICING SUMMARY:**

Bill Noe: 312 555-1212   Discount off list: 5.00%
                                                        Bar Code Label Charges: 0.00%
                                                        Emergency Order Charges: 0.00%
                                                        Restock Charges: 0.00%
                                                        Other Charges:_____   0.00%

PRICING CAPS: (These are the maximum percentage increases the supplier will levy in the relative year)

Year 1: 0%   Year 2: 0%   Year 3: 4%   Year 4: 4%   Year 5: 4%

COMMENTS:

Expected Benefits/   We can share what we have learned by working with other companies,
  Partnership Concerns: and we can benefit from early access to your forecasts

Strategic Plans: We look to implement Just in Time inventory strategies with many of our
                                long-term customers.

Distinctions: We put the customer first, and we have a long-term agreement with mills
                                to provide our raw materials at lower costs, even during shortages

EDI: Has no EDI capabilities but plans to incorporate EDI in the next 2 years

Pricing: This company will cost us $10,532 more than we currently pay, and only
                                covers 78% of our product needs

Overall Assessment: We currently use this company for about one half of our corrugated
                                needs. They do a good job, but they are overpriced and short on
                                product coverage.

CONTROL NUMBER: 3   *****American Box Inc.**   *****

Proposal Submitted By: John Sherman, Director of National Accounts   (800) 555-8923

COMPANY INFORMATION:

Type:		1994 Revenues:	$100,000,000.00
Primary Commodity:	Corrugated	1994 Net Income:	$ 5,000,000.00
Primary Service Area:	Midwest	Number of Locations:	5

PRIMARY COMMODITY SUMMARY:

Number of Products:	1,138,000
Percent of Products:	100.00%
Total Cost of Proposal:	$296,360.00

SERVICE STATISTICS:

1993 Order Fill:	90.00%	100.00% of all claims will be resolved in 30 days.
1994 Order Fill:	88.00%	
Proposed Performance:	85.00%	

CUSTOMER REFERENCES:

William Eon: 312 555-1212

PRICING SUMMARY:

Discount off list:	12.00%
Bar Code Label Charges:	0.00%
Emergency Order Charges:	0.00%
Restock Charges:	0.00%
Other Charges:_____	0.00%

PRICING CAPS: (These are the maximum percentage increases the supplier will levy in the relative year)

Year 1: 1%   Year 2: 3%   Year 3: 3%   Year 4: 3%   Year 5: 3%

COMMENTS:

Expected Benefits/ Partnership Concerns:	Added volume, commitment to order from us regularly, better forecasting will help us reduce costs
Strategic Plans:	We are the largest supplier in the country and we look to continue supplying the quality products we have in the past.
Distinctions:	We are the largest manufacturer of corrugated products in the country, we provide the most stability and the best costs, coupled with unmatched R&D.
EDI:	Has no EDI capabilities and no plans to implement EDI in the near future
Pricing:	With complete coverage, this company will save us $11,400 annually.
Overall Assessment:	This company combines covering 100% of our needs with a positive savings number. We have never used them before, so we have to carefully check the references.

CONTROL NUMBER: 4   *****Packaging Systems**   *****

Proposal Submitted By: Mike Dobbs, Sales Representative   (312) 555-7500

COMPANY INFORMATION:

Type:	
Primary Commodity:	Corrugated
Primary Service Area:	Midwest

1994 Revenues:	$10,000,000.00
1994 Net Income:	$ 500,000.00
Number of Locations:	1

PRIMARY COMMODITY SUMMARY:

Number of Products:	928,000
Percent of Products:	81.54%
Total Cost of Proposal:	$295,010.00

SERVICE STATISTICS:

1993 Order Fill:	88.00%

100.00% of all claims will be resolved in 30 days.

1994 Order Fill:	93.00%
Proposed Performance:	92.00%

CUSTOMER REFERENCES:

Mike Morris: 312 555-1212

PRICING SUMMARY:

Discount off list:	2.00%
Bar Code Label Charges:	5.00%
Emergency Order Charges:	0.00%
Restock Charges:	0.00%
Other Charges:_____	0.00%

PRICING CAPS (These are the maximum percentage increases the supplier will levy in the relative year)

Year 1: 4%   Year 2: 3%   Year 3: 3%   Year 4: 2%   Year 5: 3%

COMMENTS:

Expected Benefits/ Partnership Concerns:	By working together we can better forecast your needs and lengthen our production runs to reduce costs for both of us
Strategic Plans:	As a small player, we are looking for reduced costs via EDI and new manufacturing processes to allow us to compete with, and beat, our larger, but slower, competitors.
Distinctions:	We have the best service in the industry, we aren't the lowest price, but we are the best value
EDI:	Can accept orders and order inquiries via EDI
Pricing:	This company is proposing to cover 82% of our purchases, at essentially the same cost we pay today
Overall Assessment:	This company has much to prove because they cannot cover all of our purchases, and they are proposing a 4% price increase.

CONTROL NUMBER: 5 *****AAA Boxes Company *****

Proposal Submitted By: JoAnna Van Amiga, President   (815) 555-4357

COMPANY INFORMATION:

Type:		1994 Revenues:	$500,000.00
Primary Commodity:	Corrugated	1994 Net Income:	$ 25,000.00
Primary Service Area:	Nationwide	Number of Locations:	2

PRIMARY COMMODITY SUMMARY:

Number of Products:	1,138,000
Percent of Products:	100.00%
Total Cost of Proposal:	$280,470.00

SERVICE STATISTICS:

1993 Order Fill:	97.00%	100.00% of all claims will be resolved in 30 days.
1994 Order Fill:	96.00%	
Proposed Performance:	96.00%	

CUSTOMER REFERENCES:

Andy Andrews: 815 555-1212

PRICING SUMMARY:

Discount off list:	15.00%
Bar Code Label Charges:	0.00%
Emergency Order Charges:	0.00%
Restock Charges:	0.00%
Other Charges:_____	0.00%

PRICING CAPS: (These are the maximum percentage increases the supplier will levy in the relative year)

Year 1: 3%   Year 2: 3%   Year 3: 5%   Year 4: 2%   Year 5: 4%

COMMENTS:

Expected Benefits/ Partnership Concerns:	We are looking forward to working with someone who commits their volume to us.
Strategic Plans:	We look to add the equipment and machinery to increase our capacity over the next 2 years.
Distinctions:	We are a small company, so we are able to provide close attention to every customer. You would be a very important customer to us.
EDI:	Can accept orders via EDI
Pricing:	While covering all of our purchases, this company will save us $27,000 annually
Overall Assessment:	This is the smallest company, we would increase their sales by 50% if we choose them. But they provide 100% coverage, significant savings, and have the ability to receive orders via EDI.

CONTROL NUMBER: 6   *****Shipping Systems   *****

Proposal Submitted By: "Honest Joe," President   (708) 555-4321

COMPANY INFORMATION:

Type:		1994 Revenues:	$22,500,000.00
Primary Commodity :	Corrugated	1994 Net Income:	$ 1,125,000.00
Primary Service Area:	Nationwide	Number of Locations:	2

PRIMARY COMMODITY SUMMARY:

Number of Products: 450,000
Percent of Products: 39.54%
Total Cost of Proposal: $76,500.00

SERVICE STATISTICS:

1993 Order Fill: 98.00%   100.00% of all claims will be resolved
                                                in 10 days.
1994 Order Fill: 98.00%
Proposed Performance: 98.00%

CUSTOMER REFERENCES: **PRICING SUMMARY:**

Jack Shelter: 312 555-1212   Discount off list: 25.00%
                                               Bar Code Label Charges: 0.00%
                                               Emergency Order Charges: 0.00%
                                               Restock Charges: 0.00%
                                               Other Charges:_____   3.00%

PRICING CAPS: (These are the maximum percentage increases the supplier will levy in the relative year)

Year 1: 2%   Year 2: 3%   Year 3: 4%   Year 4: 4%   Year 5: 4%

COMMENTS:

Expected Benefits/ Partnership Concerns:	We are looking for added volume to spread our overhead over. Also, many benefits will come from working together as partners.
Strategic Plans:	We provide high quality corrugated products, at a better price than our competitors. It is a simple formula that we intend to continue using.
Distinctions:	Service, that is our motto. You will find our company the best value for your long-term needs.
EDI:	Has no EDI capabilities and no plans to implement EDI
Pricing:	Although this company only covers 40% of our shipments, they would save us $27,000 annually.
Overall Assessment:	Look into selecting this supplier in combination with another company to maximize savings potential.

Figure 9.3 is a sample rate summary report. This report might include the following information:

Field	Description
Code	The same code for the supplier that has been used in the profile control and executive summary tables. This will allow you to access the supplier's basic information without retyping.
Product code	The basic product code used in your profile.
Product description	The description of the product as listed in your profile.
Annual quantity	The total quantity bid on by the supplier.
Historical amount paid	The amount your company actually paid to purchase this product in the historical period summarized in your proposal.
Proposed amount paid	The amount the supplier is proposing to bill you to supply your annual volume of the product.
Difference	The net amount to be saved or premium bid by the supplier.

One word of caution: Do not be intimidated by this report. You will often find that the individual rate summaries do not show much in terms of dollar savings for your company. This is normal. The vast majority of the dollar savings will come from comparing amounts bid and taking the best mix of prices and rates bid by all of the suppliers.

— FIGURE 9.3 —

YOUR COMPANY PURCHASING PROJECT
RATE SUMMARY

Product Code	Product Description	Annual Quantity	Historical Amount Paid	Proposed Unit Rate	Extended Annual Cost	Savings over Historical
Supplier: AAA Boxes Company						
192	2 gallon corrugated bag	100,000	17,000	.220	22,000	(5,000)
7864	6 gallon corrugated bag	150,000	43,500	.240	36,000	7,500
11679	2' x 4' x 1.5' 1/4" Box	10,000	7,300	.770	7,700	(400)
11780	3' x 3' x 3' 1/4" Box	120,000	110,400	.960	115,200	(4,800)
12465	1' x 3' x 2' 1/3" Box	3,000	2,010	.690	2,070	(60)
15443	4 gallon corrugated bag	450,000	103,500	.160	72,000	31,500
24324	2' shrink wrap	100,000	12,000	.130	13,000	(1,000)
34653	2" packing tape	200,000	6,000	.030	6,000	0
543477	6' x 6' x 4' 1/3" Box	5,000	6,050	1.300	6,500	(450)
Total for AAA Boxes Company					**280,470**	**27,290**
Supplier: American Box Inc.						
192	2 gallon corrugated bag	100,000	17,000	.220	22,000	(5,000)
7864	6 gallon corrugated bag	150,000	43,500	.330	49,500	(6,000)
11679	2' x 4' x 1.5' 1/4" Box	10,000	7,300	.670	6,700	600
11780	3' x 3' x 3' 1/4" Box	120,000	110,400	.860	103,200	7,200
12465	1' x 3' x 2' 1/3" Box	3,000	2,010	.670	2,010	0
15443	4 gallon corrugated bag	450,000	103,500	.200	90,000	13,500
24324	2' shrink wrap	100,000	12,000	.100	10,000	2,000
34653	2" packing tape	200,000	6,000	.040	8,000	(2,000)
543477	6' x 6' x 4' 1/3" Box	5,000	6,050	.990	4,950	1,100
Total for American Box Inc.					**296,360**	**11,400**

— FIGURE 9.3 (CONTINUED) —

Product Code	Product Description	Annual Quantity	Historical Amount Paid	Proposed Unit Rate	Extended Annual Cost	Savings over Historical
Supplier: Boxes R Us						
192	2 gallon corrugated bag	100,000	17,000	.230	23,000	(6,000)
7864	6 gallon corrugated bag	150,000	43,500	.340	51,000	(7,500)
11679	2' x 4' x 1.5' 1/4" Box	10,000	7,300	.750	7,500	(200)
11780	3' x 3' x 3' 1/4" Box	120,000	110,400	.910	109,200	1,200
12465	1' x 3' x 2' 1/3" Box	3,000	2,010	.570	1,710	300
15443	4 gallon corrugated bag	450,000	103,500	.190	85,500	18,000
24324	2' shrink wrap	100,000	12,000	.110	11,000	1,000
34653	2" packing tape	200,000	6,000	.028	5,500	500
543477	6' x 6' x 4' 1/3" Box	5,000	6,050	1.100	5,500	550
Total for Boxes R Us					**299,910**	**7,850**
Supplier: Corrugated Manufacturers						
11679	2' x 4' x 1.5' 1/4" Box	10,000	7,300	.780	7,800	(500)
11780	3' x 3' x 3' 1/4" Box	120,000	110,400	.920	110,400	0
12465	1' x 3' x 2' 1/3" Box	3,000	2,010	.620	1,860	150
15443	4 gallon corrugated bag	450,000	103,500	.250	112,500	(9,000)
24324	2' shrink wrap	100,000	12,000	.130	13,000	(1,000)
34653	2" packing tape	200,000	6,000	.035	7,000	(1,000)
543477	6' x 6' x 4' 1/3" Box	5,000	6,050	1.010	5,050	1,000
Total for Corrugated Manufacturers					**257,610**	**(10,350)**
Supplier: Packaging Systems						
192	2 gallon corrugated bag	100,000	17,000	.130	13,000	4,000
7864	6 gallon corrugated bag	150,000	43,500	.290	43,500	0
11780	3' x 3' 1/4" Box	120,000	110,400	.930	111,600	(1,200)

— FIGURE 9.3 (CONTINUED) —

Product Code	Product Description	Annual Quantity	Historical Amount Paid	Proposed Unit Rate	Extended Annual Cost	Savings over Historical
12465	1' x 3' x 2' 1/3" Box	3,000	2,010	.720	2,160	(150)
15443	4 gallon corrugated bag	450,000	103,500	.240	108,000	(4,500)
24324	2' shrink wrap	100,000	12,000	.105	10,500	1,500
543477	6' x 6' x 4' 1/3" Box	5,000	6,050	1.250	6,250	(200)
Total for Packaging Systems					**295,010**	**(550)**
Supplier: Shipping Systems						
15443	4 gallon corrugated bag	450,000	103,500	.170	76,500	27,000
Total for Shipping Systems					**76,500**	**27,000**

Generating a Pricing Comparison Report

This report will provide the real fire power in your quest to select the best supplier. It will help you compare each of the suppliers among themselves and against your current purchasing practices. Although service and quality play equally important roles in your decision process, pricing is an area for which you can quantify and compare numbers in black and white. Companies that are more expensive will have to prove that their value and service are higher than from the companies that have found ways to demand lower rates. In fact, companies that offer the lowest prices often offer the best quality and service levels as well.

Figure 9.4 shows an example of a pricing comparison report for a group of suppliers in a commodity area. The following fields are included:

Field	Description
Code	This field allows you to access the information input in the profile control table as well as the other tables created.
Product code	The basic product code used in your profile.
Product description	The description of the product as listed in your profile.
Quantity	The total quantity bid on by the suppliers.
Supplier 1	Proposed price by supplier 1 to handle your business.
Supplier 2	Proposed price by supplier 2 to handle your business.
Supplier 3	Proposed price by supplier 3 to handle your business.
Supplier 4	Proposed price by supplier 4 to handle your business.
Supplier 5	Proposed price by supplier 5 to handle your business.
Best supplier name	In many database programs, you can use a minimum value function to give you the name of the supplier that has the lowest price for the product. You can use this field to see which suppliers routinely have the best price on different items.

— FIGURE 9.4 —

YOUR COMPANY

PARTNERSHIP IMPLEMENTATION PROJECT

PRICING REPORT

Product	Historical	Boxes R Us	Corrugated Manufacturers	American Box, Inc.	Packaging Systems	AA Boxes Company	Best Price Source
2 gallon corrugated bag	17,000	23,000		22,000	22,000	13,000	AAA Boxes
6 gallon corrugated bag	43,500	51,000		49,500	36,000	43,500	Packaging Systems
2' x 4' x 1.5' 1/4" Box	7,300	7,500	7,800	6,700	7,700		American Box, Inc.
3' x 3' x 3' 1/4" Box	110,400	108,000	110,400	103,200	115,200	111,600	American Box, Inc.
1' x 3' x 2' 1/3" Box	2,010	1,710	1,860	2,010	2,070	2,160	Boxes R Us
4 gallon corrugated bag	103,500	85,500	112,500	90,000	72,000	108,000	Packaging Systems
2' shrink wrap	12,000	11,000	13,000	10,000	13,000	10,500	American Box, Inc.
2" packing tape	6,000	5,500	7,000	8,000	6,000		Boxes R Us
6' x 6' x 4' 1/3" Box	6,050	5,500	5,050	4,950	6,500	6,250	American Box, Inc.

To create this report, your MIS support person will need to develop an intermediate table. In some software this step is called crosstabbing, and it is the process of making a grid out of a list of prices for a group of products. Alternatively, you can create this report manually by entering the proper numbers in a spreadsheet directly. Although this is not the most automated way to generate this report, it will give you the information you need.

Creating a Best-of-the-Best Report

This is one of your most powerful reports. By developing a single database with every supplier's bid on the products, you can produce a report that summarizes the best price bid for each item. This will provide you with a benchmark for pricing levels. Figure 9.5 is a sample best-of-the-best report. The following information is included:

Field	Description
Code	This field allows you to access the information input in the profile control table as well as the other tables created.
Product code	The basic product code used in your profile.
Product description	The description of the product as listed in your profile.
Annual quantity	The total quantity listed in the profile.
Best price offered/paid	The lower of the best price offered by any supplier who responded to your profile and the historical amount paid for the product.
Best price source	The name of the supplier who offered the best price, or historical if the best price is the current actual price paid.
Historical amount paid	The amount actually paid in your historical period to purchase that product.
Savings potential	The difference, if any, between the historical amount paid and the lower of the best offered price and the historical price.

— FIGURE 9.5 —

YOUR COMPANY

PARTNERSHIP IMPLEMENTATION PROJECT

BEST OF THE BEST

Product Description	Annual Quantity	Historical Price	Overall Best Price	Source of the Best Price	Potential Savings Estimation
4 gallon corrugated bag	450,000	103,500	72,000	AAA Boxes Company	31,500
6 gallon corrugated bag	150,000	43,500	36,000	AAA Boxes Company	7,500
3' x 3' x 3' 1/4" Box	120,000	110,400	103,200	American Box, Inc.	7,200
2 gallon corrugated bag	100,000	17,000	13,000	Packaging Systems	4,000
2' shrink wrap	100,000	12,000	10,000	American Box, Inc.	2,000
6' x 6' x 4' 1/3" Box	5,000	6,050	4,950	American Box, Inc.	1,100
2' x 4' x 1.5' 1/4" Box	10,000	7,300	6,700	American Box, Inc.	600
2" packing tape	200,000	6,000	5,500	Boxes R Us	500
1' x 3' x 2' 1/3" Box	3,000	2,010	1,710	Boxes R Us	300
Total for Corrugated Suppliers:		307,760	253,060		54,700

Tips for Generating a Best-of-the-Best Report

If you create a database that looks like the following example, then you have the basic data you need to generate a best-of-the-best report:

Code   Product Code, Description, and Quantity Supplier/Historical Amount Bid/Paid

The code field links to your profile control to give you the supplier information; and the product code, description, and quantity fields give you the product information. In the supplier/historical field, list the name of the supplier who provided the bid, or list historical for the actual amount paid. In the amount bid/paid field, list the amount you paid for the historical purchases and the amount bid by the supplier when you are listing a supplier's bid. After you create this listing, you have a database that can be summarized in the best-of-the-best report.

Generating a Supplier-versus-Supplier Report

This report, shown in Figure 9.6, allows you to show two suppliers head to head. This type of report can be useful when you have narrowed the search to a small number of suppliers and want to see how they stack up against one another. Because you may not want to negotiate with every supplier (which would be expensive and time consuming), a comparison of competing suppliers can help you determine which supplier best meets your needs. If one supplier proposes better pricing on some items, comparing that supplier with a competitor can illustrate how consistent that supplier's pricing is or if the supplier is using a loss-leader strategy. (In a loss-leader strategy the supplier will provide an item at a low price to get your business, with other products priced to make up any lost profits.) To help you make a good decision, this report should show every product you purchase in detail. The fields you could summarize in this report are explained as follows:

Field	Description
Code	This field allows you to access the information input in the profile control table as well as the other tables created.
Part number	The basic product code used in your profile.

Part description	The description of the product as listed in your profile. Be sure to list all products bid by either supplier. If only one of the two suppliers bids on a specific product, leave the unit cost, lead time, extended cost, and savings amount blank for the nonparticipating supplier.
UOM	The unit of measure for the product.
Annual quantity	The total quantity listed in the profile.
Actual historical amount paid	The actual total amount you paid for the product in the historical period.
Supplier 1 unit cost	The unit cost per unit of measure proposed by supplier 1.
Supplier 2 unit cost	The unit cost per unit of measure proposed by supplier 2.
Supplier 1 lead time	How long from the time you place an order until you receive your shipment, as proposed by supplier 1.
Supplier 2 lead time	How long from the time you place an order until you receive your shipment, as proposed by supplier 2.
Supplier 1 extended cost	Quantity times the unit cost proposed by supplier 1.
Supplier 2 extended cost	Quantity times the unit cost proposed by supplier 2.
Supplier 1 savings over actual	Actual historical cost minus the supplier 1 extended cost.
Supplier 2 savings over actual	Actual historical cost minus the supplier 2 extended cost.

— FIGURE 9.6 —

YOUR COMPANY
PARTNERSHIP IMPLEMENTATION PROJECT
AMERICAN BOX VERSUS PACKAGING SYSTEMS

Product	Unit of Measure	American Box Unit Cost	Packaging Systems Unit	American Box Lead Time	Packaging Systems Lead Time
2 gallon corrugated bag	Each	.220	.130	48 hours	36 hours
6 gallon corrugated bag	Each	.330	.290	48 hours	36 hours
2' x 4' x 1.5' 1/4" Box	Each	.670	0.000	48 hours	36 hours
3' x 3' x 3' 1/4" Box	Each	.860	.930	48 hours	36 hours
1' x 3' x 2' 1/3" Box	Each	.670	.720	48 hours	36 hours
4 gallon corrugated bag	Each	.200	.240	48 hours	36 hours
2' shrink wrap	Feet	.100	.105	48 hours	36 hours
2" packing tape	Feet	.040	0.000	96 hours	36 hours
6' x 6' x 4' 1/3" Box	Each	.990	1.250	96 hours	36 hours

Product	American Box Extended $	Packaging Systems Extended $	American Box Savings	Packaging System Savings
2 gallon corrugated bag	22,000	13,000	(5,000)	4,000
6 gallon corrugated bag	49,500	43,500	(6,000)	0
2' x 4' x 1.5' 1/4" Box	6,700		600	
3' x 3' x 3' 1/4" Box	103,200	111,600	7,200	(1,200)
1' x 3' x 2' 1/3" Box	2,010	2,160	0	(150)
4 gallon corrugated bag	90,000	108,000	3,500	(4,500)
2' shrink wrap	10,000	10,500	2,000	1,500
2" packing tape	8,000		(2,000)	
6' x 6' x 4' 1/3" Box	4,950	6,250	1,100	(200)
Totals:			**11,400**	**(550)**

DEVELOPING A SUPPLIER SHORT LIST
▼

By reviewing these reports with the members of your team, you can make a sound decision about which suppliers to invite for further negotiations. The suppliers you decide to negotiate with are, in reality, the suppliers who make your short list. As with every step you have taken in this process, your goal is to have your team make this decision, not you solely.

How to Prepare for the Selection Meeting

A typical sequence of events to accomplish includes the following steps:

1. Develop the reports as outlined in this chapter for each commodity area you are focusing on.

2. Send the group reports for each commodity area to each team member.

3. Ask the team members to review the reports. Be sure to offer to let them review any of the original proposal documents you received from the suppliers.

4. Schedule a meeting to review the suppliers as a group and to narrow the field of suppliers.

5. After the meeting, send a list of the suppliers who have been selected for further negotiations and a list of the suppliers who have been cut to each team member for review.

6. Invite the selected suppliers for negotiation.

7. Do not communicate with the unselected suppliers yet. It is unwise to exclude a supplier from the process until you have actually concluded negotiations with your new partners.

Holding the Selection Meeting

The selection meeting is critical. In this meeting, you will once again include your co-workers in the decision process so that you manage change effectively.

Figure 9.7 is a sample memo you could use in distributing the reports and scheduling the supplier short list meeting.

— FIGURE 9.7 —

MEMO RE SHORT LIST MEETING

To: Supplier Partnership Implementation Committee

From: Your Name

RE: Selecting suppliers to negotiate with

Attached to this memo is a set of reports that you might find helpful in determining the best mix of suppliers to negotiate with in our first commodity area: corrugated boxes. We chose this area to negotiate first because we anticipate significant opportunities in it and because we did not want to start with our most critical areas first. Please review these reports. If you have any questions or would like additional information from the original proposal packages we received from the suppliers, call me at your earliest convenience.

I will follow up with you to see what you think and to schedule our final meeting, at which we will select the suppliers we want to negotiate with.

Thank you,

Your Name

To follow up, call each team member one or two days after you send the memo. Be sure to ask team members what they have found by reviewing these reports. Find out if there is anything you need to provide so they can make decisions they will feel comfortable with. In addition, ask them if there are any other suppliers in this commodity area that they would like to add to the reports. If it is possible to add these suppliers or obtain their proposal, do so.

Figure 9.8 is a sample agenda you might use in your selection meeting.

— FIGURE 9.8 —

SAMPLE SHORT LIST MEETING AGENDA

Supplier Partnership Program
Suppliers to Negotiate With: Selection Meeting

AGENDA

1. Review reports for inclusion of all relevant suppliers.

2. Open meeting to discussion of the suppliers and their proposals.

3. Conduct a blind vote on which carriers to negotiate with.

4. Review vote, and confirm each supplier as one to negotiate with or one to hold communications with.

5. Schedule days to practice negotiating for the first session with a supplier.

The blind vote referenced in the agenda is a good way to get consensus without forcing peer pressure on each participant. To use a blind vote, hand out a piece of paper for each supplier with that supplier's name on it. Each person will write "negotiate with" or "don't negotiate with" on the paper. For the suppliers that the team reaches consensus on, no more discussion is needed. For the suppliers that elicited split votes, work through members' views as a team. You might find it helpful to list all the suppliers you have decided to negotiate with on the board, then go through each remaining supplier and, as a group, either add them or discard them. At the end of this exercise, review the list with the team. Does the group of suppliers you have decided to negotiate with

▼ Cover the vast majority of the product coverage you will need?

▼ Require too much time in terms of negotiating? (Do you have too many suppliers to negotiate with?)

▼ Leave you vulnerable in any areas? (Do you have too few suppliers to negotiate with?)

SUMMARY
▼

This chapter has provided you with some tools for selecting the best suppliers with whom to negotiate. To maximize your ability to make an informed decision, be sure to address the following topics:

▼ Decide which group to analyze first.

- – Areas with the most opportunity
- – Areas with the most dollar volume
- – Areas critical to your company
- – Areas with contracts that are about to expire

▼ Develop the reports to help you analyze the suppliers' proposals.

- – Develop the profile control report to help you organize the proposals.
- – Develop the executive summary report to help you consolidate the critical information about each supplier onto one page.
- – Develop a rate summary report to help you compare each proposal to last year's prices.
- – Develop a report to compare the different suppliers.
- – Develop a report to show the best price offered for each product by any supplier.
- – Develop a report that will compare two suppliers, allowing you to analyze a small number of suppliers after you have narrowed your search.

▼ After you have completed these reports, you are ready to gather your negotiating team and select the suppliers you will negotiate with.

You are now ready to prepare for the negotiations. In Chapter 10, we will review the steps you can take to prepare for an efficient and effective negotiating session.

CHAPTER 10

PREPARING FOR
NEGOTIATIONS

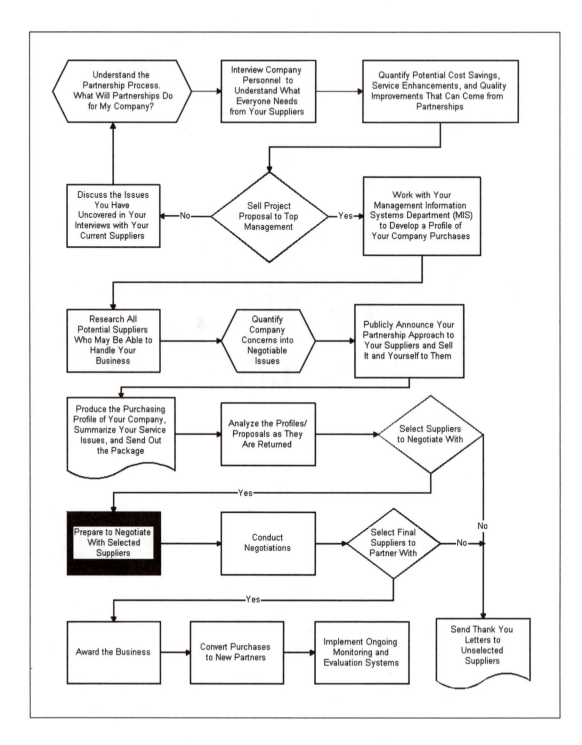

You have done your research, you have developed an idea of which suppliers you are interested in, you have really put together a good presentation, and your profile has provided good data for analysis. The suppliers have returned many bids, and you have analyzed them. Now you pull everything together and prepare to hold the actual negotiations. One way to solidify your beginning dates is to schedule your negotiations.

SCHEDULING YOUR NEGOTIATION MEETINGS
▼

Your first step in preparing for the actual negotiations is to schedule the meetings with individual suppliers. Before you meet with any suppliers, you should do the following:

- ▼ Define the team that will negotiate with the first group of suppliers.
- ▼ Establish the days and times your team will be available to negotiate.
- ▼ Decide on where you will negotiate.
- ▼ Send an invitation letter to the supplier.
- ▼ Call the supplier to discuss the invitation and finalize the schedule.

SELECTING TEAM MEMBERS
▼

You have included many people in your supplier partnership implementation process. You may have more than three of four people whom you could ask to be on a specific negotiating team for a specific commodity group. Regardless of who you pick, every negotiating team should have each of the following represented:

- ▼ A buyer or user of the primary products offered by the supplier
- ▼ A representative of top management who has the authority to negotiate on behalf of the company
- ▼ A representative of another department, not necessarily affected directly by the supplier (This person may provide some objective insights.)

▼ One or two additional team members who you might have identified as strong communicators or negotiators.

It has worked well in the past if four or five people are on a negotiation team. Once you have selected and confirmed the team that will negotiate for a specific commodity group or product area, it is time to agree on a tentative negotiating schedule.

DEVELOPING A NEGOTIATING SCHEDULE
▼

Provide a blank calendar to your negotiating team. Begin filling in the dates when everyone can meet for practice sessions and actual negotiations. Be sure to keep the following in mind:

▼ Do not schedule more than three negotiations per week. (The exception to this rule applies when your team is able to concentrate full time on negotiations for a short period of time.) This will allow each team member to spend at least two days per week on day-to-day responsibilities and will give you time to reflect on how the negotiations fared.

▼ Allow room in the schedule to bring the top supplier back for a second meeting.

▼ Schedule at least three days of practice sessions before your first negotiation.

▼ Schedule an evening or any two- to three-hour period to prepare for subsequent negotiations.

▼ Schedule two to three hours for debriefing after each negotiation.

▼ Schedule the negotiation meetings to begin early in the morning.

Once you have determined the days available for your negotiating team, you can schedule your practice sessions and, after you have determined your negotiating site, formally invite the suppliers for negotiations.

Timing the Meeting

In the beginning, you can expect that your negotiations will take much of the day. After you practice and work as a team and learn to stick to your schedule better, you will be able to trim your negotiation sessions to a three- or four-hour period (especially in your lighter commodity areas). Schedule your negotiation sessions to start at 9 A.M. This will give you the option of working throughout the day (even into the evening, if necessary) if you are negotiating with a supplier that is participating sincerely, but requires more time than usual. Some complex commodity areas will take all day because there are more issues that require deep thought and strict negotiations. In such cases, be up front with suppliers, let them know that you expect to work all day, and ask them not to schedule airplane flights that depart before 5 P.M. In the past, some suppliers have scheduled early flights to pressure companies into moving along quickly, cutting out issues that the supplier does not want to negotiate.

Determining the Negotiation Site

Although site selection might seem like a trivial matter, it can have significant affects on your negotiations. You have three basic choices in selecting a negotiation site.

1. YOUR CORPORATE OFFICES

Benefits:

▼ There will be no out-of-pocket costs for you and your company.

▼ You can take the supplier on a tour of your business to help him or her understand and conceptualize your business.

Risks and Caveats:

▼ Meeting at your office can intimidate the supplier, who might feel that because you are on your home turf, you have the upper hand.

▼ If you do meet in your offices, ask your assistant to hold all phone calls. The supplier might perceive phone interruptions as rude and indicative of a lack of concern for the supplier's needs.

2. THE SUPPLIER'S CORPORATE OFFICES

Benefits:

▼ The supplier will have no out-of-pocket costs (unless you convince him or her to pay for your travel expenses).

▼ The supplier can give you a tour of his or her operations, allowing you to get an impression of the supplier's quality and professionalism.

Risks and Caveats:

▼ You might provide the supplier with a psychological edge.

▼ You and your company may incur travel and lodging expenses.

▼ Some companies will interrupt the meeting for phone calls and emergencies. In some cases, this is done to throw the visiting company off track. (See Chapter 11 for dirty tricks and tactics and how to avoid them.)

3. A NEUTRAL LOCATION

Benefits:

▼ Neither company has the upper hand psychologically.

▼ Neither company will be interrupted by the phone.

▼ A neutral location will provide you with the best opportunity to hold a productive, win/win negotiation session.

Risks and Caveats:

▼ You may incur costs of renting a meeting room.

▼ Both companies will have to incur some travel and meal/lodging costs.

Although a neutral location provides the best opportunity for conducting fruitful negotiations, it is not always the best choice. You might decide to meet at the supplier's location if you feel it is important to see the supplier's operations or if the supplier's location is central to each of your company's team members (especially if they are spread throughout the country). In addition, if you wish to avoid any out-of-pocket expenses or are particularly proud of your offices, you might decide to hold the negotiations at your offices.

Once you have developed a negotiating schedule and location, you can send an invitation letter to the selected suppliers.

CREATING THE SUPPLIER NEGOTIATION INVITATION LETTER
▼

It is important that the suppliers you negotiate with understand the comprehensive process you undertook to select them. Making it to the final round is not something every supplier was able to do, and in the invitation letter you can communicate and reinforce the practices and attitude of the supplier that led to the selection. A sample invitation letter is shown in Figure 10.1. You might consider using this as a template for your own company.

— FIGURE 10.1 —
SAMPLE VENDOR NEGOTIATION INVITATION LETTER

Contact Name
Supplier Company Name
Address

Dear Contact:

I am pleased to inform you that you and your company have made our final list of suppliers for detailed discussions about a long-term partnership. As you could see at the supplier presentation we hosted this fall, hundreds of suppliers expressed interest in our business. From those suppliers, we have chosen a few with whom to discuss in detail the possibility of a long-term partnership. There were a couple of important characteristics that you and the rest of the successful suppliers demonstrated:

▼ A commitment to quality and customer service that is backed up by the ability and resources to deliver on your promises.

▼ A commitment to containing our mutual costs, working together to ensure our mutual success.

▼ A commitment to the future. We will be working together to streamline processes, enhance the services provided to our end customers, and continuously increase quality.

▼ A competitive pricing structure. Some companies described world-class service and quality but did not understand the importance competitive pricing plays in any market, especially to our mutual customers.

I will be following up with a phone call in the next day to schedule a meeting between our company management and your executive team. We will be discussing some specific issues and will only have one day available for negotiation. Consequently, it is imperative that you personally attend the negotiations. Please invite your company executives who can discuss and negotiate in the following areas:

▼ Engineering and quality

▼ Service and delivery

▼ MIS and EDI

▼ Pricing

▼ Top management involvement in the partnership

Once again, I want to congratulate you and your team on your proposal. We are excited about the prospect of working with you over the next couple of weeks to develop a world-class relationship and a long-term plan for success.

If you have any questions or comments, please feel free to give me a call at (XXX) XXX-XXXX.

Sincerely,

Project Leader

Depending on the amount of time you have before your scheduled negotiation days, you might decide to fax this letter to the supplier. Once you have sent this letter to the supplier, you are ready to follow up over the phone and discuss the actual meeting.

Finalizing the Negotiation Schedule

To finalize the negotiation schedule, you will need to contact each of the suppliers and confirm the actual negotiation date. As you call each of the suppliers, keep in mind the following:

▼ The negotiation session will be a complete waste of time if the supplier does not bring people with the authority to make decisions. Consequently, be sure to impress this point on the supplier contact. If the contact asks what issues you will be negotiating, explain that you are primarily looking to finalize the issues discussed in the profile. It is better to change the schedule to accommodate the supplier's top executives than to go through a negotiating session only to find that the supplier team must get approval from the home office for even the smallest decisions.

▼ You may want to avoid negotiating with the most important supplier first. In this way, you can "practice" on a smaller or less significant supplier without the risk of damaging your continued operations. This is not to say that you are inviting the smaller supplier on false pretenses; you should only negotiate with suppliers you would consider partnering with. The reality of the situation, however, is that you have less at risk with a new or smaller supplier than you might with an industry leader.

Once you have solidified the schedule for the negotiations and feel comfortable that the right people from the supplier's company will attend, it is time to practice.

PRACTICING YOUR PRESENTATION
▼

So far, you have focused on developing the message you want to deliver to the suppliers. To tie together everything you have done in preparation, you need to practice your delivery of the message. You should schedule three day-long sessions for practice. A basic list of tasks for these practice sessions might include the following:

▼ Determine specific issues to negotiate with this group of suppliers. (You will not need to negotiate every issue with every supplier. For example, you will not need to negotiate engineering support with your tissue paper supplier.)

▼ Review each of the issues and edit them relative to the suppliers you will be negotiating with.

▼ Assign roles to each team member for each issue.

▼ Practice issue negotiations and video tape.

▼ Practice issue introductions.

▼ Review videotapes and discuss how to improve your communication style.

Preparing the Agenda

As with other meetings you have led, it is important to be organized for this meeting. An agenda will help you be organized and will help you show the other participants what topics you need to review. A typical agenda is shown in figure 10.2.

— FIGURE 10.2 —

— FIGURE 10.2 —

PRACTICE SESSIONS AGENDA

Day One:

Determine specific issues to negotiate with the first group of suppliers.

Review each issue and edit relative to the product area and suppliers.

Assign each role for each issue to individual team members.

Choose one issue and videotape a practice negotiation session.

Day Two:

Review videotape from day one and adjust communication and negotiation style accordingly.

Choose three issues to negotiate sequentially, videotape, and record elapsed time. (i.e., how long does it take to negotiate all three issues?)

Review videotape and elapsed time.

Special exercise: In negotiation order, have each presenter introduce, sell, and ask for his or her position in each issue.

Choose another three issues to negotiate sequentially, videotape, and record elapsed time.

Day Three:

Review videotape and discuss appropriate revisions to issues and presentation style.

Hold a full run-through of all issues.

Debrief.

Following Through

Here are tips for handling videotape review, issue introduction, and run-through.

VIDEOTAPE REVIEW

As you review a videotape of your practice negotiating session, watch for the following:

▼ Are you working as a cohesive team? Never disagree in front of the supplier. (If a teammate is making inappropriate comments or offers, call a caucus or time out.)

▼ Are you teleprompting when you are leading the discussion to another team member? Teleprompting is the art of asking someone on your team to share an insight or story in such a way that gives him or her time to think and prepare. For example, "Now I would like to talk about ontime delivery. Bob, my esteemed colleague, has a story about how a late delivery once caused our entire plant to shut down. Bob, would you please relate that story to the group?" This introduction gives Bob a clear indication of what he is to talk about and a moment to gather his thoughts. That approach is much better than "Tell them about the late delivery, Bob."

▼ Does your team come across as a gracious host? Remember, the suppliers are your guests, and you are trying to develop a long-term relationship. Avoid remarks, body positions, voice tones, and any other method of communicating that could provide a negative message to the supplier.

▼ Are you actually asking for what you want? Often, the presenter will introduce the issue, sell it masterfully, and then not ask for what his or her company wants. Within two to three minutes of introducing the issue, ask for specifically what you have quantified as your interest and position for the issue.

▼ Are you negotiating at a swift pace? Although you do not want to ignore issues, it is important to keep the meeting moving. Few issues should take longer than 20 to 30 minutes to negotiate. For some of the smaller issues, five minutes is enough time. If the supplier refuses to work with you on an issue, say something like "Let's take a step back. For this issue, we have asked you to provide us with a dedicated customer service representative. At this time, you are unable to offer that service to us. Is that correct? Then let us mark that down and move on to the next issue." If you have time at the end of the session, go back to any issues you want to develop further.

▼ Can the presenter control the issue? Often, the supplier will attempt to take over an issue. Although it is important to let the supplier express his or her views, the meeting should not become a free-for-all. It helps to review how an order is negotiated:

1. Introduce the issue and define it.
2. Sell the issue to the supplier.
3. Ask for what you want specifically.

4. Allow the supplier to respond.

5. Record any agreements made.

6. Go back to Step 2 as needed.

7. Finalize the issue and read agreements to the group.

▼ Are you communicating effectively? This can reflect on how well you know your issues. Often, if you have not studied the issue you are presenting, you will use more nonwords, avoid eye contact, use defensive body language, etc. If this seems to be a problem, spend more time reviewing the issues before your next practice session.

▼ Are you being creative? Although you may not have much opportunity to display creativity in a meeting with your co-workers, be sensitive to how you react to alternative approaches to an issue brought up by the supplier.

▼ How are you handling transition? As you begin to negotiate more than one issue in a practice session, how well are you able to move from one issue to the next? This is a combination of practicing your introductions for each issue and teleprompting.

▼ Are you an effective listener? One of the key roles in negotiating sessions is the listener. As you review the videotape, observe how well you force the group to summarize each issue before moving on to the next issue.

ISSUE INTRODUCTION EXERCISE

Try the following exercise: Have each person present the first two to three minutes of his or her issue. In this time, the presenter should be able to define the issue, explain its importance to the supplier and to your company, and ask for the specific quantified desires (see Chapter 6). Evaluate each presenter's issues based on the following:

▼ *Content.* Are you convinced that what you are asking for is in the best interests of the supplier and your company based on what was said?

▼ *Time.* Can the presenter cover the important points of the issue in a reasonable time?

▼ *Style.* Does the presenter use nonwords, avoid eye contact, use offensive language, or maintain a defensive body posture?

RUN THROUGH ALL ISSUES

Hold a full run-through. This final exercise will help you get a feel for the actual amount of time you will need for each issue. After you have run through all of the issues for the group of suppliers you will be negotiating with, you are ready to prepare specifically for each supplier, in the order you will be negotiating with them.

CONDUCTING SPECIFIC SUPPLIER REVIEWS
▼

In addition to preparing for negotiations in general, you will need to review each individual supplier and his or her proposal. The main focus of this specific preparation is to be aware of the offers, capabilities, biases, past performances, and other relevant factors about suppliers you will be negotiating with. The following tasks and exercises will help you prepare to negotiate with each individual supplier:

▼ Collect all the reports (see chapter 9) that relate to the supplier and provide a copy to each team member for review.

▼ Photocopy all useful pages in the supplier's proposal and provide a copy of those pages to each team member. You might include the following:

– Pages in which the supplier answers specific service, quality, and pricing questions.

– Brochures that describe EDI capabilities, quality focus, strategic direction, or other features of the supplier.

– The most recent annual report or other financial summaries that can help you understand the supplier's financial stability.

▼ Hold a two- to three-hour preparation session for that supplier the day before the meeting. At the meeting, review these materials as a group. Specifically, review the materials to understand the supplier's view of each of the issues you will negotiate. For example, review the supplier's quality brochures to understand his or her commitment to quality. In addition, you will find it particularly powerful to quote the supplier's materials as you present your issues. (Suppliers may find it difficult to argue with their own words.)

▼ Prepare the blank memos of understanding for each issue. (This is discussed in Chapter 11.)

▼ Prepare a clean set of negotiable issues and issue indexes for each team member. (This is discussed in Chapter 11.)

SUMMARY
▼

As you can see, preparing for the negotiations brings together all of the individual steps you have finished to date. In Chapter 9, you pulled together the analysis of each of the suppliers. You are now able to make intelligent decisions about how to negotiate. In this chapter, you began the process of preparing for specific negotiations. To prepare to negotiate, you need to perform the following steps:

▼ Schedule the meeting with your co-workers to prepare for the negotiations. In that meeting,

– Select the negotiating team for your first commodity group.
– Develop your negotiating schedule.
– Determine your negotiation site based on
  – Your location
  – The supplier's location
  – A neutral site.

▼ Create the supplier invitation letter.

▼ Confirm your negotiating schedule with the suppliers and your teammates before you commit to any neutral site reservations.

▼ Practice your presentation of issues to the suppliers. Focus on how you deliver the message of the partnership to the suppliers. Although this step will not guarantee success, lack of it will prevent success. Among the other topics to focus on in the practice sessions, be sure to emphasize the following:

– Practice on videotape so you can review your performance.
– Practice introducing each issue to make sure your team is presenting a cohesive front.
– Run through all issues without breaking stride.

▼ Finally, before you get ready to negotiate with a specific supplier, conduct team reviews of the scheduled supplier.

This leads us to the day of negotiating. In Chapter 11, we will detail some tips and tasks to maximize the effectiveness of the actual negotiating session.

CHAPTER 11

CONDUCTING
NEGOTIATIONS

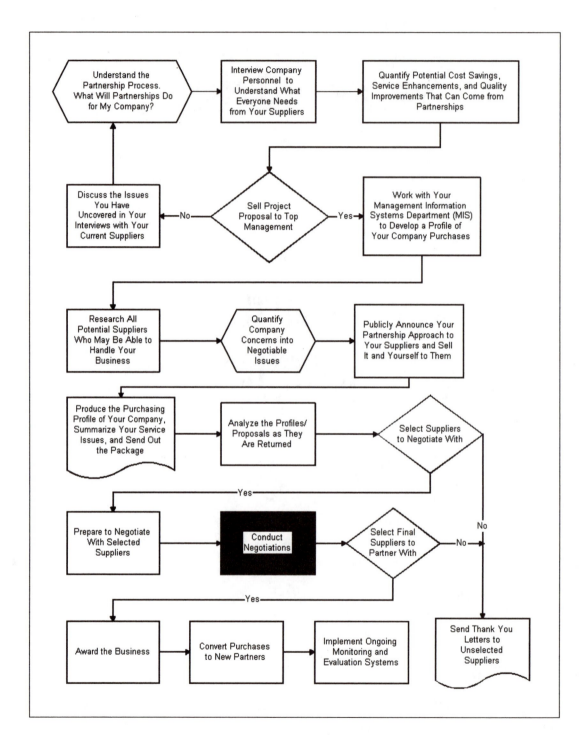

It has been said that in negotiations, 90% of success is driven by preparation and only 10% stems from your ability to horsetrade. So far, you have done the following:

▼ Uncovered and quantified your company's and customer's interests

▼ Prepared your issues

▼ Put yourself in the supplier's shoes to understand his or her interests

▼ Set yourself up to greet the suppliers in the most competitive way possible through your supplier presentation

▼ Done the research to know that you are negotiating with the best suppliers in the country who can handle your business

▼ Gathered the support of your organization

▼ Provided the supplier with all the information needed to make an intelligent business decision about how much of your business the supplier wants, and at what pricing levels.

You have built a powerful and fine-tuned machine. It's gassed up and idling, and now it's time to put it in gear and execute.

This chapter will give you tips for conducting a fair and positive negotiating session. In addition, it will discuss how the day will be organized, agendas, tours, breaks, lunch, caucuses, phone calls, and dirty tricks.

MAKING FINAL PREPARATIONS BEFORE NEGOTIATION BEGINS
▼

Before you begin negotiating, you must follow a few remaining steps to finish your preparations. These steps will ensure that you are organized and ready for the suppliers when they arrive to negotiate your partnership.

Materials to Provide

To manage the day efficiently, have the following materials available for the actual negotiation session.

THE ISSUE INDEX

This is a list of each issue that you will negotiate, in the order that you plan to negotiate them, and who will be negotiating each issue. You should distribute this list to your negotiating team (see the discussion of issue quantification in Chapter 6).

ISSUE DIAGRAMS

This is a detailed printout of each issue that summarizes your interests, goals, issue discussion outline, supplier benefits, and team roles. Give a copy of each issue diagram to your negotiating team. (Refer to Chapter 6 for a review of the issues diagram.)

THE BLANK MEMO OF UNDERSTANDING

During negotiation, you will need to summarize the agreement for each issue. Print out a blank memo that includes only the issue description on each page; leave the balance of the page for writing the actual agreement on that issue as you and the supplier negotiate. After you print out the blank pages for the memo of understanding, distribute to each of your negotiation team members the pages that relate to the issues for which they are the listener. The listener can record the agreement during the actual session.

GIVEAWAYS AND TOKENS

Handing out mugs, pens, shirts, or other tokens that feature your company logo is a good ice breaker and a gracious way to open or close the meeting. In addition, this shows suppliers that you appreciate their time and effort.

Preparing the Conference Room

In a negotiation session, you can control the setup of the meeting room, the comfort of the suppliers, how welcome they feel, and their initial impressions of your professionalism. There are a number of factors to attend to: the table setup, the seating arrangement, the room temperature, the frequency and quality of the meals, breaks, and refreshments, and your overall graciousness. Each of these factors can influence significantly how the supplier perceives you and your company. If you are good or bad in one of these areas, it will affect your negotiations seriously. For example, if you set the temperature too high or too low, the supplier will be too uncomfortable to give you his or her full attention.

SELECTING THE TABLE

You have three basic choices in terms of the table you use in the negotiating session—the round table; the U-shaped table; and the rectangular table. The round table has worked well in the past because it tends to make everyone equal. There is no head of the table, and everyone can see everyone else. Many conference rooms, however, have a rectangular table. Although this is not as conducive to open-minded communications, you can make a rectangular table work. Instead of having people sitting at the head or the foot of the table, try to keep everyone on the sides and as close together as possible. In this way, more people can see other people's facial expressions and reactions.

In some cases, you will have a U-shaped table. This is common in classroom settings because there is room in the front for a lecturer or presenter. If you find yourself with a U-shaped table, work with it as you would a rectangular setup, and do not use the front podium or lecture area. Remain seated; this is a discussion, not a lecture.

ARRANGING THE SEATING

Many of us can remember seeing clips on the TV news of union negotiations in which labor and management sit on opposite sides of a wide table. Some explain this setup as a means to prevent fist fighting during negotiations. In your negotiations, however, the supplier is not an adversary but a potential partner in your business. Avoid "our side, your side" arrangements. Instead, have your team members sit in every other seat so the supplier's people can sit in the remaining seats. Before the meeting, get the names of the supplier's people who will be attending your negotiations, make name cards for them, and place the cards so the supplier's people will be interspersed with your team members. This will increase camaraderie and break down defenses.

CONTROLLING THE ROOM TEMPERATURE

Be careful to keep the room temperature comfortable. One common tactic of unethical negotiators is to manipulate the temperature to affect endurance. For example, a warm room in the afternoon, after you have eaten lunch, will make you sleepy and tired and more likely to agree with negotiation issues so you can go home quickly. Other negotiators make the room too cold to achieve the same end. Keep the temperature between 70 and 75 degrees. If you have a problem controlling the room temperature and it becomes uncomfortable, explain your predicament to the supplier and offer to move to another room.

HANDLING MEALS, REFRESHMENTS, AND BREAKS

This is one opportunity for you to be a gracious and polite host to the suppliers. When you design your menu for a meal, avoid heavy food that will cause everybody to fall asleep (don't order prime rib). Appropriate choices include sandwiches, deli trays, and pizzas.

Another option is to make refreshments available. Bring donuts in the morning; have cookies, vegetables, or fruit brought in the afternoon. Have drinks and coffee available throughout the day. This will let the supplier know that you are sincerely trying to be a good host and that you are a thoughtful company.

Similarly, make it clear that anyone can call a break at any point to use the restroom or for any other personal need. You want to avoid the feeling that this is formal session in which people must sit uncomfortably until a formal break is called.

BEING A GRACIOUS HOST

I have mentioned the word *graciousness* often throughout this book. So far, we have talked about room temperature, meals, and refreshments; these are all ways to make the supplier feel more comfortable and at ease. The main point is to remember that the supplier is your guest. You invited the supplier to negotiate with you. Always remain calm, polite, and friendly and always try to provide for the creature comforts of your guests. This is not done as a tactic to make the supplier more amenable to what you're asking for, but it is basic humanness, and anything less will take away from your message and will cause the supplier to doubt your sincerity.

In addition, being gracious has strong benefits beyond demonstrating your sincerity. It shows that although you are professional and prepared, you are humane. In my experience and study, over 80% of buying decisions are based on emotion. Only 20% are based on facts. Although you might think that the supplier is meeting with you solely to sell his or her company, that is not wholly true. You are asking the supplier to buy into a partnership and to invest in the infrastructure of a long-term relationship. You are asking the supplier to take a risk politically because this is not the type of relationship that many suppliers have invested in historically. If you are polite and take care of the supplier's needs, if you are gracious, calm, friendly, and sincere, the supplier will recognize this and will want to work with you on a long-term basis.

CONDUCTING THE MEETING
▼

You have completed everything you need to do to implement a successful supplier partnership. In this section, we will review the steps you can take on the day of the negotiation to maximize the benefits of negotiating with the supplier.

What to Do Just before the Meeting

On the morning of the negotiation, make sure that everyone is comfortable with their role in the negotiations. Try the following exercises to loosen up your team.

THE HOT SEAT

In the hot seat exercise, each of your teammates is sitting in a circle, and a facilitator points to different people and shouts an issue. The teammate then describes the interest and position for that issue, and the rest of the team reviews the issue diagram to ensure that the person is in line with the team. This exercise will eliminate any impression that you have a disjointed team.

THE INTRODUCTION

In this exercise, each person runs through his or her issue, from the introduction to the request for the team's position. This is a powerful exercise because it refreshes the issues in everyone's minds and will help team members to be succinct during the negotiating session. (If you are not familiar with your issue, you might need additional time to state your point during the negotiation.)

THE FINAL BOOST

About 15 minutes before the suppliers are to arrive, give your team a pep talk. Let them know how well they are prepared, that they are as prepared as anyone in the country would be for this negotiation. Remind them that these suppliers are their guests for the day and are to be treated with warmth and politeness.

Opening the Negotiation Session

As the project leader for this process, you are responsible for introducing your team of negotiators to the supplier as well as introducing the day's agenda. It is important that you prepare your introduction and incorporate the following ideas:

▼ This is your first chance to sell for the day, so bring up what you perceive as the main benefits for the supplier. For example, for many suppliers these benefits may include the following:

  – A five-year expected purchase amount for the supplier's commodity area.

  – A five-year agreement with a company that is dedicated to reducing mutual costs through paperwork reduction, process reengineering, quality control, and other methods.

  – A chance to secure your company's business for five years, thus eliminating the need to assign sales resources to the account.

  – Forecasts and strategic plans that will help the supplier prepare for the future.

▼ Although this is a negotiation for a five-year contract, you look forward to a partnership that will be mutually beneficial for a much longer time—perhaps a lifetime.

▼ Provide an overview of your company. Although the supplier is most probably familiar with it by now, an overview is a good ice breaker and might help you provide suppliers with additional insights. Keep this description to less than a minute. Talk about your locations, number of employees, growth, and what you are excited about within your company (e.g., this partnership process).

▼ Introduce each of the people on your team and explain why they have been invited to the negotiation session. For example, you could introduce the buyer who has been responsible for purchasing the supplier's commodity in the past. You could introduce an end user who would be the recipient of the contract—the goods that are purchased through this contract. You could introduce someone from accounting and finance to ensure that the supplier's financial needs are discussed and that his or her commitment to the process and his or her needs are well understood. You could introduce someone from the engineering department to make sure that any technical issues are discussed competently. For each person introduced, mention his or her name, title, years with the company, and a short story about that person or explanation of that person's strengths.

▼ After you have introduced your team, ask the supplier team to introduce themselves.

▼ Go over the agenda. Explain that you will be going through a number of issues (the same ones summarized in the profile). Although the suppliers have provided high-level answers to your company's basic service, quality, and pricing questions, set aside time to discuss exactly how these issues would be treated under a partnership agreement.

▼ Discuss and explain the memo of understanding. Let suppliers know that you plan on taking detailed notes that describe the understanding achieved on any individual issue. In that way, at the end of the day, you can review what you have agreed to, make any final adjustments, sign a copy of the agreements, and provide a copy to both parties.

▼ Ask suppliers if they have any questions at this time.

▼ Introduce the presenter for the first issue. For example, "Now that we have introduced ourselves and have gone through the basic events for the day, I would like to introduce Bob. Bob is going to take us through our first topic for the day: product line coverage. It is important that we understand how much of our product needs you can supply to us."

How to Negotiate an Issue

Although we have discussed this in earlier chapters, this concept is so important that we discuss it here as well. For any issue you negotiate, the basic outline looks like this:

1. Introduce the issue, describing the current situation and what your interest is in fixing or enhancing it.

2. Sell the issue, trumpeting the benefits of the issue for both your company and the supplier.

3. Ask for your position.

4. Allow the supplier to respond. Do not alter your position before the supplier responds. (We are often inclined to change our request if the other party makes us uncomfortable by failing to respond. If the supplier refuses to answer, simply say "It seems you need time to think about this issue; we will offer a 10-minute caucus.")

5. If the supplier agrees with your request, the listener then summarizes the issue. After each team agrees with the summary, the listener introduces the next issue.

6. If the supplier does not agree with your request, sell the issue over again, and then ask what the supplier would have in mind to satisfy your basic interest. This is where most of the creativity comes into play.

You will find appropriate points for breaks and caucuses scattered among the issues. Your goal is to balance the time schedule for everyone's comfort level.

How to Close the Negotiating Session

The way in which you close the negotiation session will provide supplier representatives with their last impression of your company. It is important that you prepare for this part of the meeting as well as any other part. A negotiation session can end in one of three ways:

1. If the negotiating session goes well, you can end the session because you have negotiated all of the issues. After you have negotiated your final issue, you may do the following:

   ▼ Let the suppliers know that you have discussed all of the issues you identified.

   ▼ Ask the supplier if they have any additional issues they would like to negotiate or discuss.

   ▼ When all the issues you or the supplier wish to discuss are settled, have the executive representative from each company review and sign each page of the memo of understanding.

   ▼ Ask the supplier team members if they would like help getting to their next destination or if you can get them anything.

   ▼ Thank the supplier for his or her time, and adjourn.

   As with every other part of the negotiating session, it is important that you treat the supplier with graciousness as you close the meeting. Refrain from any expression of victory; this is unprofessional and could embarrass the supplier.

2. If the negotiating session goes poorly and the supplier is not willing, able, or interested in negotiating the issues in good faith, you may ask the supplier to leave. This usually happens for the following reasons:

   ▼ The representatives of the supplier do not have the authority to negotiate for the supplier discounts and pricing issues.

▼ The supplier is more interested in learning your agenda, with the hopes of coming back at a later date with counteroffers.

▼ The supplier is trying to hold out to see if you really expect to get all of the concessions you are asking for.

▼ The representatives of the supplier are unprepared.

As it becomes apparent that this might be an appropriate course of events, remember that you do not need to be anything less than gracious. Remind the supplier that in your phone calls you specifically expressed that you would be discussing the issues raised in the profile in more detail and that decisions would need to be made at this meeting. After this gentle reminder, ask the supplier if he or she needs to regroup with the home office before any further discussions. If so, offer to call to reschedule another meeting as appropriate. This scenario may happen in as many as one out of four of your negotiating sessions.

3. If the negotiating session is going well but you simply run out of time, you can end the session and schedule a continuation. As it becomes clear that you will not have sufficient time to complete the negotiations, ask the group to schedule the next meeting. Then continue to negotiate as many issues as you can in the time remaining.

OTHER TOPICS TO CONSIDER
▼

Here are a number of miscellaneous topics that you may encounter in your negotiations.

Holding a Caucus

A caucus is a private meeting called during a negotiation session for one or both parties to discuss, privately, some issue. You or the supplier might call a caucus under the following circumstances:

▼ A disagreement occurs within a party. This disagreement could be over what your position is in an issue or the tactics you use to negotiate it. Whenever there is a disagreement on your team regarding your position, do not argue or allow anyone on your team to argue in front of the supplier. If you have a concern, call a caucus: "Excuse me, but I think we need to step out for a few moments and discuss exactly what it is we're talking about here." When you get to a private room, then you can discuss it, argue, and disagree. The last thing you want to show the supplier is a divided team.

▼ The supplier employs, or seems to employ, a dirty trick. For example, the supplier is playing a good cop/bad cop role: One of the supplier's people is sympathetic to what you're asking for and another one starts saying that you don't deserve it, he can't do it, it's too expensive, or there's no profit left. If the supplier is doing this, and you recognize it, call a caucus diplomatically: "Maybe we should step out of the room and allow you to discuss exactly what it is you are willing and able to offer on this issue. Does this sound agreeable?" This is polite and gracious, yet you get to the point and do not let the supplier use a dirty tactic or trick against you in a negotiating session.

▼ The supplier needs to follow up on an issue with the home office. Sometimes you will ask a supplier to agree to something, and he or she will not know if it is possible and will have to make a call to the home office or to a technical advisor. Calling a caucus to allow the supplier to confer with his or her company will help the supplier make a good business decision. In addition, the supplier will not ask to leave the meeting, study the topic, and come back at a later date. It is important that you get through the entire negotiation session on this day and come to closure on every issue. Some suppliers may not be able to do this, but fight hard to maintain this level of completeness. Otherwise you will be negotiating for the rest of your natural life.

In general, call a caucus anytime that you feel unsure about what you are interested in. For example, if you ask the supplier for something specific in a negotiation issue and the supplier makes a counteroffer, it may be wise to call a caucus. It is possible that the new option will solve your interest even though it was not your original position.

Keeping Your Issues List Private

Although you explain at the beginning of the negotiating session that you are simply going to go over the issues that you raised in the profile, some suppliers will ask you for a copy of your index or agenda of issues. It is not normally in your best interest to give this to the supplier because people tend to look ahead and jump around to the issues they find most interesting. The most powerful reply to this question is, "If there are any issues you wish to discuss after we have finished our issues, we will take the time to go over them with you. The notes we have are really no different from the issues raised in the profile we sent you."

Using Visual Presentations

Many suppliers prepare a slide show or a videotape to present their company to you. Well, these can take a lot of time and give the control of the meeting to the supplier. Both of which we are not interested in doing. Most importantly, all of the questions and issues that you are looking to discuss will provide you a detailed understanding of their company. And, if at the end of the day they are still interested in showing the presentation, you will be glad to stay and watch it. In short, politely ask the supplier to wait until the end of the day after you have gone through all the issues.

Avoiding Dirty Tricks

Although you have prepared soundly for this negotiation and preparation accounts for well over 90% of the success of the negotiating session, you must be able to communicate effectively with the supplier on this day. You must be able to work through options and get to your interests and the interests of the supplier. Sometimes you will run into suppliers who will try to detract from that cause for their own perceived benefit; they will try to use tactics which will distract you from your position and interests. The following are some of the more common tactics and how to counter them.

GOOD COP VERSUS BAD COP

As discussed earlier, you may run into a supplier that has one person who listens sympathetically to your position, continuously expressing support for your idea, and someone who opposes your request, giving statistics, examples, and many reasons why it cannot work. (One is the good cop, and one is the bad cop.) After a while the good cop, who has hopefully gained your trust, will give in: "I guess we can't do it; that's too bad." Your best response to this situation is to bring it into the open. As stated earlier, offer the supplier some private time to caucus and come to terms with its capabilities.

EMPTY PROMISES

Generalization is another tactic that might be used. Although you have come to this negotiation prepared to ask for specific, quantifiable items for each issue, some suppliers will attempt to get you to accept commitments, promises, or generalizations. For example, you may bring up the idea of EDI. You may ask the supplier to provide you with the software, training, and hardware for three computer workstations equipped for EDI. The salesperson in the supplier group may say, "We can get into the specifics of this later, but I want to let you guys know here right now I am putting commitment on the table to you. We will take care of you guys on this issue. We will go back, study this, and see what type of hardware you need and whether or not we have some of it in-house, or if we need to provide it, but I will assure you that we are interested in doing this and we will accomplish this for you. That's my commitment." This sounds good and it might bring tears to your eyes, but it's valueless. In essence, you have given the power to decide this issue to the supplier. For any issue, do not allow a supplier to come at you with a generalization. Always require that you negotiate the specifics. If the supplier cannot answer you specifically, then call a caucus and allow the supplier to make a phone call back to the home office. Do not accept generalizations. (In this example, you can decide to set up a joint committee to decide the best EDI setup at your locations, but make sure you attach a schedule, and attach the final resolution of the issue.)

THE DELAYING TACTIC

Some suppliers use a delaying mechanism. They may stay to listen to all of your issues, but they are noncommittal on any specific issue and say that they will have to get back to you. Do not be too easy on suppliers if they use this tactic. You have provided them with a profile that outlines the issues you are discussing today. They have had plenty of time to review their pricing and service capabilities. In addition, in your invitation to this meeting you specifically requested that suppliers bring their decision makers. If suppliers refuse to negotiate specific issues, send them home politely.

THE CHIP-AWAY TECHNIQUE

Some negotiators will offer you something and in later discussions change their offer slightly. This puts you in an uncomfortable position because you do not want to argue every point. Your best defense is to write down everything you agree to, and have both parties sign it. If you do not, or if you do not record the agreements in detail, you are vulnerable to this tactic.

OTHER TACTICS

Many other dirty tricks or unscrupulous tactics may be used. Rather than review the subtleties of each tactic, focus on a few basic concepts that will eliminate a supplier's ability to take advantage of you:

▼ Keep alert for instances in which the supplier is not being honest with you, is trying to distract you, or is trying to bully you.

▼ Anytime you feel uncomfortable with the negotiation style, call attention to it. Say something like, "Mr. Supplier, I want to make it clear that we are here to share information and to set up a long-term partnership. I get the feeling that you are uncomfortable with this approach. Should we reschedule this meeting for another time when you might be more at ease?" Notice that although this gets to the point, it is polite. Regardless of what words you use, point out the supplier's actions and halt the meeting.

▼ At the most basic level, work to provide yourself and the supplier with a meeting in which you share information openly and honestly and decide how best to work together in the long run.

Recognize Your Successes

We have gone over many details that you must control if you are to maximize the results of your negotiating sessions. After the supplier has departed from your first negotiating session, have a celebratory meal or dinner with your teammates, celebrating the fact that you have begun your execution. It's important that you recognize this effort and success on the part of your teammates. Remember that your role in this project is more than just a coordinator—you are also a manager, a leader, and a motivator. Thank your team members for their efforts. In addition, summarize what you have negotiated in this session and make a presentation to your president. (You may wait until you have finished a complete commodity area.) Summarize the key concessions the supplier has made—especially if you have negotiated a rebate for past overpricing or have won better discounts. These types of concessions are dramatic, and although other service issues may be more important for the long-term competitive nature of your company, money issues provide a quantifiable success measure.

SUMMARY
▼

In this chapter, we have reviewed some of the key elements of successful negotiations. For each commodity or product area, follow the steps listed in this chapter. If you do, you will maximize the benefits available to you.

To get ready for the negotiations, you need to prepare the documents and materials you will need, including the following:

▼ Issue index

▼ Issue worksheets

▼ Blank memo of understanding

▼ Items to give suppliers in appreciation of their efforts.

As these documents are prepared, take some time to confirm the negotiations schedule with the supplier and with your team. Once you have confirmed the schedule, you can prepare the meeting room. To address all the details that could affect your negotiations, pay attention to the following:

▼ The shape of the table

▼ Seating arrangements

▼ The temperature of the room

▼ Meals, refreshments, and breaks

▼ An overall attitude of graciousness.

Now you have arrived at the day of the negotiation. You are ready to communicate with the suppliers about working together in a long-term partnership. To maximize your ability to do this effectively, focus on the following tasks on the day of the negotiating session:

▼ Loosening-up exercises, including the hot seat, the introduction, and a pep talk

▼ Opening the negotiation session

▼ Negotiating specific issues

▼ Closing the negotiation session.

In addition to these steps, consider the following topics as you negotiate:

▼ How and when to hold a caucus

▼ Keeping your issues list private

▼ Using visual presentations

▼ Avoiding dirty tricks and tactics, including

- Good cop versus bad cop
- Empty promises
- The delaying tactic
- The chip-away technique
-- Other tactics

▼ Recognizing your success

After you negotiate with the suppliers, you are ready to go through the process of selecting the suppliers to partner with.

CHAPTER 12

AWARDING
THE BUSINESS

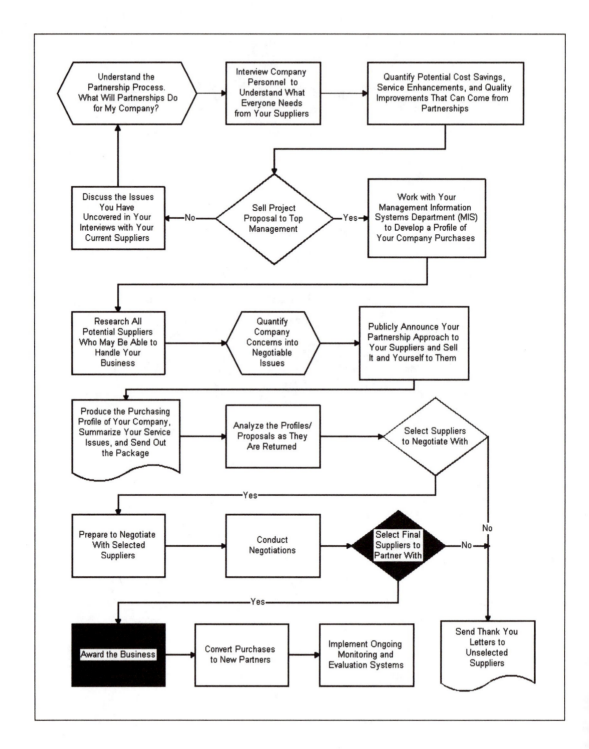

Now that you have negotiated with your short list of suppliers, it is time to make the final decision and then launch your new supplier partnerships. In this chapter, we will walk through the partner selection process and discuss the following:

- ▼ Selecting your new partner(s)

- ▼ Communicating with your new partner(s)

- ▼ Hosting an "Awarding the Business" dinner or banquet

- ▼ Finalizing your partnership contract

- ▼ Beginning to plan to convert your business.

How to Make Your Selection
▼

Now that you've negotiated with each of the suppliers in a specific commodity group or product area, it is time to meet with your council or negotiating team and vote for the supplier(s) to whom you will award the business. How do you decide? How do you make a good decision?

Reviewing Your Supplier Data

You have a major task ahead of you. Although many of the suppliers you have used in the past and many of the alternative suppliers you have negotiated with could make valuable partners, you must select which companies to contract with and which to send away. This can be an emotional and difficult step. However, you have already taken the following steps to ensure a good decision:

- ▼ Your interviews have provided you with a keen insight into the important features that your company seeks in a supplier.

- ▼ Because you have included other people in your company in your negotiating team, you have built a foundation of support for whatever decision is made. Many people have taken ownership of the process and, therefore, the results.

- ▼ You have a quantified summary of each supplier's offer for pricing, including discounts, base prices, payment terms, future pricing caps, and total annual cost. This knowledge will help you compare competing suppliers.

▼ In addition to pricing issues, each supplier has committed to specific service issues. This allows you to rank suppliers based on their ability to satisfy your most critical service and quality levels.

▼ You have financial statements from each of the suppliers. It is critical that you partner with a supplier who will be in business 5 or 10 years from now.

▼ You may also consider history. If you have worked with a supplier in the past, consider your impressions of that supplier. Before you dismiss a supplier based on past performance, however, be sure to temper your memory with a realistic assessment of how good of a customer you were.

Gaining Consensus

Based on the work you have completed, you are ready to gather your team and select your supplier partner base. The following are some steps you might take to gain consensus and choose your partners.

DISTRIBUTE MATERIALS

For each supplier you are considering, provide a copy to each team member of the memo of understanding based on the concessions in the negotiation session, the supplier's original proposal, and any related materials. In addition to this information, rerun the cost analysis reports discussed in Chapter 9 based on any new pricing terms negotiated. For example, you might print the supplier-versus-supplier report for the suppliers you are considering with any new negotiated discount information. If the supplier proposed a 20% discount off list prices in the original proposal, and you negotiated a 25% discount, you should incorporate this change in your price comparison reports.

In some cases, you will be able to estimate the effects of price concessions, especially when the pricing is based on base prices and discounts. If, however, you have negotiated with a supplier that incorporates complex pricing algorithms, you may need to ask the supplier to provide you a new pricing proposal based on the terms negotiated in your meeting.

SCHEDULE THE SELECTION MEETING

Schedule the selection meeting at your earliest convenience, allowing each team member to review the documents for at least one or two days. You still have some additional steps to complete before the selection meeting, so you should consider scheduling it to allow one or two weeks of lead time.

Follow Up before You Hold the Meeting

Before the meeting, follow up with each team member and ask if they need any additional information. If you can provide the information, do so as soon as possible. If you cannot satisfy the request, discuss it to work out an alternative. It is important that people review the information they need to make a decision.

If you do not complete this step, you face two risks. The first is that you might be surprised in the meeting. By talking with each of the participants before the meeting, you will understand which suppliers they favor and what their concerns are. This will give you an opportunity to address these concerns before the meeting. If you do not, you can be sure that you will not be able to gain consensus in the meeting and you will have to schedule another meeting in the future.

The second risk is that some of the participants will have legitimate requests for additional information or reports, but you will be unaware of those requests until the consensus meeting. If this happens, you will have to schedule another meeting at a later date, after team members have reviewed the requested information.

Develop Your Consensus Meeting Agenda

The basic format for a meeting agenda is shown in Figure 12.1.

— Figure 12.1 —

Partner Selection Meeting Agenda

---

1. State your objectives. For example, "The clear objective of this meeting is to select our core group of supplier partners for the _____ commodity group/product area."

2. Hold an initial blind vote for primary and secondary suppliers. (Make sure you partner with enough suppliers to cover your business.)

3. If the vote is not unanimous, discuss each supplier and related good and bad points.

4. Redo the blind vote.

5. Repeat Steps 3 and 4 as necessary until all products are covered by a group of core supplier partners.

6. Assign roles to each supplier.

7. Develop closing issues for each new partner.

Holding the Consensus Meeting

Now that you have followed up with each of the participants and have prepared the information that was requested, you are ready to hold your consensus meeting. The following are some major points you should consider in running this meeting.

TAKING THE VOTE

Your goal is to reach a unanimous decision. The risk of a split decision is that minority voters might sabotage, at some level, the partnership with the suppliers they did not vote for. If a unanimous decision is not likely, make sure everyone agrees on a method for selecting the partners (e.g., a simple majority vote or a two-thirds vote). In addition, you can give extra weight to the vote of the people who work more intimately with the suppliers in the commodity group or product area you are voting on.

INTEREST VERSUS POSITION

As you deal with dissension in the meeting, it is important to remain aware of the difference between an interest and a position. For some questions, you might involve some of the suppliers in the discussion over the phone. For example, a client had a choice between two suppliers for a five-year partnership. One of the suppliers had a superior offer for dollar savings and service levels but had a weaker balance sheet, which caused some team members to doubt the supplier's ability to handle the business on a long-term basis. After a team review, the supplier's long-term financial stability was still unclear. The next step was to call the supplier and say, "We love your offer, we're very interested in it; however, we feel uncomfortable about your financial position. Is there something that you can tell us to ease our fears? Do you have an investor coming in? Did you have a profitable year this year? Why should we believe that you are going to be in business five years from now?" This put the ball in the supplier's court. As it turned out, the client was not convinced of the supplier's stability and therefore decided to offer that supplier a position as a secondary partner in the commodity group/product area.

ASSIGNING THE SUPPLIER'S ROLE

For each commodity group/product area, you can select one primary supplier (who has the first choice on all sales) and one secondary supplier (who supplies what the primary cannot) or divide the business among a larger group of suppliers based on some criteria. For example, if you chose three corrugated suppliers, you might provide the following guide for sourcing a specific order:

1. For corrugated boxes smaller than 2.5 cubic feet, order from supplier A.

2. For corrugated boxes larger than 2.5 cubic feet, order from supplier B.

3. For any orders that cannot be serviced timely by supplier A or supplier B, order from supplier C.

You can develop your own criteria based on the capabilities and capacities of each of the suppliers you are considering.

Normally, the more volume you can give to a single supplier, the more benefits you can receive from this process—whether it's from better pricing because you order in bigger volume, or from simplifying the process by having one supplier taking care of all of your needs, thus reducing your paperwork. However, it does not make sense to force this situation if there are mitigating factors which must be considered.

Splitting the Business

You may need to split your purchases to mitigate business risks or to take advantage of special characteristics of a particular supplier. Valid reasons for splitting your business include the following:

▼ One supplier provides superior quality in certain product areas.

▼ One supplier whom you like and would select as your primary supplier does not cover certain product lines that you need.

▼ One supplier provides superior service in a given area that is not matched by another supplier.

▼ There is an atmosphere of instability that compels you to select a backup supplier.

▼ Your primary supplier does not have the capacity to meet your needs 100% of the time.

Selecting the Suppliers

As you gain consensus in your meeting and select specific suppliers to handle parts of your business, you can prepare to appoint that supplier as your partner. As soon as you reach consensus on a supplier, be sure that the decision is clear to the entire team, write down the selection, and move on. In addition to writing down the name of the suppliers you select and what role they will play, write down any lingering concerns about the supplier or the supplier's offer.

Developing Closing Issues

Your final task before inviting your selected suppliers to the awards banquet is to develop any closing issues you wish to negotiate with the supplier based on the concerns you recorded about the supplier in the consensus meeting. These issues may have surfaced during negotiations with other companies and pertain to areas in which the supplier is weak (e.g., service or pricing). Typical issues include the following:

VOLUME INCENTIVES

If your business exceeds expectations and goes above a certain level defined by you and the supplier, then you will get an additional discount or rebate based on that purchase volume. For example, if you negotiate with your supplier of corrugated goods, you might stipulate that, although you expect to buy about $200,000 worth of corrugated, if you buy 30% more in a given year ($260,000), you will receive an additional 2% discount on your purchases. The following options are possible:

Option 1: If we exceed our estimated purchases from the supplier in any one-year period by more than 30%, the supplier will provide us a rebate of 2% of total purchases. This rebate will be payable within 30 days of the year end.

Option 2: If we exceed our estimated purchases from the supplier in any one-year period by more than 30%, the supplier will increase our discount by 2%. This increased discount will be applicable to all future purchases throughout the life of the partnership.

The primary benefit to the supplier in this issue is the incentive it will provide your company to increase purchases from this supplier. At the same time, the supplier is not at risk by providing additional discounts if the business doesn't grow. In addition, this issue assures the supplier that if your business grows quickly in the future, you will still want to remain in partnership with that supplier. If volume discounts were not offered, it might be financially enticing to open the business to other suppliers at the end of the contract period.

REFUNDS OF OVERPAYMENTS

For supplier partners who have worked with you in the past, you can negotiate to recover some portion of the amount you paid to them in excess of your new negotiated rates. For example, if the corrugated supplier you wish to partner with is a current supplier, and what he or she used to charge you $1 for is going to cost you $.80 under the partnership agreement, you may request that you recover part of the 20% excess you paid in the past. If you spent $100,000 with the supplier at the old rates, you could calculate that you overspent by $20,000 based on the new rates offered.

This issue tends to provide an enormous boost to the partnership process and to team morale. It enables you and your team to present to the president of your company a check that was a direct result of your negotiating efforts. However, it is important that you calculate the exact amount you are proposing that the supplier rebate to you for past business. By comparing the rates you have negotiated with the supplier in this partnership agreement with the rates the supplier charged in the past, you can calculate the difference. As part of the partnership agreement, ask the supplier to present you with a rebate for the amount paid in excess of current rates over the past year. Ask the supplier to present this check within 30 days of the commencement of your partnership. (Although you ask for the entire amount of the discrepancy, negotiating even a 10% rebate is still a major victory.)

When a supplier has charged you rates well in excess of the negotiated rates you secured in the partnership process, the numbers will be demonstrable. In this issue you are, in essence, asking the supplier to refund inappropriate amounts charged to you over the years. If the supplier does not agree to the refund, he or she may not be fully committed to the partnership process. Although you might begin by asking for the entire amount you can show that the supplier overcharged you, your goal is to bring a check for some amount to your president. In the past, some suppliers have settled for 25% to 60% of the total amount!

COST EQUALIZATION

If you find in your analysis of the supplier's proposal that his or her price quotes, as they stand, require that you pay higher prices in some areas (more than you did before the partnership), you can show the analysis to the supplier and ask him or her to adjust the pricing accordingly.

To calculate the amounts, summarize the total amount for the year that you will pay for each product you bought in the previous year. If you find that for some products you will pay more than you did before the partnership, then you need to ask the supplier to equalize the cost for that product with the cost you paid the previous year. Although you would be happy with any movement on the part of the supplier, you are looking for the supplier to match any prices you received before the partnership.

This can be important to the supplier as well if he or she is at risk of pricing a certain location or product area at a level that will make your buyers source the purchases elsewhere. The goal of the partnership is not to force your buyers to use your new partners but to negotiate an agreement that will make them want to use the partner.

Other Issues

Any issues are appropriate as closing issues. If you have new information or would like to negotiate something more meaningful than the supplier offered, then you should reopen the issue. Regardless of which issue you decide to open in the closing meeting, be sure to explain to the supplier why you want to discuss the issue. Typical reasons include the following:

▼ We have received new information about this issue since we last talked.

▼ This is a new idea we have developed based on discussions with other suppliers.

▼ We wanted to discuss this issue again because we did not gain closure in our previous discussions.

▼ This is an issue we did not bring up in our previous meeting, but on review, we think our partnership could benefit if we addressed it.

CONDUCTING THE AWARDS CEREMONY
▼

After you have made your decision and developed your closing issues, it is time to award the business to your new partner. To schedule the ceremony, call your main contact at the supplier. Explain that you have enjoyed working with him or her in these discussions and that you would like to offer the supplier your business, subject to the discussion of a couple of issues. Based on the resolution of those issues, you plan to award the business the same day in a banquet or ceremony.

You need to decide where to hold the banquet. Unlike the actual negotiations, there is no threat of biasing your team's decision, so you might feel comfortable having the banquet at the supplier's location or your own. Nearby banquet halls or hotels often provide a suitable atmosphere as well as a neutral location.

Issuing the Invitation

After you discuss the award ceremony verbally, send a follow-up letter reiterating logistics of your meeting, where it's going to be, when, at what time, and for how long. A sample invitation letter is shown in Figure 12.2.

— FIGURE 12.2 —

SAMPLE AWARDS CEREMONY INVITATION LETTER

Supplier Contact
Supplier Company
Address
City, State, Zip

Dear Supplier:

As we discussed on the phone, each of us at our company has enjoyed work-ing with you and your company in developing what will be a world-class strategic partnership. Based on your initial proposal and the modifications we agreed to in our discussions, we have selected you and your company, sub-ject to a discussion of three closing issues, to be our long-term partner. In anticipation of this event, we would like to invite you and your teammates to join us for a working session, which will be followed by a dinner and award ceremony.

We have chosen your company to be our long-term partner because you have shown a keen understanding of the importance of superior quality and customer service as well as the importance of working together to reduce our mutual costs.

I will follow up with you to confirm our date and location, but if you have any questions or concerns, please call me directly at (XXX) XXX-XXXX.

Sincerely,

Purchasing Manager

Preparing for the Ceremony

It is thoughtful to select a gift for the supplier. The gift should be pre-sentable—a plaque, a statue; something that can be displayed proudly in the sup-plier's lobby or office. Make this gift professional, not too gaudy or ostentatious; do not spend more than $100 or so. Have both your name and the supplier's name engraved on the gift. In addition, if you hold the meeting at your company site, set up a tour so your guests can become more familiar with your business facilities.

A sample agenda for a business award ceremony is shown in Figure 12.3.

— FIGURE 12.3 —

THE AWARD CEREMONY AGENDA

▼ Introduction and welcome

▼ Issues discussions/closing issues

▼ Caucus

▼ Discussion of the portion of your business that the supplier is to receive

▼ Award ceremony

▼ Presentation of the awards or gifts

▼ Small celebration cocktail hour with champagne or sparkling grape juice

▼ Discussion

▼ Setting up of the conversion task force

▼ Departure

INTRODUCTION AND WELCOME

Your introduction/welcome is important, and you should take the time to script it before you present it. Keep in mind the following when you write your introduction:

▼ Thank the supplier for the time, effort, and creative thought that went into the proposal and negotiation sessions.

▼ Make the introduction upbeat and exciting, stating that you chose the supplier because of his or her energy, commitment to customer service, and commitment to innovation.

▼ Point out that the supplier was not the best in terms of price; other companies offered better prices on some items, but you looked at the overall cost and this supplier came out ahead because of service, quality, and innovation. If the supplier did have the best cost on every item, you still should emphasize the service and quality issues you considered in choosing them.

Closing Issues

At the end of your introduction, present the first closing issue. The key is to remember your frame of mind. If you have decided to award the business to the supplier regardless of his or her answers to your closing issues, do not feel pressured to obtain your position. Be sure to sell the benefits of the issues to the supplier; you want to keep the meeting positive.

Holding a Caucus

After you have discussed the closing issues, take a recess to discuss the outcome of the closing issues negotiation. During this caucus, confirm with your team that you are ready to partner with the supplier. As you reach this agreement, print a new copy of the memo of understanding. Just as in the original negotiation session, have a representative from both companies sign each page.

Reaffirming the Supplier's Role

Earlier in this chapter, we reviewed your choices in assigning to the supplier a role for your business. It is critical that the supplier understands this role— whether it is that of a primary supplier, with the right to first refusal on all relevant purchase orders, or a secondary supplier, responsible for specific purchase items or for acting as a backup to the primary supplier.

After you explain the role the supplier will play, ask the supplier to confirm that the role is satisfactory. If the supplier is to be a secondary, give him or her the opportunity to amend the bid as appropriate. The supplier may want to adjust pricing or other service issues based on the actual amount of business he or she will receive.

Making the Award

After you return from your caucus, go to the podium or back to your seat and ask for everyone's attention: "Ladies and gentlemen, based on the commitments made by the supplier through their proposal and all of our subsequent discussions, and based on the abilities displayed, we are happy and excited to extend to the supplier our commitment to a five-year strategic partnership." Then begin the applause or standing ovation, and ask the supplier's main contact person to accept the plaque or gift.

This would be a good time to break out the champagne or the sparkling grape juice. Take time for everyone to mingle and relax. Although you and your team have broken away from the traditional relationship type of buying, it is still important to develop a good relationship with your suppliers. You did not choose them because of a relationship, but developing a relationship will improve your partnership.

SCHEDULING THE CONVERSION MEETING

Now that you have finalized the agreement for working together for the next five years, it is time to begin talking about converting your business. Set a firm date for a joint task force to plan a smooth transition (to anticipate, minimize, and avoid problems). This conversion process is the focus of the next chapter.

CLOSURE AND DEPARTURE

After you have settled the date for your conversion task force, ask the supplier if he or she has any questions. Based on the answer, you are ready to conclude your meeting. As you have throughout this process, leave with a gracious "thank you" and a warm smile.

Writing the Contract

The final step is to develop the contract from the memo of understanding. Although you need to work this out with your legal counsel, it is important to remember the following as you write the contract:

- ▼ All the points of the contract must be included in the memo of understanding, and all the points in the memo of understanding must be included in the contract.

- ▼ Make sure that any tariffs, retail price lists, or public indexes that will be the basis for pricing are specifically named in the contract.

- ▼ For some contracts, make sure you file with any required governmental agencies.

It is important to develop a document that will represent the understanding of both parties in terms of the partnership. Whether you put this understanding in the form of a formal contract or simply detail the service and pricing issues you have agreed on is up to you and your legal department. At the least, however, you must record your understanding in writing.

SUMMARY
▼

This chapter helps you bring all your efforts to a climax. You have taken all the preparation and turned it into a supplier contract. As you might expect, it is not easy to consider all the negotiations with all the suppliers and decide which ones to partner with. To make the decision as clear as possible, it is important to keep in mind the following:

▼ You have already completed many tasks that will ensure that the best supplier will be evident and your decision will be a good one.

▼ As with every other step in this process, it is vital to the long-term success of the partnership that you select the supplier partners as a team. Each of the people on your negotiating team should have input about which suppliers are selected. If you make the decision by yourself, you risk losing the support of the rest of the company.

▼ To gain consensus, you should give each person on your negotiating team a copy of the information he or she will need to make an informed decision.

▼ Before you hold the supplier selection meeting, meet with each participant in the negotiation process and discuss their views and concerns (this will prevent surprises and delays).

▼ During the supplier selection meeting, remain aware of your real interests in each issue.

▼ For each supplier who you choose to become your partner, determine his or her ongoing role. Is the supplier going to be the primary supplier or the secondary supplier? Which products will the supplier be asked to cover?

▼ After you have assigned roles to each supplier, address any additional issues that you need to cover with each supplier before finalizing the partnership.

At this point, you have chosen your suppliers and are ready to hold your awards ceremony. Consider the following steps:

▼ Send the supplier an invitation for the ceremony.

▼ Welcome the supplier and thank him or her for the time and effort expended in developing this partnership.

▼ Prepare to negotiate the closing issues you developed earlier in this chapter.

▼ Hold a caucus to allow you and the supplier to react to the negotiated closing issues.

▼ Explain the role the supplier will have in providing your product.

▼ Award the business and the gifts to the supplier.

▼ Schedule a meeting to begin converting the business to the supplier.

▼ Close the meeting and thank the supplier again for his or her time and effort.

▼ Based on the memo of understanding developed during the negotiating session and the closing issues in the awards ceremony, develop a written contract or memo that documents your agreement.

In this chapter, you have selected your suppliers and officially awarded the business to them. Although this is a tremendous relief and calls for celebration, your job is not over. If you want to enjoy the benefits that you deserve from negotiating this world-class partnership, you must make sure that the execution is as good as your preparation has been: You must manage the process of converting your business to the new supplier. In Chapter 13, we will review methods to ensure a smooth transition into your new partnership.

CONVERTING TO YOUR NEW SYSTEM

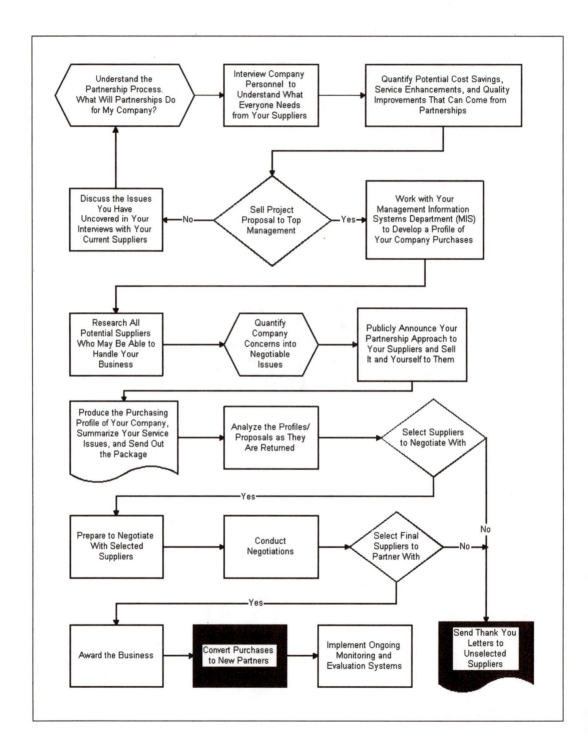

Now that you have awarded the business to your supplier partner, you may experience an early sense of euphoria; you have accomplished something! You have started the process in which your company will save many dollars and gain new competitive advantages. However, you have only begun the process; your next task is conversion—changing your current system to your new one.

One of the more common examples of a conversion is changing a computer system. For example, if your company has been working on a mainframe and is now upgrading to a more powerful computer system with new software, you will be converting to the new system. In this conversion, you will test the new system before you rely on it. You should follow the same logic in converting to a new supplier partner. To avoid costly failures in the field, you are going to work with the new partners to test their services and quality. In addition, you want to manage your company's perception of the new supplier partner. This is especially important for your first conversion. You are setting the stage for your whole approach to buying as well as for the specific supplier.

SELECTING THE CONVERSION TEAM
▼

The first step in this process is to appoint a conversion team: a task force from your company and from the supplier's company who will work together to convert the business and minimize problems. The new team should include the following people:

- ▼ A buyer, preferably one who has been responsible for buying those goods in the past.

- ▼ A line worker who is affected by that supplier. For example, if it's a raw material supplier, you might include someone from the receiving docks who receives the steel.

- ▼ An engineer who designs what will be done with the purchased products.

- ▼ A representative from manufacturing who uses the purchased products to make your final output.

- ▼ The following people from the supplier:

  - – A representative from the negotiating team who is knowledgeable in all aspects of the contract.

  - – An MIS expert who can identify the steps necessary to implement any EDI or system-related issues.

- A design engineer who can review your manufacturing process to determine if there will be any compatibility problems.
- A packaging expert who can review the potential for damage.
- An executive who can review the overall ability to handle the business in the time allotted for conversion and can authorize additional resources that might be needed. (Access to top management is important because it will give you a link to a powerful level in the supplier's company. If there is a recurring service problem, you will need access to someone who has the authority and creativity to solve it.)
- An executive or other employee who has been familiar with your account if you have done business together in the past.

With this team, you will be able to attack potential problems from all angles, eliminating them at their source, before they take effect.

HOLDING THE TASK FORCE MEETING
▼

Hold this meeting as early as you can after the awards banquet so you will have as much time as possible to handle potential problems. A sample meeting agenda is shown in Figure 13.1. Of course, you will need to customize it to fit your business.

—— **FIGURE 13.1** ——

CONVERSION TASK FORCE MEETING AGENDA

▼ Welcome and personal introductions

▼ Discussion of specific conversion issues

▼ Plant tour

▼ Identify next steps to take and make a list of things to do

---

Offering the Welcome and Personal Introductions

Begin the meeting by introducing each person who is participating. Present each person to the group, giving his or her name, position, and role on the conversion task force. In addition to these introductions, it is important, as with every meeting, that you describe the objectives of the meeting. To do this, you can review the agenda and the list of issues that you will discuss.

Discussing Specific Conversion Issues

Although you may find more issues to focus on during conversion, the following issues are critical.

SUPPLIER CAPACITY

With the supplier team present, explain as clearly as possible your detailed order volume in the first two months of your partnership. Look each supplier representative in the eye and ask the following:

- ▼ Can you deliver the quantity we expect to order of each of these products?

- ▼ Will you have any quality issues in trying to fulfill these orders?

- ▼ Are there any foreseeable obstacles to delivering these products on our expected schedule?

- ▼ How much lead time do you need to deliver these products to us?

- ▼ Do you understand the specifications we have provided for each product?

- ▼ Do you need any additional information to understand the products we intend to order?

INBOUND FREIGHT

Review the modes of transportation that the supplier will use to ship your orders. Specifically,

- ▼ Make sure the carriers are aware of the business and are prepared for the volume you expect to order.

▼ Review the past performance of the carrier with other customers your sup-plier/partnerships to in terms of ontime delivery, damage claims, and over-all reliability.

DELIVERY PROCEDURES

If you have any preferred procedures for incoming shipments, review them with the supplier and carriers (before shipping). Examples include

▼ Time of day to deliver products

▼ Unloading procedures

▼ Paperwork

▼ Plant shutdown deadlines (if the product is not delivered on time).

QUALITY INSPECTION AND CERTIFICATION

▼ In addition to reviewing the product specifications and any related blue-prints with the supplier, review the supplier's process for ensuring quality.

▼ In addition to recognizing your technical needs, the supplier should review his or her process for confirming that your orders meet specifications.

▼ Find out the name of the person ultimately responsible for inspecting your orders, and be sure that he or she understands your product and processes.

PRODUCT SPECIFICATIONS AND REQUIREMENTS

▼ With your engineering department, list and explain all of your product spec-ifications to the technical representative of the supplier.

▼ If you detect any hesitation on the part of the supplier representatives, yell early and loud. Call in the supplier negotiating team so you can work out any problems.

REVIEWING INITIAL ORDERS

In addition to product specifications and any special conditions you might have, discuss quantity, delivery locations, special customer expectations, and any specific aspects of your first 60 days of orders.

FORECASTS

▼ Invite a representative from your sales and marketing department to review any sales forecasts you can provide to the supplier.

▼ This task should be implemented in alignment with the negotiated agreement. As discussed in Chapter 6, sharing sales forecasts with your suppliers will help them plan appropriately for any shifts in volume you might experience.

ORDERING PROCEDURES

▼ It is possible to implement any EDI modules you have negotiated with the suppliers in the short run. However, for the short term, you need to set up a method for communication and ordering.

▼ Invite your MIS specialists to meet with you and the customer service representatives from the supplier and work out a paperwork method.

EDI COMMUNICATIONS AND INSTALLATION

▼ Although your main concern at this time is to develop paperwork procedures to ensure a smooth transition, you can still lay the foundation to implement EDI after the critical conversion time is past.

▼ If you have included your MIS expert in the meeting, you can discuss the following issues with the supplier:

– *EDI protocol and standards.* Make sure the language the supplier uses in its EDI applications can be imported by your system.

– *Hardware requirements.* Based on your negotiations, either you or the supplier is responsible for verifying that your systems are capable of EDI links with the supplier and arranging for any defects.

– *Business requirements.* Discuss the use of the information that will be transferred via EDI. Some applications may require additional programming, daily uploads, or other special handling that must be planned for.

– *Next steps.* Because of these discussions and the respective plans made, schedule the implementation of hardware installations, software installations, programming time, and system testing.

SPECIALIZED FIELD SUPPORT

If, during the negotiations, the supplier agreed to provide specialized support, schedule initial meetings with the affected people and define tentative tasks and work plans. Examples of specialized support can include a design engineer, a packaging engineer, a programmer, an analyst, a dispatcher, or any other skilled aid.

PERFORMANCE REPORTING

During the negotiations, you outlined reports and statistics the supplier would provide so that you could "grade" the supplier's performance. During the conversion, make sure that the supplier provides layouts and definitions of the specific reports he or she will generate periodically.

ROUTINE AND PREVENTIVE MAINTENANCE

Have the supplier inspect for immediate needs any equipment on which he or she will perform continuing preventive maintenance. This will help prevent any emergency situations in the short term.

TEST RUNS

Have the supplier provide samples of the products you will be ordering. This will allow your engineers and inspectors to review the result, not just the controls that will be in place to ensure quality products that meet your specs.

OTHER ISSUES

Review all the issues you have negotiated with the supplier. Be sure to discuss any issues that could affect your orders in the short term.

Conducting the Plant Tour

In addition to discussing the specific issues, it is important to walk through your plant with the technical people from the supplier. This will allow the experts to detect any potential problems or opportunities that you may not have identified internally. You might want one of your engineers to guide the supplier through your plant to answer any questions about design or specifications of the machines.

Many companies do not allow outsiders into their plant for fear of exposing industrial secrets. If you are concerned about showing your plant to your supplier, be sure to weigh this concern against the benefits of gleaning the supplier's viewpoint on your operations.

Identifying the Next Steps to Take

Based on your plant tour and specific issue discussions, you have developed several tasks. Before you adjourn as a group, consolidate all the tasks and responsibilities for each party and review them as a whole. Specifically, obtain agreement on the following:

1. The definition of the task
2. The major steps involved in the task
3. Who has responsibility for the task
4. When the task is due for completion
5. Any open points in relation to the task
6. Who will absorb any costs related to the task.

Examples of tasks you might identify in corroboration with the supplier include the following:

▼ Provide the supplier with a complete forecast of your purchasing needs for the next two weeks.

▼ Provide the supplier with specifications for specific parts or components of parts.

▼ Have the supplier accompany one of your sales representatives on a sales call to see customer requirements first hand.

▼ Provide the supplier with examples of products that you have in stock that are similar to what the supplier will be selling you. This allows the supplier to review the product and the supplier product's compatibility.

▼ Begin a routine maintenance program with an initial equipment analysis and checkover.

▼ Have the supplier deliver a shipment of sample products for your engineering and manufacturing departments to review.

These ideas are based on the specific experiences of other companies. Your needs could produce a completely different set of tasks.

ESTABLISHING A SYSTEM FOR ONGOING COMMUNICATION
▼

Although you have prepared to complete a world-class supplier relationship, you need to remain flexible. If there is an opportunity to bring added services or satisfaction to your customers, it is important that you discuss it immediately with the supplier. It is vital that you establish a communication link with an executive vice president from the supplier. Regardless of his or her title, the contact must have the ability and authority to make things happen. Although you do not want to call your high-level contact every time a shipment is late, do not let any repetitive problems or major opportunities slip by without a discussion.

NOTIFYING UNSELECTED SUPPLIERS
▼

After you have converted your business to your new supplier partners, it is time to notify the unselected suppliers of their situation. Although you may tell these suppliers at any point that you have not selected them, after you have converted your business to your new partners you need to inform every supplier that engaged in the process. Figure 13.2 shows a sample letter for unselected suppliers.

— FIGURE 13.2 —

SAMPLE UNSELECTED SUPPLIER THANK YOU LETTER

Dear Supplier:

On behalf of our company, I would like to thank you for your participation in our strategic supplier partnership program. At this time, we have selected other suppliers to be our partners for the next few years. Our choice was complex and difficult and was based on a combination of service and pricing issues. Although we do not have any immediate needs to work together with your company, we look forward to future opportunities.

We will preserve a copy of your proposal in the event that we need to consider alternative suppliers to our current partners. Each of us at our company would like to thank you for your proposal and wish you much success in the future.

Best Regards,

Your Name Here

SUMMARY
▼

Initial impressions can last a long time. If your partnership starts strong, your company will tend to view the partnership favorably in the future. If the partnership starts with problems and breakdowns, your company will view the partnership with distrust and will wonder why you changed in the first place. To manage your company's perception of the partnership, it is vital that you control the quality of the products and services you receive from your supplier partners. To accomplish this goal, you need to work with your supplier to convert your purchases to him or her, and you might consider taking the following steps:

- ▼ Select a team composed of employees from your company that will use the supplier's products or services as well as experts from the supplier.

- ▼ Hold a task force meeting to plan how to convert the business. Specifically, you can review the following issues with the supplier to control as many variables as possible:
  - Supplier capacity
  - Inbound freight
  - Delivery procedures
  - Quality inspection and certification
  - Product specifications and requirements
  - Initial orders
  - Forecast of requirements
  - Ordering procedures
  - EDI communication and installation
  - Specialized field support
  - Performance reporting
  - Routine and preventive maintenance
  - Other issues that are unique to your company and situation.

- ▼ After you have reviewed these issues with the supplier, you might consider giving the supplier a tour of your operations.

- ▼ Your final step in this meeting is to summarize the next steps that each party is to complete.

- ▼ After you have held your task force meeting, you need to focus on ongoing communication issues.

▼ After you have successfully converted the business to your new partner suppliers, it is time to notify the unselected suppliers about their status.

You have now set the stage for a successful transition to your new partners. Although you have performed the most demanding steps in this process and you have locked in a world-class relationship, you still have important steps to complete. Before you breathe a sigh of relief and go on a well-deserved vacation, you need to implement the ongoing systems to monitor your new partnerships.

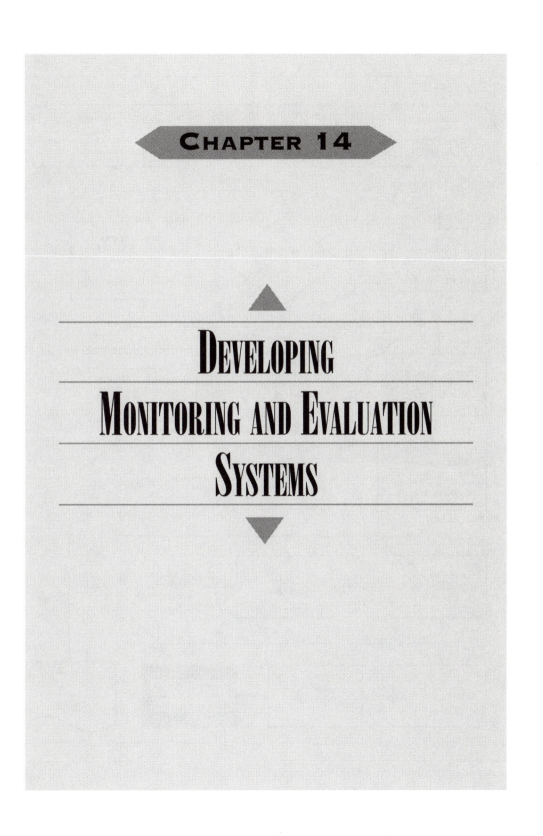

CHAPTER 14

DEVELOPING
MONITORING AND EVALUATION
SYSTEMS

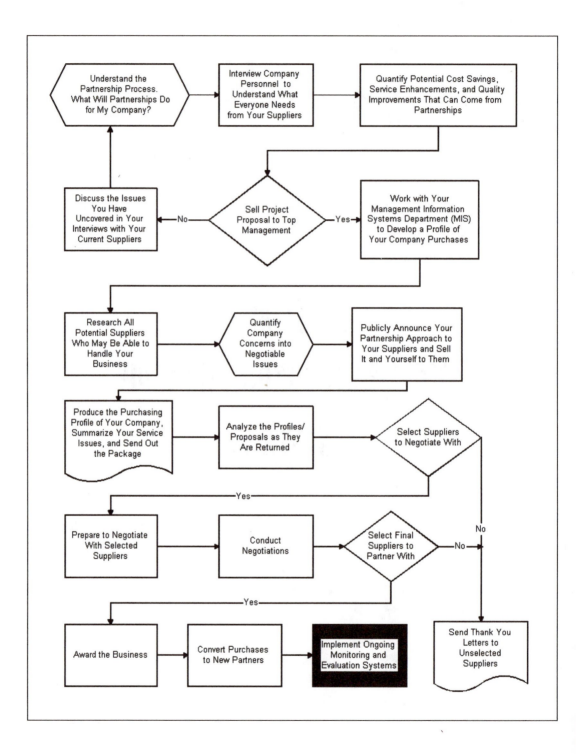

At this stage, you are completing the final tasks required to set in motion a world-class supplier relationship and all the benefits that go with it. You have selected your partner(s) and placed your initial orders, beginning the conversion process. To take advantage of everything you and your supplier partners have agreed to, you need a method to monitor service and evaluate performance. Through management reports, internal discussions, and third-party information, you will be able to manage your new relationship effectively and with a minimum of ongoing, repetitive effort.

Recently I asked a co-worker if he could complete a computer program design we were working on, and he replied in his habitually witty style: "Of course I can finish it if you give me three weeks of uninterrupted time to focus on the program." So it is with monitoring and evaluations systems: Can you set up one that will let you know when a relationship is suffering or when one of your peers declines to use your new partner? Of course you can, but the real question is, can you do it without spending the majority of your work day making phone calls, reviewing purchase orders, and meeting regularly with each department in your company? This chapter will review a number of management techniques that will alert you to problems without requiring that you spend an inordinate amount of time reviewing purchases.

The following management tools will support you in analyzing the effectiveness of your supplier relationships:

▼ Reports prepared by the supplier

▼ Reports prepared by you and your company

▼ Exception reports that display all service, quality, and pricing failures

▼ Supplier focus groups and strategy meetings

▼ Feedback from within your company

▼ Customer feedback

▼ Departmental communications.

DEVELOPING SUPPLIER REPORTS
▼

Some information can be collected and reported by your supplier and organized into a report much easier than by you, the buyer. For example, the supplier can (and often does) record the day you place your order and the day it is delivered.

This information can be used to provide ontime delivery statistics as well as back-order summaries. In addition to any custom reports you might innovate with your supplier, the following reports typically provide helpful information from the supplier.

The Ontime Delivery Report

Many suppliers track the day an order is placed as well as the day it is delivered. A supplier cannot invoice an order until the product is delivered, so he or she knows the actual delivery date. With this information, the supplier can summarize the actual lead time from point of order to point of delivery. To make this report as useful as possible, work with the supplier so the following information is included in the ontime delivery summary report:

- ▼ product description
- ▼ purchase order number
- ▼ order date
- ▼ shipment date (if available)
- ▼ promised delivery date
- ▼ actual delivery
- ▼ production lead time (number of days from order date until ship date)
- ▼ calculated delivery lead time (delivery date - shipment date)
- ▼ calculated overall lead time (delivery date - order date)

The Price-per-Unit Purchased Report

During your negotiations, you negotiated specific prices for each product, or you negotiated a specific formula for determining prices. By summarizing the actual amount you paid for each product, the supplier can provide you with information to confirm that you were invoiced correctly. The following fields or information should be included in the report:

- ▼ product description
- ▼ purchase order number
- ▼ actual price paid
- ▼ quantity purchased
- ▼ price per unit

The Returns Summary Report

Many suppliers are able to provide a summary of all the product deliveries that your company rejected and returned to the supplier. Returns could include quality rejections, late deliveries refused, incorrect products returned, as well as other inappropriate deliveries. Reviewing this report will help you recognize any repetitive quality problems originating from the supplier or your purchasing process. The following information will help you understand the number of returns you suffered in a period of time:

▼ product description

▼ purchase order number

▼ quantity purchased

▼ date delivered

▼ date returned

▼ reason for return

GENERATING INTERNAL REPORTS
▼

Although the supplier has the information to produce the aforementioned reports, the following reports need to be developed by you and your MIS department. Whereas the supplier has the information for the reports you ask him or her to generate, these reports will be generated from information that is available only on your computer system.

Supplier Purchases Report

This report summarizes purchases by supplier, allows you to understand the volume purchased from each supplier, and enables you to review purchases from nonpartner suppliers. This will help you track your performance with the suppliers you committed your volume to and will indicate if you are buying the right products from the right suppliers. When you find inappropriate purchases from a supplier, you can work with your buyers and investigate their purchasing decisions. This report should include the following information:

▼ supplier name

- ▼ product description
- ▼ quantity purchased
- ▼ total amount paid
- ▼ average cost per unit
- ▼ total purchased by supplier (in dollars)
- ▼ back order percentage

Buyer Purchases Report

In addition to monitoring which suppliers you are using, you can summarize the purchases made by each buyer. As you review this report, look for buyers who consistently use multiple suppliers for the same product or who pay varying rates for the same product. This report should include the following information:

- ▼ buyer name
- ▼ product description
- ▼ supplier name (list the suppliers used for each product)
- ▼ quantity purchased
- ▼ total dollars paid (by supplier for each product)
- ▼ average price paid by product

Price-per-Purchase Report

If you are able to produce this report internally, consider generating it to provide a comparison to supplier reports. You can then use this report to confirm supplier reports and to audit their invoices. Include the following information in this report:

- ▼ product description
- ▼ purchase order number
- ▼ actual price paid
- ▼ quantity purchased
- ▼ price per unit

Returns-by-Supplier Report

This report can provide significant information for evaluating supplier quality. You might design this report with your receiving department, asking them to record any returns they process. Request that they capture the following information so you have all the information you need to investigate returns:

▼ product description

▼ purchase order number

▼ quantity purchased

▼ date delivered

▼ date returned

▼ reason for return

▼ name of receiving agent who refused delivery

EXCEPTION REPORTS
▼

Exception reports are your most powerful tool in monitoring your suppliers and your partnerships. An exception report does not summarize all your purchases and shipments, but only those that fail to meet your needed service, pricing, or quality concerns. Computers can do much of your analysis for you by filtering out "normal" data. By removing all the shipments that were delivered on time, all the purchases from preferred suppliers, all the purchases bought at the approved prices, and all the shipments that met all quality specifications, you are able to review all of the problems, or exceptions, in a short time. Review these reports with your MIS department and with your suppliers to develop a method for creating these reports. These reports are worth the programming time necessary to create them. Some examples of exception reports follow.

Late Deliveries Report

For each supplier, you have negotiated a lead time or delivery schedule to be maintained. List every late delivery on this report. Often the supplier is best able to produce this report (because the supplier must know the dates of missed deadlines). By reviewing this report, you can get a feel for repetitive late deliveries by specific suppliers; this will allow you to solve the problem with the supplier (or look for a new one if necessary). The following fields will give you the information you need to make these decisions effectively:

▼ product description

▼ purchase order number

▼ quantity ordered

▼ date scheduled for delivery

▼ actual delivery date

▼ days late

▼ total number of late deliveries by supplier

▼ total number of deliveries by supplier

▼ on time/late delivery ratio for each supplier

▼ buyer responsible for purchase

Rejected Shipments Report

List every product returned to any supplier. Unlike late deliveries, which shows only slow production, quality failures may not be found until your finished products are in the hands of customers. In addition to working with the supplier responsible for any repeated quality problems, work with the buyer responsible for the purchase and any internal engineers who can help you understand the problem. Incorporate the following fields in this report:

▼ product description

▼ purchase order number

▼ quantity ordered

▼ description of quality failure

▼ delivery date

▼ total number of rejected shipments by supplier

▼ total number of rejected shipments by supplier

▼ accepted shipment/rejected shipment ratio for each supplier

▼ buyer responsible for purchase

Purchases-from-Nonpartners Report

You and your team have implemented a partnership program that was intended to provide the best possible mix of quality, service, and pricing to your company. It stands to reason that the vast majority of all purchases should come from partner suppliers. When buyers avoid the official partner supplier, there may be something wrong with the relationship that needs to be addressed. Consequently, it is important to review all purchases from nonpartners by buyer. The following fields will help you generate a report of nonpartner purchases:

▼ buyer

▼ supplier actually purchased from

▼ product description

▼ date ordered

▼ quantity purchased

▼ price paid

▼ price agreed to with appropriate supplier-partner

▼ amount paid in excess of partnership price

▼ summary of total purchases from nonpartners made by the buyer

Purchases-above-Expected-Prices Report

Regardless of whether the supplier you actually use is a partnered supplier, it is important to confirm that you are paying the price that you agreed to in the negotiating process. To the extent that you can calculate expected prices online, you can compare actual invoice prices. When the price charged by the supplier is higher than the price you expected to pay, this report should reflect that. For all material differences, investigate the problem with the buyer. Often a customer does not compare the actual charged amount with the contracted rates. This report should include the following information:

▼ supplier name

▼ product description

▼ quantity

▼ expected unit price

▼ invoiced unit price

▼ differential

▼ extended differential

▼ total differential by supplier/buyer

Back-Orders Report

One of the critical parts of reducing inventory is counting on your suppliers to ship all of your order when you request it. Consequently, it is vital to track all of the instances when a supplier fails to ship a full order. By reviewing back orders by supplier, you can assess the supplier's adherence to your lead-time agreements, and you can determine how to adjust your purchasing policies to compensate for undependable suppliers. To make this assessment, include the following information in your report:

▼ supplier name

▼ product description

▼ quantity ordered

▼ quantity shipped

▼ quantity on back order

▼ total orders completed on original orders

▼ back-order percentage

How to Use Focus Groups to Evaluate Your Supplier Partnerships
▼

Every six months, according to your partnership contract, you and the supplier get together to discuss your partnership. In this meeting, you can ask the supplier questions that will help improve the partnership, and you can discuss your ideas about improving the partnership. In addition to your specific needs, you may want to discuss the following topics:

▼ excessive back orders

- ▼ excessive rejections

- ▼ excessive late deliveries

- ▼ overcharges

- ▼ changes to management reports that can help provide better information to either company

- ▼ changes to paperwork procedures that can streamline or simplify procedures

- ▼ changes to delivery/receiving procedures that can simplify or streamline the process

- ▼ updates on engineering internships or consulting assistance and plans for additional coefforts

- ▼ cosponsored customer surveys or joint advertising issues.

In addition to these issues, you may decide to ask the supplier the following questions:

- ▼ What aspects of our partnership have been successful in your eyes?

- ▼ What areas can we work on now to improve our partnership?

- ▼ Are you doing any innovative things with other customers that we might implement?

GETTING FEEDBACK FROM WITHIN YOUR COMPANY
▼

As important as it was to gather the input of people throughout your company as you were developing the partnerships, it is also important to incorporate the thoughts of other people in your company in the ongoing partnership issues. You are looking for two primary types of input. The first is strategic planning, through which you, your company, and the supplier can work out innovative methods to add quality and reduce the cost of working together. The second type of company involvement is to focus on fixing and enhancing specific operational issues. Each of these input types is described next.

Holding Top Management Meetings and Strategy Sessions

If your partnership is to achieve long-term success, the top management of both companies must gather for an annual strategy session. In this session, the executives can make decisions that middle managers could not consider, such as the following:

▼ Capital expenditures that can increase the collective competitive advantages of both companies

▼ Further commitments that could enable the other party to minimize risks or increase capital commitments

▼ Opportunities for joint marketing, research and development, customer calls, etc.

These meetings, more than any other area since the original negotiations, provide for ongoing creative innovations and commitments. Whether you are the executive or you bring your executive to this meeting, this interaction with the supplier will provide additional dramatic results.

Holding Meetings with Other Employees

One of the reasons that consultants are in demand is that many companies do not actively seek and act on employee ideas. Regularly meet with line workers, engineers, buyers, and other employees that interact with the suppliers or their products. At the most basic level, use the questions from Chapter 3 to organize your interviews and discussions.

COLLECTING EVALUATIONS FROM YOUR CUSTOMERS
▼

Regardless of your internal reports, supplier reports, and joint meetings, you need your customers to confirm that you are providing the quality and service they need. Some companies develop a "call-a-customer-a-day" program. Regardless of the tactic you choose, you need to collect customers' opinions on the quality and service you are providing. This can be done jointly with the supplier or on your own. You can utilize surveys, phone calls, focus groups, on-site visits, or other communication methods, including the following:

▼ Call the customer after every major delivery to ask about the quality of the product, the service you provided, and the status of the delivery when it was received.

▼ Have a company executive call a customer at random once a day to ask about the quality of your products and services and to solicit ideas for improvement.

▼ Send out a customer survey on a periodic basis in which customers rate your service, quality, and pricing.

SUMMARY
▼

In this chapter, you have begun to undertake the final steps in maintaining a world-class, long-term partnership. The underlying critical success factor is that by setting up a system for monitoring suppliers, you will be able to keep your relationship sharp. Unlike the purchase of technology that becomes obsolete within years or months, you can keep your relationship intact and beneficial by continuing to redefine and improve your supplier relationships. The only way to do so is to review the important factors, to seek the insights and ideas of your employees, and to strategize with the supplier's executives. Specifically, you need to do the following:

▼ Request the following reports from the supplier:

  − Ontime delivery
  − Price per unit purchased
  − Returns summary.

▼ Prepare the following reports internally:

  − Summary of purchases by supplier
  − Summary of purchases by buyer
  − Price per unit purchased
  − Returns summary.

▼ Develop the following exception reports that display all service, quality, and pricing failures:

- – Summary of late deliveries
- – Summary of rejected shipments
- – Summary of purchases from nonpartner suppliers
- – Summary of purchases made above expected pricing levels
- – Summary of back orders.

▼ Hold supplier focus groups and strategy meetings.

▼ Get feedback from within your company.

- – Get feedback from the executive level to develop strategic issues that will involve your suppliers.
- – Get feedback from your line people to develop innovations or changes to assist in more efficient and effective operations.

▼ Obtain customer feedback.

Now is the time to celebrate! You have accomplished your goal, you have set your partnership in gear, and you are speeding down the road to sustainable competitive advantages.

The next chapter discusses when you may want to use consultants in implementing partnerships.

CHAPTER 15

THE ROLE
OF CONSULTANTS

There was much debate at my consulting firm about this book. "Why should we give away all of our secrets; are we shooting ourselves in the foot?" You can implement a successful supplier partnership without a consultant. At the same time, you may find that a consultant would be helpful. In this chapter, we discuss five main topics:

- ▼ When not to use a consultant
- ▼ When to use a consultant
- ▼ What role the consultant can play
- ▼ How to select the best consultant
- ▼ How to work with a consultant after you have retained one.

WHEN NOT TO USE A CONSULTANT
▼

In the past, many consultants simply determined your opportunity to save money or increase sales if you made the changes they suggested in their report. You would be responsible for implementing the changes on your own. However, in deciding to enter supplier partnerships, you have already identified the changes you are going to make. You do not need a consultant to help you with that.

In addition, if you have an internal project manager and can focus on specific projects such as this, you have the blueprint (this book) and are ready to go. You do not need a consultant. If you do not have an internal project manager but feel that you could take the time to lead this endeavor, you might consider reading about project management. One of the main benefits of knowing how to manage a project is that you can manage change effectively. As we mentioned throughout this book, people resist change, and the way you manage the project and include others in the process can act as a catalyst or an inhibitor.

The toughest question to answer is, Do you have the time to dedicate to this project? Even with the help of an MIS representative and various departmental people in your company, you can expect to spend 30 to 50 hours per week managing this process. If you can dedicate this time, then you can do without a consultant.

WHEN TO USE A CONSULTANT
▼

Given the fees of some consulting firms today, why would you ever want to use a consultant? Can consultants provide value at such high prices?

Value Calculation

In the following sections we will review areas that consultants can help you implement supplier partnerships. One factor that will limit how much you would ever want to spend on a consultant is how much you would expect to save in implementing the partnerships. For example, if you spend $200,000 per year on total purchases, it will not make sense for you to engage a consultant who would charge you even $50,000. It would take years to recoup your costs. At the same time, if your company purchases over $50,000,000 annually and your annual savings could reach $2,000,000 annually, even a million dollar fee structure would be conceivable.

The following sections will describe different situations where you can consider the value of consultants. Although these topics will help you recognize the need for consulting assistance, the idea of how to use a consultant is a separate issue discussed later in the chapter.

Limited Resources

One misconception about consultants is that they are primarily hired because they are the experts in a given field. In reality, the most common reason consultants are hired is the lack of company resources to accomplish a task internally. How long would it take your company to implement the program without consultants? If it would take you 24 months, what is the dollar amount of savings and other benefits that you would have realized 18 months sooner if you had hired consultants? With a consultant, you can expect to implement partnerships for most of your commodity groups within six months. Would your company be able to focus on this program without a consultant and still accomplish all of its day-to-day activities? If you plan to hire one or more people, how long will it take you to find the right candidates? What is the cost of recruiting them? Can you attract the same talent that a reputable consulting firm could offer? What will these people do when the project is concluded? Another area to consider is MIS support. If your MIS department is too busy to assist you in data gathering and generating the reports you need, you might consider a consultant to assist you in those areas.

Guarantee of Completion

Another reason to consider consulting assistance is consultants' ability to guarantee completion of the project. For internal employees, any emergency can halt the implementation of the project. A consultant is shielded from this concern and is paid to complete the project. This issue is important to consider when the consultants' fees are smaller than the savings you expect to receive. One feature of your relationship with the consultant is the consultant's ability to guarantee the savings your company will receive in the year following the implementation process. (This is discussed in detail later in this chapter.)

In addition, the service and quality enhancements you hope to receive from the partnerships may make hiring consultants advisable. When your company cannot offer the same levels of service and quality offered by your competition, supplier partnerships offer one of your best opportunities to increase competitive advantages. A consultant can help you initiate such partnerships.

Market Intelligence

Experienced consultants who have implemented supplier partnerships before, or who have significant industry experience, can provide intelligence about the suppliers you could partner with. A good consultant can help you with the following:

▼ Identifying alternative suppliers to your current supplier base.

▼ Helping you understand what the best suppliers are doing with their best customers to maximize competitive advantages.

▼ Helping you understand how other companies have reduced cost or enhanced services with their suppliers.

▼ Identifying alternative ways to satisfy your needs rather than through conventional methods. (For example, in the transportation industry, many companies have replaced over-the-road trucking service with rail service, which can reduce cost significantly for some companies.)

▼ Identifying the real costs of your suppliers. Suppliers will often charge what the market will bear—a price that may have little to do with real costs. If you work with a consultant who can identify actual supplier costs, you will be in the best position to negotiate dramatic savings from the supplier. In one case, I recommended that my client stop purchasing the product and begin making the product because the actual cost to produce was much lower than the market price. On an annual budget of $20 million, the client ended up spending $8 million less than before—a 40% reduction in cost.

Outside Perspective

A knowledgeable consultant can also challenge current company policies, beliefs, and practices. Some companies do make a regular practice of engaging consultants so they have someone who can challenge the status quo. Often, people are tempted to do things the same way they have always been done, because it works. An outside perspective can help a company identify the current practices that take away from its ability to service customers.

This outside perspective also raises the expectations for a partnership program. Company employees typically do not expect much from partnership programs. Their expectations are clouded by years of doing things a certain way and getting the same results; by what they assume to be true; or by what they "know" the suppliers are thinking (without ever asking them).

Research has shown that the higher people set their goals, the more likely they are to achieve high goals. This may seem like simplistic or circular thinking, but it holds true. The realists in your company may be right more often, but do they ever achieve the lofty goals of the dreamers? Jack Welch, the renowned CEO of General Electric, calls this principle "stretch." If you are comfortable shooting for your goals and you know exactly how to get there, you are not stretching enough. A consultant can help in opening the eyes of realists, showing them that aggressive goals are not always far-fetched—especially if the consultant has implemented supplier partnerships in the past and has war stories, specific examples, and other pieces of evidence of positive supplier partnerships.

ROLES CONSULTANTS CAN PLAY IN IMPLEMENTING
SUPPLIER PARTNERSHIPS
▼

There are different roles a consultant can play in your supplier partnership project. The following four roles can be considered if you decide to engage consultants:

Opportunity Assessment

In this case, the consultant (sometimes called the "report" consultant) helps you identify opportunities for implementing supplier partnerships. The consultant reviews current practices, benchmark studies, current rates and prices, and additional information in an attempt to quantify how much your company could benefit from supplier partnerships.

This can be important if you are unable to convince your company that supplier partnerships are necessary. In most cases, however, this type of consulting is of dubious value. Often, the consultant's report sits on the shelf, ignored.

You may want to look for an implementation-focused consultant who will perform a high-level review of your opportunities in supplier partnerships at little or no fee. The idea is simple: the consulting firm is interested in implementing supplier partnerships for you and is not interested in producing a report. In some cases, you can ask the consulting firm to provide the high-level review at no cost, with the understanding that the consultant will have the first opportunity to bid on the implementation phase of the project. In other cases, you will be required to pay a fee, but that fee will be refundable if you hire the consultant to assist you in implementing partnerships. Either method is a good way to minimize your cost and risk in assessing the benefits of supplier partnerships.

Full Implementation by the Consultant

In this type of project, consultants implement the supplier partnerships for you. They interview your people to find out your needs, review the market, and negotiate on your behalf. These projects can be beneficial to your company because you don't have to spend much time but gain the benefits. However, there is one major large drawback: The consultant will go away after the project is over and may not have an inherent interest in making the partnership work. In addition, you will need to call the consultant back every time you want to negotiate other commodity groups or when you need to renegotiate your contracts. This can prove to be expensive in the long run.

Full Implementation by Your Team Administered by the Consultant

In this approach, the consultant will work with you and your negotiating team to implement the supplier partnerships. This approach is the best value in the long run for the following reasons:

- ▼ Your team will learn how to implement supplier partnerships so you will not be dependent on consultants in the future.

- ▼ The consultant will be responsible for making sure the project is completed on schedule.

- ▼ You will get an outside perspective on your project without losing control.

- ▼ You will be able to tap the market intelligence of the consultant while gaining the experience necessary to implement future supplier partnerships.

- ▼ By working with the consultant, you can gain a basic understanding of project management.

▼ You can negotiate that the consultant guarantee the results of the project based on fees (the consultant only gets paid when the project is completed and the savings and service enhancements are realized).

Facilitation by the Consultant

This type of consulting assistance is similar to the type just described, but the consultant does not accept any responsibility for completion or for results. You will not pay the same fees you pay for a full implementation assistance, but you will not receive any guarantees. You may find that the extra time it will take to implement supplier partnerships under this scenario is more expensive than the reduced fees you pay.

HOW TO PICK THE BEST CONSULTANT FOR YOU
▼

Now that you are familiar with the different types of assistance consultants can provide, the following lists features to look for in any consultant you might consider:

Start with Word of Mouth

If you decide that hiring outsiders is an attractive option, it is time to find the right firm. A good way to begin your search for good consultants is through friends, business associates, and other contacts who have direct (positive) experience with a given firm. Remember that you are buying people and expertise.

In addition to word of mouth from your business associates and friends, you can also call some of the associations listed in Chapter 5 to ask for references about different consultants.

Implementation versus Report Focus

Before you hire a consultant to help you in any part of your partnership process, be sure to find out how well he or she can implement the process. This is true even if you plan to use a consultant only to provide you with a report. If you are going to implement the consultant's suggestions, you clearly want to use an implementation-focused consultant.

Train Your People in the Process

Although some consultants will implement supplier partnerships for you, there is a major difference between projects in which you are trained to implement future partnerships and projects in which you simply watch the consultant in action. If the consultants do not train you to implement the partnerships yourselves and to negotiate with suppliers, you run the risk of being dependent on the consultant whenever you need to work with the supplier.

A Long List of References

All consultants have to get their start. But you do not want to be the guinea pig. Always work with a consultant who has experience that can be backed up by past clients. Even if a new consultant is willing to discount his or her fees, you are putting your business on the line. The risk that a neophyte consultant might contaminate or deoptimize your relationship with your suppliers is too high.

HOW TO WORK WITH THE CONSULTANT
▼

There are ways of working with your consultants that will affect the success of your project. Each of the following suggestions is based on experience, and you should consider them as you set up your consulting arrangements.

Fixed Fee versus Contingency Fee

This is a controversial topic. In a fixed fee environment, the consultant charges a flat amount that will not be affected by the actual amount your company saves through supplier partnerships (subject to any fee guarantees you might negotiate with the consultant, of course). In a contingency fee arrangement, the consultant gets a percentage of the savings you receive for the first one or two years of your partnerships.

At first look, the contingency fee arrangement might seem like a good risk for your company because you pay only if and when you save money. There are two risks you must consider, however. The first is that you might end up paying extremely high fees if your company saves a lot of money. Although you might be happy to pay $500,000 if you save $1,500,000, you might have been able to pay a fixed fee of only $200,000 to complete the project. This outcome is related to the second risk. When a consultant is paid based on dollar savings, the consultant loses independence. The consultant is rewarded directly based on who the contract is awarded to. This puts your company in danger of selecting suppliers based more on price than on service. Although dramatic in the short term, this approach can cost you much more than the cost of your purchases.

Guaranteed Savings

If a consultant assists you in implementing supplier partnerships, you should negotiate with the consultant to guarantee the annual results of the partnership. For example, if the consulting firm estimates that you will save $300,000 per year and its fees are $150,000 for the project, it should guarantee the completion of the project and its results. In this example, for every two dollars the actual savings falls below $300,000, the consultant should reduce fees by one dollar. With this guarantee, you can feel certain that the consultant will provide the value you seek.

Encourage Company Interaction

Throughout this book, we have discussed the importance of managing the change process. People become comfortable with the way things are and are nervous about change. Consultants can help you make people feel more comfortable with the changes you implement. One of the ways they can help is to spend time interviewing your line workers and other employees. In addition, since the consultants have experience with many other companies, if your employees are able to talk to the consultants regularly, the employees might learn a lot about what other progressive companies are doing.

Assign One Person to Be the Liaison/Project Leader

If you work with a consultant, be sure that he or she reports to one person. This will allow you to keep control of the consultant and effectively manage his or her progress. In addition, it will give someone in your company the best chance to learn what the consultants do. In many cases, the person the consultant reports to is later able to implement partnerships in other areas of the company.

Periodic Updates

To keep the project from getting out of control, it is important to ask the consultant to provide periodic updates to the management team. Often, consultants will go off track, investigate in areas other than they agreed to, or move too slowly to finish the main project. Periodic updates will keep you informed of the consultant's progress.

When outsiders enter your company, they carry their own set of assumptions and face information gaps regarding your company, people, marketplace, history, etc. Halfway into a consulting project, a consultant may find that these initial assumptions have changed and, thus, the scope of the project needs to change as well. Insufficient dialogue between management and the consultant is an expensive way to drift off course.

Summary
▼

Using a consultant to help you implement supplier partnerships can mean hundreds of thousands of dollars for your company. In this chapter, we reviewed the following points regarding consultants:

- ▼ You should avoid using a consultant when you do not have enough savings on the table to justify consulting fees. In addition, if you have the resources to implement the partnerships on your own, consulting support will be of limited value.

- ▼ You might consider using consultants when
  - – You have insufficient resources to implement partnership internally.
  - – The potential savings justify consulting fees, especially when you hire a consultant that will guarantee the completion of the project.
  - – You feel you would benefit from additional project management experience.
  - – You could benefit from an experienced consultant's market intelligence.
  - – An outside perspective will provide additional firepower to win company-wide support.

- ▼ If you do decide to use a consultant, what role should the consultant play for you? Options include
  - – Having the consultant help you identify and define your opportunities to benefit from supplier partnerships
  - – Having the consultant implement supplier partnerships for you

  – Having the consultant implement supplier partnerships with you and your negotiations team, leaving you able to implement partnerships independently in the future

  – Having the consultant facilitate supplier partnerships but not handle the administration of the project and not guarantee the results.

▼ Once you decide to use a consultant, the following will help you to choose the best consultant:

  – Start by asking people you respect if they have used any consultants that have been effective and fairly priced.

  – Find a consultant who specializes in implementation, not in writing reports.

  – Find a consultant who will train your people in the process.

  – Require a long list of references from the consultant, and call them.

▼ As you hire the consultant, the following will help you maximize your benefits and minimize your costs:

  – Evaluate the benefits of negotiating a fixed fee instead of the potentially high and damaging contingency fee.

  – Negotiate that the consultant guarantee the savings and the completion of the project.

  – Encourage the consultant to interact with your company personnel on a regular basis.

  – Assign one person to be the liaison between your company and the consultant.

  – Have the consultant provide periodic updates to you.

This book has given you the knowledge to implement a supplier partnership with or without a consultant. By following the points in this chapter, you will be able to choose the best way to move forward and how to use consultants, if at all.

APPENDIX A

NEGOTIABLE ISSUES

This appendix provides an overview of many of the issues you may negotiate with suppliers. For each issue, a general definition is provided along with generic but specific points to negotiate and some related basic tactics or supplier issues. Although your company may not need to address each of the issues, reviewing them all will give you many ideas that could relate to your company. The issues are grouped into categories based on substance:

▼ Communication issues

▼ Paperwork issues

▼ Legal issues

▼ Pricing issues

▼ Quality issues

▼ Service issues.

As you enter negotiations, remember to determine the best answer to each negotiable issue based on the supplier's profiles and any suppliers you are aware of. There is no reason to limit yourself to the service levels your company was held to in prior supplier relationships.

COMMUNICATION ISSUES
▼

Forecasting

In addition to the commitment of purchasing all your products from the supplier, this is one of the more powerful issues you offer the supplier: your sales forecasts. For example, "We will provide our annual, quarterly, and other forecasts to you as they become available." (Specify the actual frequency that your company produces forecasts.) The supplier would then read the forecast and follow up with your company's sales force as needed to prepare for anticipated sales levels.

Your challenge in this issue is to communicate the power of the forecasts to the supplier. Although the forecasts will maximize the supplier's ability to plan for upcoming sales demands, you are placing yourself in a vulnerable position by providing this information to parties outside your company. You are doing it because you want a true, long-term partnership.

Research and Development

Many companies research new technologies and develop innovative products. You can negotiate with supplier partners to direct some of their R&D budget to target projects that could help you. In addition, you can negotiate to be a beta site for any new technologies the supplier develops. (A beta site is a company/location that tests a new product for the company that developed the product.) You could ask the supplier for the following in your negotiations:

▼ You as the supplier will notify our company of any developments you innovate and offer to let us act as a beta site for appropriate technologies.

▼ As a beta site, we will not be charged for the use of any new technology and will be given a credit toward the purchase of the final technology as it is released. In exchange, we agree to work with your engineers to provide feedback on the features of your new technology or product.

▼ You, the supplier, will direct some of your R&D in our industry, developing new products that could affect our business. (In regard to this issue, it is critical that you have a specific idea for the supplier to pursue. To the extent that you can, work with the supplier to develop an agreement for its level of commitment to the project you decide on.)

This is another issue that helps you develop strong ties with a core supplier group. Sharing in the supplier's technology can provide you with a competitive advantage and give the supplier helpful feedback in its testing process.

Strategic Planning

In this issue, you negotiate mutual involvement in, and understanding of, each other's strategic plan. This can be critical to maximizing the benefits of a long-term partnership. The supplier can prepare for any significant changes in the buyer's business that will affect how much of which products the buyer will purchase in the future. The buyer will understand any developments in the supplier's market before the competition is aware of these developments. You can negotiate the following with the supplier:

▼ You, the supplier, will make your top executives available to our strategic planning group for up to three days per year to provide insights on how we might work better with our suppliers.

▼ We will make our top executives available to work with your strategic planning group for up to three days per year.

▼ Excluding some parts of our respective strategic plans that may be inappropriate to share, we will provide each other with a copy of our strategic plans on an annual basis.

Many suppliers will love this issue. You are offering to let the supplier deep into your company. Sharing information at this level is a key to true partnerships, and suppliers are yearning for this communication. Understanding your strategic vision will help the supplier prepare proactively for changes in your business. This is a key issue in developing trust between partners.

Training

Each year, more and more companies uncover the benefits of continuing education for their employees. You can take advantage of your supplier's expertise and training facilities to educate your employees. The following are some options to negotiate with the supplier:

▼ Make your training library available to our employees. Please provide a list of all books, videos, tapes, and seminars you maintain in your library.

▼ Train five (customize this number based on your company needs) of our employees each year at your training facilities. We will pay for airfare, while you will provide the tuition, room, and board free of charge.

▼ Send five of our employees to one third-party seminar annually. These seminars will relate to our mutual industry and areas so we can bring new ideas and relationships to our partnership. We will pay for the airfare and lodging and are asking that you pay for the tuition and registration fees.

As with most issues, this issue is best initiated with a question: "What types of training do you, or can you, provide to your employees or customers?" These training sessions can become a strong source for new innovative options that you and your supplier can implement to reduce mutual costs or develop a competitive advantage.

Paperwork Issues
▼

EDI: Capability

EDI, or electronic data interchange, is a system that allows parties to communicate directly from computer to computer, with no paperwork. These systems can be as simple as two computers with a modem link or as complicated as a $40 million satellite system with multinode communication abilities. In this issue, you are determining the supplier's capabilities and plans in terms of EDI. You can raise the following questions and requests with the supplier:

▼ What capabilities do you have in terms of electronic communications between our companies? (Some common capabilities include the ability to accept orders, deliver invoices for payment, accept payments, allow the buyer to track orders, and perform inventory look-ups online.)

▼ The supplier will make all capabilities available in the partnership.

▼ The supplier will provide the technical expertise to install and test the software.

▼ The supplier will provide technical assistance to link the EDI software with our current MIS system.

▼ What plans does the supplier have to implement additional EDI capabilities in the future?

▼ What specific type of EDI communications does the supplier support? (This issue may be important as you set up EDI applications with multiple companies and try to maintain a single system. You may need your MIS representative to help you define which EDI communication standards are right for your company.)

Begin this issue by asking an open-ended question such as, "What are your company's EDI capabilities? Is this type of paperless communication important to you and your company?" This will provide a spirited start to the issue because companies that have EDI capabilities have invested a lot of time and money and are anxious to explain EDI's benefits.

EDI: Hardware

Often, you will find that you need additional hardware to implement EDI with some suppliers. Because of the strong benefits available to both companies through EDI, you can negotiate for the supplier to provide some of the hardware for you. For example,

▼ For each location where we will use EDI,

- The supplier will provide a 486-based computer system with a 250-megabyte hard drive, a 14,400-baud modem, a printer, and any other peripherals necessary to maintain the supplier's EDI application.
- This hardware will remain the property of the supplier but will be used by the company for the period of the partnership.
- The supplier will be responsible for necessary upgrades and maintenance.

As mentioned earlier, this issue is beneficial for both parties in a partnership. You can demonstrate this importance: On a flip chart or overhead, multiply the number of annual orders you would place with the supplier by $30 per order to cover paperwork charges. (This $30 represents the cost to process the paperwork that relates to a specific order; $30 is considered a minimum amount that any company would spend to process an order. Many companies spend as much as $100 per order to process paperwork.) This will provide the supplier with a budget number that could make a computer seem like a trivial investment compared to the benefits both companies would receive.

EDI: Training

In this issue, you negotiate how your people will be trained to use EDI. Most veteran implementers of EDI have found that even the best-designed applications require assistance in installation. Based on that premise and the fact that the benefits of using EDI only accrue after it is installed, negotiate the following points with the supplier:

▼ The supplier will provide EDI training for each software module installed within one month of the contract award.

▼ The trainer (list the name of the trainer at this time; you want to avoid salespeople as trainers; you want the supplier's EDI expert) will carry out the training at your company locations.

▼ There will be no charge for the training.

▼ The supplier will provide additional training for new modules as they are implemented.

▼ The supplier will provide continued training as requested by the buyer.

The requests you make in this issue are necessary for the effective use of the systems implemented by the supplier. If the supplier has alternatives to these requests, look at how effective those alternatives would be in enabling your people to use EDI on a daily basis.

EDI: Beta Site

This issue finishes off the EDI issue by ending on a positive, forward-thinking note. By requesting that the supplier consider your company as a beta site in the development of new applications, you will provide the supplier with a built-in test market. In addition, being a beta site will provide you with the latest capabilities and access to the latest developments. You can negotiate the following:

▼ The supplier will offer to use our company as a beta site for all new applications being developed for EDI.

▼ There will be no charge for the use of the new application.

Providing the supplier with a beta site can help the supplier work out bugs and technical problems before unleashing the product on other customers. In addition, the new application may provide you with a new service or a new way of communicating—a competitive advantage.

Order Forms/Procedures

For many companies, the cost to process orders can exceed $30 per order (sometimes as high as $100 in some areas). Depending on the extent of the EDI link you develop with your suppliers, you will have manual paper orders flowing through the system. In this issue, you work with the supplier to ensure that the process is as efficient as possible for both parties. You can negotiate as follows:

▼ During the first month of our partnership, MIS, order entry, and order placing representatives from each company will meet to go through the ordering process and develop any modifications to maximize efficiency.

▼ Each company will bear the cost of the changes at their respective companies.

▼ The time frame for modification implementation will be set forth in the meetings.

Although some suppliers may not show immediate interest in changing their order processing system, you are only negotiating that both companies research the possibility that there may be better options than the status quo.

Legal Issues
▼

Audits

If your pricing is on a cost-plus basis or if the supplier is asking for additional increases, you need to review the supplier's accounting records and costs. Negotiate as follows:

- ▼ For any price increases or changes, the buyer has the right to request to review and audit the records.

- ▼ To the extent that an independent audit is not conducted on the pricing assumptions made for our partnership, the buyer reserves the right to review and audit accounting and costing records.

Some suppliers may object to this if they are privately held. Avoid negotiating this issue unless your prices are based on the supplier's costing information.

Contract Enforcement/Cancellation

The contract is intended to last for a three- to five-year period. However, some events could alter the ability of either company to adhere to the contract. Negotiate as follows:

- ▼ Events that make the contract voidable might include

  - – The supplier is unprofitable for more than one year in a row (making it financially unstable and therefore a risky partner).
  - – Either party becomes insolvent.
  - – The supplier ships products that fail to meet the predetermined quality standards more than two quarters in a year.
  - – The supplier or your company fails to meet any of the quality or service levels defined in the contract.
  - – In addition, if either party decides to secede from the contract, it must provide 60 days' notice to the other party. (This will allow you time to find and convert to a new supplier if your selected partner withdraws from the partnership.)

This issue provides protection for both parties. Although the intention is to develop a long-term, three- to five-year agreement, the prudent businessperson prepares for the unexpected. Having a prestructured framework will protect both the supplier and buyer in case of contract cancellation.

Exclusions from the Contract

In this issue, list any items that explicitly fall outside the contract (e.g., products you buy from another supplier or separate agreements you already have with the supplier). The specific items you might negotiate in this area are completely dependent on your specific circumstances but could include

- ▼ Products that the supplier can provide but you purchase from another supplier.

- ▼ Special purchases of proprietary products from other suppliers that you may require.

- ▼ Seasonal peak periods that you might need to source additional purchases from outside suppliers.

Of course, the best option is that there are no exclusions to the contract. If, however, you do need to exclude some portion of your business from the supplier, it is smart to identify those exclusions up front and avoid surprises.

Government Regulations and Compliance

In many industries, the government levies regulations. These regulations place responsibilities on you and on your supplier. The primary issues include compliance with regulations, proof of compliance, and the cost of compliance. Specific points to cover with the supplier include the following:

- ▼ Both the supplier and our company will comply with all government regulations regarding our products and services.

- ▼ Based on formats agreed to by our legal counsels, we will provide each other with documented proof of compliance with all industry or government regulations.

- ▼ Each company will be responsible for its own costs of compliance.

- ▼ In a joint meeting, we will determine if there are any areas in which we can work together to develop needed documentation and save time and effort.

This issue will not cause any celebration or excitement, but it can help you and your supplier avoid potential compliance problems down the road.

Unionization/Strikes

Many industries are prone to strikes and unionization. Although unionization itself may not be your concern, developing a backup plan in the case of a strike is. In addition, some companies that are not unionized are more flexible in their ability to cut costs and implement innovative ideas. For these reasons, it is important that you understand the status of your supplier's work force before you enter a long-term partnership. You can negotiate as follows:

▼ At the first hint that your company might by threatened by a strike that would hinder your ability to service our product needs, you will inform us of the situation.

▼ In addition, we will work together to develop a plan to provide continuous service to our company in the case of a strike. Options include

  – Alternate suppliers who could provide our products
  – Stockpiling inventory in the months preceding the threatened strike
  – Third-party shipments administered by the supplier.

This is another example of reducing your risk when consolidating suppliers. In fact, negotiating this type of issue could provide you with more protection than maintaining multiple suppliers for a given product area or commodity group because many unions will span multiple companies in the same industry.

PRICING ISSUES
▼

Changes and Additions

If every order placed was free from customer cancellations and changes, suppliers would be happy. Since orders are not free of change, it is important to understand the true costs associated with changes and cancellations. Negotiating this issue will protect you, as the customer, from paying the sometimes unjustifiably high change fees, and it will protect the supplier from losing money. Specific points you can cover with suppliers include the following:

▼ In the rare case that we need to alter an order that is already placed, we will notify the supplier as soon as we identify that need.

▼ The supplier will not assess any additional charges based on these changes.

▼ If the supplier, at any time during our partnership, feels that this issue has become a burden, we will reconvene to develop alternative pricing or procedural changes.

In addition, the following option could be considered:

▼ After reviewing the actual costs the supplier incurs, we will jointly develop a matrix of charges based on the timing and quantity of those changes. (This should be your minimum acceptable option for this issue. If the supplier incurs real costs when you change an order after, for example, it enters production, you, as a partner, do not want to injure the supplier, but do not want these penalties to be a source of additional profits for the supplier.)

Begin this issue by asking the supplier about his or her change policy: "How long before an order is shipped can we call to make a change?" Then discuss the importance of working together to minimize changes (discussed on page 290). (The specialized field support issue could be helpful here because the supplier's experts might be able to reduce your internal need for changes.)

Claims and Disputes Settlement

Regardless of how well you anticipate the needs of the partnership, you may end up with problems. Therefore, it is important to develop an agreed-upon approach to settle disputes and claims. You can negotiate as follows:

▼ Whenever a dispute arises between the supplier and our company, our respective personnel will strive to work out the problems internally.

▼ If the dispute is not resolved by the normal operational personnel within 30 days, the original negotiating committee from each company will meet to resolve the issue.

▼ If this committee is unable to resolve the issue within 30 days, the respective company presidents will meet to resolve the issue.

▼ If the company presidents are unable to resolve the issue, the contract will be voidable after 30 days.

This approach is only one option. Any reasonable method that can be used to settle disputes could be substituted. The important thing is to have a plan to control disasters if they arise.

Commitment of Supply

Although your company should avoid guaranteeing specific volumes, you can commit your loyalty to the supplier's products. For example,

▼ In the areas we have negotiated, we will present every opportunity to our partner supplier to provide those products and services.

▼ Only when the supplier is unable to meet the demand or specific request will our company solicit bids from alternative companies.

If your supplier could request any single issue to be negotiated, this would be number one or two on the list. The commitment of supply is the most powerful single item you can offer the supplier. In short, you will buy all that you need from the supplier as long as he or she can supply you with the agreed-on levels of service and quality.

Consignment Inventory

Another option to reduce the carrying cost of inventory is not to pay for it until you use or sell the inventory. You can negotiate as follows:

▼ The supplier will maintain one week's (only an option; you may ask for as much as a month or two based on production lead times) worth of inventory at our location but will not charge us for the inventory until we actually use the products.

▼ Any slow-moving inventory will be picked up by the supplier either at the supplier's desire or at our company's request.

▼ The supplier will store consignment inventory at his or her location.

This option guarantees safety stock levels while reducing your need for warehousing space. This option allows you to test new products (especially if you are a distributor) more easily than if you had to invest up front in every product you want to present to your customers. This arrangement could lead to sales increases for both companies.

Discounts/Pricing Levels

The most commonly negotiated issue is pricing. Few people are unaware that they can negotiate price in almost any business situation. You may want to raise the following points when selling the supplier on giving you the discounts you are asking for:

▼ We are putting five years, or $_____ worth of business, on the table in one negotiating session; those who are not competitive are locked out for at least five years.

▼ Once you win our business, you will have our commitment to work with you as our partner for the next five years. We will not solicit or accept any bids from other companies.

▼ The issues we have negotiated will provide cost savings to the supplier as well as to us in the form of

– Paperwork reduction and EDI
– Forecasting
– Reduced quality exceptions.

Guaranteed Volume

Many suppliers will ask you to guarantee volume if you enter into a partnership. Avoid this if at all possible. Instead, provide the supplier with a commitment of supply. For example,

▼ Our company will not guarantee a specific volume of purchases. But the purchasing levels provided in the profile represent our best estimate of our future business needs.

▼ We will commit our supply needs to the supplier.

There are market forces and developments that can make a specific product obsolete. In addition, if your company fails, a commitment to purchase additional inventory can be difficult and expensive to honor. If you are uncomfortable with refusing to guarantee purchasing levels with the supplier, review the commitment of supply issue to determine an appropriate solution.

Insurance

Products you purchase from the supplier may end up in the hands of your customers. You want to make sure that these products are insured in case of any accidents or defects that lead to lawsuits or claims. For example,

▼ The supplier will provide proof of insurance before the beginning of the contract.

▼ The supplier's insurance must meet any governmental regulation levels.

In addition to the quality and certification issues you will negotiate, this issue provides a safety net against defective products that could harm end users and customers.

Loaner Equipment

When your equipment breaks down (e.g., fork lifts or other machinery), you can negotiate for the supplier to provide loaner equipment while repairing the original equipment. Negotiating this issue up front in a supplier partnership can prevent significant costs down the road. In addition, you can negotiate for the supplier to provide loaner equipment during your peak periods, which will help you maintain a lean level of equipment inventory. For example, you can negotiate the following points:

▼ If one of the pieces of equipment breaks down that you, the supplier, sold to us, you will provide us with a piece of loaner equipment that can provide the same functions as the serviced equipment.

▼ This service will be provided at no cost to our company. (Another option is to offer to split the cost of delivery and the labor for installation.)

▼ For up to ___ weeks per year, the supplier will provide us up to ___ pieces of equipment. We will use this equipment during peak periods. (For example, one client negotiated that the supplier provide up to five loaner fork lifts during annual physical inventory counts.)

▼ For this peak-period loaner equipment, we will provide 30 days' lead time to allow the supplier to prepare for the loan as inexpensively as possible.

One way to communicate this issue is to explain the costs related to plant shutdowns and other effects of nonfunctioning equipment. Working out a smooth method to bring in loaner equipment is key to minimizing the risk of consolidating so much business in a core group of suppliers.

Obsolete and Slow-Moving Inventory Buyback

For many reasons, companies often accumulate inventory that they either will not use for many months or will never use again. Some items may have no channel for liquidation. You can negotiate for supplier partners to buy back excess inventory. Some of the inventory they will sell back to you as you need more, and some they will simply have to sell to other customers or liquidate themselves. This issue can provide a tremendous psychological boost to your partnership process, team, and company. You can negotiate as follows:

▼ The supplier will buy the products and quantities listed below for the cost we paid for them. (Then list the product descriptions, quantities, and costs related to your slow-moving and obsolete inventory. Recovering the actual costs you originally paid is the best you can do. It is your option to negotiate a smaller percentage in order to obtain agreement with the supplier.)

▼ The supplier will provide a check for the appropriate amount at the official contract kickoff meeting and banquet.

This issue is easier to negotiate if the supplier is the one that sold you the inventory. But you can negotiate it with alternate suppliers as well, especially for slow-moving inventory that they will eventually sell back to you. For obsolete inventory that you will not be buying back, ask if the supplier has other customers to whom it could sell your obsolete inventory. If not, another option is to accept less than one dollar on the dollar for obsolete inventory. Even if the supplier pays you 10 cents on the dollar, you may be better off than continuing to pay the carrying costs associated with the inventory.

Over/Under

Many suppliers reserve the right to add or subtract units up to 10% of an order. This causes the buyer to alter orders to receive the actual amount needed. For this reason, it is helpful to inform the supplier that you will order exactly what you need—no more and no less. For example,

▼ The supplier will not, as a matter of normal business, add to or subtract from the quantity we order.

▼ Any amount of our order not shipped will be classified as a back order.

Explain this issue to the supplier as no more than nuisance control. Tell the supplier how your buyers learn the patterns of each supplier and alter their orders accordingly. For example, some buyers might say "this supplier always adds 10% to our order, I need 100, so I will order 91."

Overtime Payment

The key to this issue is to define how much you will pay for overtime required to finish your product or service. This is especially relevant for construction, printing, or other job shop suppliers. For example,

▼ Overtime charges will exclude the following items that are not affected by overtime hours:

– Fringe benefits

– Insurance

– Union dues

▼ Overtime charges may include

– Amounts actually paid to workers

– Actual Federal Insurance Contribution Act (FICA)

– Actual Social Security.

This issue points out the importance of understanding how a company that provides specialized service develops its costing formula. Overtime is one instance in which the unwary buyer could pay more than he or she is led to believe. Many times a buyer will be asked to pay for overtime charges incurred by the supplier. They will ask, for example, that you pay double their normal labor rate because they pay their employees double time for overtime. While this seems reasonable on the surface, it is not. A supplier's labor rate includes the actual amount paid to a worker, plus other costs that are not affected by overtime. For example, the supplier will not have to pay double medical insurance for overtime hours. Other items that are included in labor rates that are not affected by overtime could include:

▼ Union dues

▼ Fringe benefits

▼ Supplier profits

▼ Overhead charges

Payment Terms

This issue can be significant over the term of your partnership. Basically, you are negotiating when you will pay for the products and services you receive from the supplier. You can either try to extend payment, and use this issue to save money internally, or you can pay quickly to provide a good-faith benefit to the supplier. This decision can be based on how quickly your customers pay you, your cash position, and your supplier's cash position.

▼ *Due date.* Negotiated in days from the time you receive their invoice. The most common level is 30 days. Depending on your accounts payable system, you might be able to go as low as 20 days. Going the other way, you can negotiate as many as 45 to 60 days. Your best gauge is how quickly your customers pay you and what the normal industry standards are.

▼ *Days to pay to qualify for a discount.* Some suppliers will offer an additional discount if you pay within a certain number of days. The most common level is 10 days. You can negotiate as high as 30 days, however.

▼ *Discount level.* The range for the discount is 1/2% to 2%.

If you negotiate to get the best terms for your company, your best approach might be to explain why you cannot pay more quickly (e.g., you cannot pay faster than your customers pay you). Alternatively, you can decide to offer quicker payment terms to the supplier (this is especially important for smaller suppliers with a tighter cash flow).

Price Increase Caps

This issue allows you and the supplier to determine the cap for any annual price increases over the life of the partnership. It will provide you with the ability to develop a financial plan for the future years of the partnership. For example, you can negotiate as follows:

▼ For each of the years of the partnership listed below, the price of the products and services will not increase more than the respective percentage. (The numbers provided are only examples; the actual numbers you use should be based on historical price increases as well as current market conditions. In fact, some commodity areas have fallen in price and the price caps could include negative increases.)

  – Year 1: 0%
  – Year 2: 2%
  – Year 3: 2%
  – Year 4: 3%
  – Year 5: 4%

In this issue, it is important to discuss the impact of the cost-cutting measures each of you will be taking to reduce mutual costs throughout the partnership. For example, paperwork reduction and the elimination of sales calls will control costs. Because of this, you will be able to control price increases and would like to document that now. This will help both companies plan for the future. In addition, you can communicate your commitment to the supplier's long-term success and will not refuse to discuss any needed price changes.

Pricing of Future Items

Often, you will add to the list of products and services you purchase from a specific supplier. Therefore, it is important to set up the method of pricing those new products at the beginning of the partnership.

Option 1: If a supplier has a retail price list

▼ The same discount levels negotiated for current purchases will apply to any products the supplier will add during the course of this contract.

Option 2: If a supplier does not have a retail price list

▼ The pricing for new products will be based on the prices for similar or substitute items provided today.

▼ If no similar item exists, both companies will meet to decide on the price based on the prices charged to other customers, market prices, and profit margin levels.

This issue primarily minimizes any quarrels that could occur one or two years into the partnership.

Fixed Cost + Fixed Profit

If the supplier's costs are available to you, you can negotiate pricing on a cost-plus basis. This requires full disclosure from the supplier but can reduce the risk that the supplier will not be profitable or that it will price gauge you. You can negotiate as follows:

▼ The supplier will provide us with a complete audited accounting of its costs.

▼ The pricing for any specific product will be set by a joint committee between our company and the supplier's. This committee will determine which costs should be included in our price and what level of profit is reasonable.

▼ The pricing will be reviewed annually throughout the partnership.

▼ Whenever significant business factors change the effective costs of the products, either company can request that the pricing committee reconvene to review the new circumstances.

This approach to pricing should always be tempered by and compared to market prices. In addition, only negotiate this type of pricing if you have an expert who can analyze the costing information provided by the supplier.

Title Passage

This issue relates to who owns the products you order at different points in the process. For example, if products are damaged en route from the supplier to your location, who assumes the cost? This depends on when the title passes. Title can pass at any of the following points:

▼ When it leaves the supplier's dock

▼ When it arrives at the buyer's location

▼ When the buyer inspects the products and places them into inventory

▼ When the product is used in the production process

▼ When the buyer pays for the product.

Essentially, you might expect to accept title for the products when you obtain control over the products. This issue is important so you do not accept responsibility for the safety of a shipment before you have control over the handling of that shipment.

Work with the supplier to decide the best point at which title should pass. Chances are that this issue will become a problem in your partnership. If it does, you will avoid arguments and lawsuits.

QUALITY ISSUES
▼

Deming's Principles

Deming's fourth of his 14 points for the transformation of management states, "End the practice of awarding business on the basis of price tag. Instead, minimize total cost. Move toward a single supplier for any one item, on a long-term relationship of loyalty and trust."[1] Thus, the partnerships you are creating are, inherently, an integral part of implementing Deming quality principles. Points you could negotiate to enhance your Deming approach to quality include the following:

▼ Both the supplier and our company will share information, unless forbidden by law, that could help the other company reduce costs or increase efficiency. Examples include market research, R&D developments, forecasts, etc.

▼ We must negotiate regarding

– Top management involvement
– Strategic planning
– Forecasting
– Quality inspections and certification
– Specialized field support
– Length of the contract.

This issue should please suppliers. Communicate your commitment to a true partnership in which the supplier, as well as your company and customers, benefits.

ISO 9000

ISO 9000 is the emerging world-wide quality standard. Issues you can raise to manage ISO 9000 compliance include the following:

▼ The supplier will obtain the materials, practices, and applications necessary to obtain ISO 9000 certification within the first three years of the partnership.

▼ The supplier will lend its engineers to review our processes and use of the supplier's products for opportunities to increase quality.

Other issues that are required to qualify for ISO 9000 certification include the following:

---

[1] Rafael Aguayo, *Dr. Deming, What Every U.S. Business Person Should Know About Successful Management and Bringing Quality Back Home.* Page 149. Fireside, Simon & Schuster, Rockefeller Center, 1230 Avenue of the Americas, New York 10020. 1991.

▼ Obtain a copy of the supplier's quality policy book.

▼ Obtain a copy of the supplier's claims procedure and settlement agreement.

▼ A top-level technical executive needs to join your ISO 9000 steering committee to aid in creating action plans and corrective steps.

▼ The supplier will assist in your ISO 9000 internal company training. (Negotiate the same details for this issue as negotiated in the training issue.)

▼ After ISO 9000 certification is achieved, the same top-level technical executive will participate in your semiannual review and self-assessment.

This issue can become one of the most memorable in the long run. Three to five years into the partnership, the effects of working together to develop world-class quality levels will begin to pay off. Of course, this issue will be much more palatable to suppliers who already understand the importance and power of quality. In addition, this issue is, at its most basic level, about communication. You are asking the supplier to become entrenched in your operations. This should be an exciting prospect for the supplier.

Just-in-Time Delivery

Just-in-time (JIT) delivery is a method of reducing the amount of inventory you maintain. To make this approach a success, it is imperative that your suppliers have the ability and desire to support your production (or distribution) schedule and inventory levels. You can negotiate as follows:

▼ The supplier will deliver our purchases daily (or some other frequent periodic level).

▼ We will provide our production schedule and product requirement forecasts to help the supplier determine its production schedule.

▼ Other issues that support the implementation of a JIT delivery schedule include

  – EDI links between our companies
  – Supplier safety stock levels
  – Quality certification and/or ISO 9000 (the higher the quality of the products supplied, the less time your company has to spend inspecting deliveries).

JIT is an ideal way for the supplier to provide your company with a significant cost savings without having to reduce price. You will find that some suppliers are more prepared for this and can provide the required levels of service and quality within their current infrastructure.

Quality Certification/Inspection

This issue is important on two levels. First, every shipment you receive should be exactly what you order. The supplier should certify that it has delivered what you have asked for. Second, the shipments you receive should be to your specifications and free of defects. Your interest is to eliminate on-site inspections of shipments from your supplier partners. This can only occur if you are certain that the supplier sends you quality products. You can negotiate as follows:

▼ The supplier will self-certify deliveries and will provide documentation that every shipment was inspected and matches the order placed by our company.

▼ The supplier will guarantee a percentage (99.5%, for example) of defect-free products.

▼ The supplier will provide a copy of its quality control procedures to our company so we can understand the supplier's methods.

This will also benefit the supplier due to reduced returns (which cost money to process, ship, and replace). In addition, providing quality products and shipments will be the type of issue that will turn this five-year partnership into a lifetime partnership.

Replacement of Defective Materials

When a defective product does slip through the system, you can save time and money by specifying up front how those products will be handled. For example,

▼ Defective parts will be picked up by the supplier and disposed of at the supplier's discretion and cost.

▼ A replacement will be sent immediately, or on the next order, depending on our company's choice and at no cost to our company.

Other topics to negotiate include

▼ When the product will be picked up

▼ Penalties for defective shipments in excess of predetermined levels.

This is another issue that will benefit both parties by eliminating future disagreements.

Specialized Field Support

This could be one of the most dramatic issues for your company. In this issue, you negotiate for the supplier to provide expert help in the design, manufacturing, or distribution of your products. For example,

▼ The supplier will provide a design engineer to work (on our premises) exclusively on our company's processes, procedures, and products, especially as they relate to the supplier.

▼ The engineer will work to design quality and cost controls into our mutual products and processes.

Stress the opportunity to reduce mutual costs through this issue. Many suppliers have great ideas about how to improve your products. This, in turn, will increase your sales and demand for the supplier's products. In addition, this is another method for the supplier to reduce your costs without reducing price.

Total Quality Management

Many companies have embarked on an effort to empower their employees to make good decisions as part of a team and thus help the company improve quality or reduce costs. One name for this effort is total quality management (TQM). In line with this approach to management, you can negotiate the following with your suppliers:

▼ As part of a partnership agreement, selected employees of the supplier will join your TQM teams to add the supplier's perspective to the management issues addressed. In this way, the supplier can provide additional insights to your TQM effort. One option would be to ask the supplier to make members of its engineering staff available to your TQM teams.

▼ In addition, you can offer to make some of your customer service representatives, line workers, salespeople, or other employees available to the supplier's TQM efforts.

In this issue, you are providing another long-term quality check. Instead of always reacting to quality problems, by working together in teams you and the supplier can work to avoid problems and increase efficiency. This issue costs little money for either party and can provide a method for extending communication links deep within your companies.

Warranty

Warranty is another issue that can prevent misunderstandings throughout the partnership. Specifically, what type of warranty will the supplier provide on its products? To determine this, you can negotiate the following:

- ▼ How long will the warranty be effective?

- ▼ What paperwork will we have to process to collect on a warranty?

- ▼ Will the warranty cover parts and labor? How long for each?

- ▼ If we return a product under warranty, are there any charges we could be assessed?

- ▼ The warranty needs to cover lost production time and lost profits caused by your products.

- ▼ The warranty should cover any subsequent claims by customers caused by your products.

In addition, this is a protection issue that reduces the risks of relying on a core group of suppliers.

SERVICE ISSUES
▼

Acts of God (Force Majeure)

Many things can happen to the supplier and its products that the supplier has no control over (e.g., lightning, hurricanes, floods, car accidents). In this issue, you define steps to take in these circumstances. For example,

- ▼ When acts beyond the control of the supplier prevent the supplier from fulfilling an order or group of orders,

- Those orders will not be counted in performance measurements.
- The supplier will notify our company at the earliest time it has knowledge of the event, thus allowing our company to make alternative plans.

This issue shows your desire to enter into a true partnership: You understand that the supplier will be affected by events outside its control.

Blueprints and Schematics

At times, you may need or want to allow another company to work on the machinery purchased from a specific supplier. By obtaining a copy of the design and specifications for the equipment, you are able to solicit help from alternate companies. You can negotiate as follows:

▼ The supplier will provide a copy of the schematics, specifications, and blueprints for all equipment and machinery purchased.

Emergency Maintenance

In addition to routine maintenance visits, you can negotiate how emergency maintenance will be handled. For example,

▼ The supplier will respond to emergency maintenance situations within four hours of notification of the problem.

▼ The supplier will maintain a safety stock of the most common items needed to repair our machines.

▼ The supplier will charge normal labor rates and spare part charges for repairs not covered in our warranty.

▼ The supplier will charge nothing for repairs covered by the warranty.

It is critical that the supplier minimize any downtime caused by equipment problems. This issue must be negotiated up front so you will know the supplier's capabilities.

Freight on Board

This issue addresses the responsibility of controlling the delivery of the goods from the supplier to your location. How this is negotiated will affect who pays for the freight on board (FOB) and who is responsible for damage. To clarify this issue, negotiate the following:

▼ *FOB loading dock.* This indicates that the supplier will get the product to its dock, but you and your carrier are responsible for getting the product to your location. This method could be your choice if you have carrier partnerships.

▼ *FOB customer.* This means that the supplier will be responsible for getting the products to your dock. Any problems with the product will automatically become the supplier's responsibility.

Joint Advertising

This issue provides another opportunity to increase mutual sales because you negotiate to work together with the supplier to feature each other's products in advertising and press releases. For example,

▼ The supplier will work with its public relations department or consultant to publicize the partnership relationship in industry periodicals that would be read by customers of both parties.

▼ The supplier will feature your product in an advertisement and will run the ad in industrial periodicals that service each company's markets.

Lead Time

This is the amount of time it takes for an order to arrive at your locations after you place the order with the supplier. The major components include the order or paperwork lead time, the production lead time, and the distribution lead time.

▼ *Order lead time:* With today's technology, most orders should be processed on a same-day basis, which allows stock items to be available for next-day delivery.

▼ *Production lead time:* For nonstock items that must be produced by the supplier, work with the supplier to understand his or her constraints and abilities. Based on that discussion, define the normal production lead time you can expect from this supplier. Finally, based on your physical distance from the supplier, define a normal delivery time or schedule.

Begin this issue by asking the supplier about internal cycle or lead times. How long does the supplier's order processing take? How quickly can the supplier set up and change production lines to manufacture your products, and what are the supplier's options in delivering the product to your locations? Based on these answers, you can quantify the expected lead times for your partnership, explaining any issues that may require faster lead times.

Performance Criteria

In this issue, you define the basic standards of service over the life of the partnership. Establishing measurable criteria lays the groundwork for your ongoing monitoring and evaluation of the partnership and is yet another practice that will minimize any risks you face by partnering with a finite number of suppliers. In this issue, address the following points:

▼ On a monthly basis, we would like to receive a report from the supplier that quantifies actual lead time (the average, lowest, highest, and median time elapsed from the point of order to delivery at our docks).

▼ For each of the following statistics, provide the percentages of total orders as well as total line items:

– Returns

– Back order

– On-time delivery (absolute percentage disregarding the effects of early deliveries)

– Claims (this could cover damaged materials and shipments that were not returned to the supplier).

Ongoing monitoring and evaluation is a critical factor in the long-term success of a partnership. These statistics will provide a quantifiable basis for reviewing the partnership.

Promotions

This is a double issue. First, you want to negotiate that the supplier will automatically give you credit for any manufacturer promotions or coupons. Second, you are trying to schedule a number of promotions for your customers and are looking for a cosponsor. For this issue, consider the following points:

▼ Credit our account for the promotions and coupons sponsored by you or by your suppliers.

▼ Pass on any promotions you have control over that we can offer to our customers.

▼ We will cosponsor one promotion per year for our mutual customers. To determine the specifics, we will form a committee between our marketing departments to work out the details. In principle, we will agree to split the costs.

Routine and Preventive Maintenance

Everyone saves money if the process doesn't break down. Based on this truth, you want the supplier to provide preventive maintenance. You can negotiate the following:

▼ The supplier will inspect each piece of its equipment that we have purchased on a monthly basis.

▼ As part of these inspections, the supplier will provide routine and preventive maintenance.

▼ These inspections and maintenance reviews will be completed by an engineer or mechanic, not by a salesperson.

▼ There will be no charge for these visits, or the supplier will provide these services for the cost of supplies.

▼ Uncovered nonroutine problems will be fixed by the mechanic with no visit charges.

Remind the supplier about the goodwill it can buy by providing equipment and machinery that does not break down. In addition, communicate to the supplier your desire for the supplier to be profitable—but that profit should come from sales, not from breakdowns and ancillary charges.

Spare Parts

For many products, people say that "the cheapest thing about this darn thing was buying it." This can be true about the supplier's machines and equipment as well, based on the availability and price of spare parts. You can negotiate as follows:

▼ As a partner, our company will be able to purchase spare parts at a discount of ___% off the list price.

▼ The same lead time and performance standards that are applied to other products will apply to the purchase of spare parts.

▼ The supplier will maintain a safety stock for each spare part we might reasonably need in the operation of its equipment.

This issue will be important to many suppliers as well because of the repeat business it can provide. This can be a critical issue in the automobile industry.

Stockouts

Often, suppliers are not able to forecast the demand for their products. Because of this, they may run low on specific items and not be able to fulfill all of their customer orders. As a preferred customer and partner, you are looking for special treatment during these stockouts. Negotiate as follows:

▼ Our orders are for any stock available, regardless of competing customer orders.

▼ Maintain a safety stock of one to two weeks of inventory for each of our critical purchases.

▼ Critical products will be defined by a joint committee between the supplier and our company.

The supplier will benefit from this issue primarily because it is a key factor in reducing the risk of consolidating business. If the supplier is able to eliminate stockouts or delayed shipments, you will not be forced to use other suppliers during the partnership.

Substitutions

If you place an order for a specific product, can the supplier arbitrarily substitute a similar product? Sometimes this can save both companies money; sometimes you have a reason for requesting a specific product. You can negotiate as follows:

▼ The supplier will not substitute any product in any order without the express consent of our buyers.

▼ The supplier will pass along the savings any substitutions bring to the table.

Negotiating this issue up front will help minimize misunderstandings down the road.

Tooling Movement Penalty

Even if you own the tools and have paid for them, some suppliers will charge you a penalty for moving the tools to another supplier (this acts as a built-in barrier to market entry). Negotiate as follows:

▼ For all tools that our company has paid to have produced or has paid for through capitalization, we shall not be charged a movement fee if our contract becomes violable in the future.

This should not be a major issue. The key is that if the supplier does not live up to its agreed service and quality levels and you are forced to find another supplier, the supplier cannot hold your tools hostage.

Tooling Ownership and Maintenance

If your supplier uses tools and dies to manufacture your products, you might consider formalizing who owns them. This affects your ability to switch to new suppliers in the future as well as the costs you bear or avoid in the case of broken or worn-down tools.

Option 1: Supplier owns the tools

▼ The tools and dies used in the production of our products will remain the property of the supplier.

▼ The supplier will maintain the tools and dies and will be responsible for repairs.

▼ The supplier will capitalize the cost of the tools and dies over the useful life and include the expense in its normal pricing.

Option 2: Your company owns the tools and dies

▼ Our company will maintain ownership of the tools and dies.

▼ Our company will be responsible for the initial creation of the tools and dies, but the supplier, who has physical control of them, will be responsible for routine maintenance and repairs.

This is another issue that is best to clarify up front. In many cases, the issue will never surface, but it could. Your focus is to avoid any potential for misunderstandings.

Tooling Quality, Size, and Cost

As part of the specialized field support approach, you can have the supplier's engineers review your end products, manufacturing process, and distribution process to see if costs can be trimmed by changing the quality, size, or material of the tooling. For example,

▼ The supplier will review our uses of the products manufactured with the tooling and make any recommendations to trim costs and enhance quality through the actual tools themselves.

▼ This review will begin within one month of the initiation of our partnership.

▼ The engineer must be approved by both companies.

This is another area in which the supplier can work to make your products the low-cost leader and the quality leader without taking price cuts.

Transportation

If you have a preferred mode of transportation for delivery of your product, you can negotiate that the supplier honor that preference. For example,

▼ Our company will provide the supplier with an inbound routing guide that will identify the carrier we would like the supplier to use when delivering our product.

▼ If the supplier does not comply with our inbound routing guide, it will be responsible for the difference between our negotiated rates and the rates the supplier incurred on our behalf. (This issue assumes you are charged for freight by the supplier or by the carrier.)

Another option is to negotiate that the supplier pays for all freight. The assumption is that the supplier will make its profits in the pricing of its main products. This issue will be more important to suppliers who have negotiated partnership contracts with their own carriers. If they have, compare their rates to your own to assess the most economical choice.

OTHER ISSUES
▼

Based on your interviews with company personnel, suppliers, competitors, and other associates, you will need to develop customized issues. Refer to Chapter 6 to identify and define additional issues.

APPENDIX B

PROJECT TASK LIST

Many steps and tasks are discussed throughout the book that must be completed to develop a world class supplier partnership. In order to help simplify these steps, and to show the relationships between them, the following Task List is provided. A Task List is helpful because, in addition to listing the tasks that need to be performed to achieve a goal, it also shows the relationship between tasks, the relative length of each task, and the timing of each task.

In general, the order of the tasks down the page indicates the order in which the tasks should be completed. Some tasks can be completed concurrently. However, when a description is listed in the "Predecessors" column, it indicates any tasks that must be completed before that task can begin. For example, Task 7, "Develop Survey", and Task 9, "Schedule interviews with each person selected" must be completed before you can begin Task 10, "Conduct Interviews". The following legend will help explain some of the technical abbreviations used in this Task List:

TASK LIST LEGEND
▼

ID	Task Number
Task Name	Task Description
Duration	d=day, w=week, h=hour
Start	Task Starting Date
Finish	Task Finishing Date
Predecessors	The number in this box refers to the Task ID Number that must precede task.
	FS means "Finish to Start", indicating that the task must begin after the preceding task modified by the number of days listed. For example, "FS-2d" means that the current task should start two days before the end of the preceding task.
	SS means "Start to Start, indicating that both tasks should begin at the same time.

This Task List assumes a 6-7 month implementation cycle, and each task's estimated length is represented duration. For purposes of illustration, a starting date of "June 10" was selected, with an ending date of "December 9"

You can use this Task List to help you plan the actual steps you undertake to implement your supplier partnership. As with most examples in this book, this is based on a generic company and will need to be customized based on unique circumstances at your company.

Task List

ID	Task Name	Duration	Start	Finish	Predecessors
	IMPLEM2.MPP	**130.69d**	**Jun 10**	**Dec 9**	
1	**Understand Partnership Process**	1d	Jun 10	Jun 10	
2	Compare company performance to industry	1d	Jun 10	Jun 10	
3	**Develop an estimated savings analysis**	1d	Jun 10	Jun 10	
4	Estimate Annual Purchases	1d	Jun 10	Jun 10	
5	**Data Gathering**	15d	Jun 10	Jun 30	
6	**Perform Internal Interviews**	15d	Jun 10	Jun 30	
12	**Gain Company Wide Support (see chapter 4)**	8d	Jul 1	Jul 12	11
13	Prepare summary of issues discussed in interviews	3d	Jul 1	Jul 5	11
14	Prepare presentation to top management and/or peers	3d	Jul 6	Jul 8	13
15	Review presentation with the department head to gather support and incorporate their views	1d	Jul 11	Jul 11	14
16	Hold top management presentation and work to gain the support to implement supplier partnerships	1d	Jul 12	Jul 12	15
17	**Prepare your Purchasing Profile**	7d	Jul 13	Jul 21	
18	Write introduction letter to suppliers	1d	Jul 13	Jul 13	16

ID	Description	Duration	Start	Finish	Pred.
19	Generate historical database of annual purchases by product for each commodity area	4d	Jul 13	Jul 18	
20	Work with your MIS department to summarize all purchases	3d	Jul 13	Jul 15	
21	For each commodity area (or product type) summarize annual purchases	1d	Jul 13	Jul 13	16
22	Show each buyer the summary of product purchases so they can review them for unreasonable data	1d	Jul 14	Jul 14	21
23	Compare the summary of purchases to financial records to make sure that your data is reasonable	1d	Jul 15	Jul 15	22
24	Create the report to give to the suppliers in the profile	1d	Jul 18	Jul 18	
25	After the data is reviewed for reasonableness, print a report showing the annual quantity purchased	1d	Jul 18	Jul 18	23
26	Develop the Service, Quality and Pricing Issue sections of the profile	3d	Jul 13	Jul 15	
27	Review interview notes for issues to include	1d	Jul 13	Jul 13	16,13
28	Review list of issues in Appendix A for additional ideas	1d	Jul 13	Jul 13	27SS
29	For each issue identified, develop a question that will help you to understand the supplier's commitment	1d	Jul 14	Jul 14	28
30	Review the sample profile in Chapter 8 for additional ideas and formatting options	1d	Jul 15	Jul 15	29
31	Prepare the profile for promulgation	4d	Jul 18	Jul 21	

ID	Task Name	Duration	Start	Finish	Predecessors
32	Take your draft of the qualitative and quantitative sections and prepare one complete draft of the profile	1d	Jul 18	Jul 18	30
33	Ask each of your team members to review the profile for corrections or additions	1d	Jul 19	Jul 19	32
34	Merge the profile letter with your list of contacts	1d	Jul 20	Jul 20	33,41
35	Send out the profiles	1d	Jul 21	Jul 21	34
36	**Research Alternative Suppliers**	**3d**	**Jul 13**	**Jul 15**	
37	Develop list of all possible sources for alternative suppliers	1d	Jul 13	Jul 13	16
38	Review interview notes for alternative suppliers mentioned	1d	Jul 13	Jul 13	37SS
39	Review other sources listed to collect alternate suppliers	1d	Jul 13	Jul 13	38SS
40	For each supplier identified, collect pertinent information in a database	1d	Jul 14	Jul 14	39
41	Print out a list of all suppliers identified and have each buyer review to add to, or edit, the list	1d	Jul 15	Jul 15	40
42	**Develop Negotiable Issues (see chapter 6)**	**17d**	**Jul 6**	**Jul 28**	
43	Review interview notes for issues to be developed	1d	Jul 6	Jul 6	13
44	Collect the team you would like to include in developing the issues. (Should be a cross-functional team)	1d	Jul 7	Jul 7	43
45	Review each issue and develop the interests, positions, supporting facts, issue outline, and supplier issues	3w	Jul 8	Jul 28	44

ID	Task Name	Duration	Start	Finish	Predecessors
46	**Supplier Presentation**	**44d**	**Jun 10**	**Aug 10**	
47	Develop list of suppliers to invite to the presentation	1d	Jul 6	Jul 6	13
48	**Send out supplier invitations**	**5d**	**Jul 6**	**Jul 12**	
49	Write invitation letter	1d	Jul 6	Jul 6	13
50	Review list of invitees with other buyers and company executives	1d	Jul 7	Jul 7	47
51	Finalize invitation letter and mail merge with invitee list	1d	Jul 8	Jul 8	50
52	Update invitee list for any positive or negative RSVP's	1d	Jul 11	Jul 11	51
53	Call any suppliers that do not respond, or who do not plan to attend to give them another chance to participate	1d	Jul 12	Jul 12	52
54	**Prepare the presentation**	**24d**	**Jul 8**	**Aug 10**	
55	Identify Presenters	1d	Jul 8	Jul 8	44
56	Work with each speaker to develop their presentation	2w	Jul 11	Jul 22	55
57	Develop visual aides to support each presentation	2w	Jul 20	Aug 2	56FS-3d
58	Work with each presenter to practice their speech prior to the actual presentation	1w	Aug 3	Aug 9	57

ID	Task Name	Duration	Start	Finish	Predecessors
59	Hold a full dress rehearsal the evening before the actual presentation	1d	Aug 10	Aug 10	58
60	Prepare a name tag for each supplier contact who indicates their participation in the presentation	1d	Jul 25	Jul 25	
61	**Secure the facility**	**5d**	**Jul 13**	**Jul 19**	
62	Based on responses to supplier invitations, estimate the number of attendees you expect	1d	Jul 13	Jul 13	53
63	Compare different locations based on atmosphere, quality of service and food, and price	1d	Jul 14	Jul 14	62
64	Items to include in your presentation room: writing tablets and pens, ice water, mints, a coffee break with rolls, a registration	1d	Jul 15	Jul 15	63
65	Work with Audio Visual Representatives to setup the appropriate A/V equipment	1d	Jul 18	Jul 18	64
66	Test all visual aides and A/V equipment to be used the night before the actual presentation	1d	Jul 19	Jul 19	65
67	**Hold the presentation**	**2.13d**	**Jun 10**	**Jun 14**	
68	2 minute run through. Have each presenter practice their first two minutes of their speech	1h	Jun 10	Jun 10	
69	Greet your guests as they arrive. Introduce yourself to new suppliers, and welcome current suppliers.	1d	Jun 10	Jun 13	68
70	Hand out any materials you have prepared for the attending suppliers.	1d	Jun 13	Jun 14	69
71	**Send Profile to Suppliers**	**3d**	**Jul 7**	**Jul 11**	**47**
72	Generate a list of suppliers to send a profile	1d	Jul 7	Jul 7	67

ID	Task Name	Duration	Start	Finish	Pred
73	Take master copy of the profile and make a copy for each supplier you will send one to.	1d	Jul 8	Jul 8	72
74	Prepare a profile control database, as described in chapter 9	1d	Jul 11	Jul 11	73
75	**Analyze Returned Profiles**	**21d**	**Jul 12**	**Aug 9**	
76	Prepare Reports illustrated in Chapter 9	3w	Jul 12	Aug 1	74
77	Copy relevant material from each supplier's proposal to distribute to team members	3w	Jul 19	Aug 8	76SS+5d
78	Distribute reports and proposal copies to each team member	1d	Aug 9	Aug 9	77
79	**Select Suppliers to Negotiate With**	**3d**	**Aug 10**	**Aug 12**	
80	After each team member has a chance to review the materials you have distributed, hold a meeting to select suppliers	1d	Aug 10	Aug 10	78
81	During the meeting develop a list of suppliers to negotiate with based on the materials reviewed.	1d	Aug 11	Aug 11	80
82	Work towards a unanamous decision for the selected suppliers	1d	Aug 12	Aug 12	81
83	**Conduct Negotiations**	**42.75d**	**Aug 15**	**Oct 12**	
84	**Invite the suppliers**	**3d**	**Aug 15**	**Aug 17**	
85	Write your invitation letter (See chapter 10)	1d	Aug 15	Aug 15	82

ID	Task Name	Duration	Start	Finish	Predecessors
86	Send the invitation to the selected suppliers	1d	Aug 16	Aug 16	85
87	Follow up with a phone call to each supplier to confirm their attendance and the schedule for the meeting	1d	Aug 17	Aug 17	86
88	**Secure the meeting room and make related arrangements**	**4d**	**Sep 19**	**Sep 22**	
89	Decide where to hold your negotiating sessions (see discussion of neutral sites in chapter 10)	1d	Sep 19	Sep 19	
90	Secure the appropriate date based on discussions with supplier and your team	1d	Sep 20	Sep 20	89,87
91	Work with the management of the room to setup table structure (see discussion in chapter 10)	1d	Sep 21	Sep 21	90
92	Set up the room for details such as coffee, tablets, handouts, promotional material, audio/visual support	1d	Sep 19	Sep 19	
93	Review the room setup the night before the negotiations to make sure everything is set	1d	Sep 22	Sep 22	92,91
94	**Prepare for each supplier negotiation (See chapters 10 and 11)**	**3d**	**Aug 25**	**Aug 29**	
95	Review materials relating to the supplier	1d	Aug 25	Aug 25	87FS+1w
96	Prepare index of issues to negotiate for that specific supplier	1d	Aug 26	Aug 26	95
97	Review any issues specific to that supplier or their industry	1d	Aug 29	Aug 29	96
98	**Conduct the actual negotiation meeting**	**0.59d**	**Oct 10**	**Oct 10**	
99	Welcome the suppliers	0.25h	Oct 10	Oct 10	

ID	Task Name	Duration	Start	Finish	Pred
100	Bring the meeting to order and give introduction presentation	0.5h	Oct 10	Oct 10	99
101	Begin going through your list of issues	4h	Oct 10	Oct 10	100
102	**Develop the memo of understanding**	**2.16d**	**Oct 10**	**Oct 12**	
103	As you close each issue, summarize the agreement in writing and ask for verbal agreement after each issue	0.25h	Oct 10	Oct 10	101
104	At the close of the meeting have the lead negotiator from each team sign each page of the memo of understanding	1h	Oct 10	Oct 10	103
105	Type the memo of understanding and send it to the supplier	1d	Oct 10	Oct 11	104
106	Ask the supplier to modify the memo as they understand it	1d	Oct 11	Oct 12	105
107	**Select Suppliers to Partner With**	**8d**	**Oct 12**	**Oct 24**	
108	Update supplier proposals for new rates negotiated and reprint comparison reports discussed in chapter 9	1w	Oct 12	Oct 19	106
109	Provide a copy of the memo's of understanding and the updated comparison reports to each of the team members	1d	Oct 19	Oct 20	108
110	Schedule a meeting to select the supplier	1d	Oct 20	Oct 21	109
111	As discussed in chapter 12, conduct the selection meeting with the goal of a unanimous decision	1d	Oct 21	Oct 24	110
112	**Award the Business**	**13.44d**	**Oct 24**	**Nov 11**	

ID	Task Name	Duration	Start	Finish	Predecessors
113	For the selected suppliers, convert the memos of understanding into contracts	1d	Oct 24	Oct 25	111
114	Have your legal department or counsel review your contracts	1d	Oct 25	Oct 26	113
115	Call your contact at the supplier an congratulate them on their selection	1d	Oct 25	Oct 26	114SS
116	Send the supplier a formal letter inviting them to the Award dinner (see example in chapter 12)	1d	Oct 26	Oct 27	115
117	Develop any closing issues you need to discuss with the supplier before you award the business	1w	Oct 27	Nov 3	116SS+1d
118	Secure and prepare a banquet setting for your dinner	1d	Nov 3	Nov 4	117
119	**Hold the award dinner**	**0.44d**	**Nov 10**	**Nov 11**	
120	Welcome your guests	0.25h	Nov 10	Nov 10	117FS+1w
121	Discuss any remaining closing issues	1h	Nov 10	Nov 10	120
122	Sign a letter of intent or revised memo of understanding	1h	Nov 10	Nov 11	121
123	Schedule your first conversion task force meeting	0.25h	Nov 11	Nov 11	122
124	Have dinner and celebrate with your guests	1h	Nov 11	Nov 11	123
125	**Convert Business to New Partners**	**5.5d**	**Nov 18**	**Nov 25**	

126	Hold initial conversion task force meeting	0.5d	Nov 18	Nov 18	
127	Take supplier on a plant tour so they can see how their products are used	1h	Nov 18	Nov 18	124FS+1w
128	Review order quantities for the initial 2 to 3 months with the supplier in detail to identify potential problems	2h	Nov 18	Nov 18	127
129	Review order specifications and technical requirements to make sure the supplier can deliver	1h	Nov 18	Nov 18	128
130	Order initial quantities from the supplier	1w	Nov 18	Nov 25	129
131	Review initial deliveries for specification and quality exceptions	1w	Nov 18	Nov 25	130SS
132	Set up timelines and plans for implementing each of the different issues according to the memo of understanding	1w	Nov 18	Nov 25	131SS
133	**Implement Ongoing Monitoring and Evaluation Systems**	15d	**Nov 18**	**Dec 9**	
134	Develop management reports and exception reports with your MIS department	3w	Nov 18	Dec 9	132SS
135	Schedule top management meetings between your company and the supplier	1d	Nov 18	Nov 21	134SS
136	**Notify Unselected Suppliers**	1d	**Nov 25**	**Nov 28**	
137	Write the thank you letter (See chapter 12)	1d	Nov 25	Nov 28	132
138	Merge thank you letter with the list of unselected suppliers	1d	Nov 25	Nov 28	137SS

Index